# Aston Martin

THE COMPLETE STORY

GN57 BZS

# Aston Martin

## THE COMPLETE STORY

MATTHEW VALE

THE CROWOOD PRESS

First published in 2022 by
The Crowood Press Ltd
Ramsbury, Marlborough
Wiltshire SN8 2HR

enquiries@crowood.com

**www.crowood.com**



**British Library Cataloguing-in-Publication Data**
A catalogue record for this book is available from the British Library.

ISBN 978 0 7198 4118 7

Typeset by Simon & Sons

Cover design by Blue Sunflower Creative

Printed and bound in India by Parksons Graphics

# CONTENTS

# ACKNOWLEDGEMENTS

This book would not have been possible without the assistance of many people, including private owners, the Aston Martin Heritage Trust (AMHT), the Aston Martin Owners Club (AMOC) and Aston Martin, as well as well regarded experts including Ecurie Bertelli and Chicane.

The owners of the cars I write about are always a great source of information. I'd like to thank Chris Bland, Jeff Sears, Rob Smith, Richard Loveys, Zara and Jerry Doughty, Tim Slow, Edward Hollaway, Mark Seligman, Phil Taylor, Chris Youell, James Bevin, Rodney McMahon, Roland Long, Mark Holmes and Alan Cambridge for giving me access to their cars and allowing me to tell their stories.

So a special thanks to John Watson, the managing director of Chicane (Ford Lane, Bramshill, Hook, RG27 0RH, *see* chicane.am) and Robert Blakemore, the managing director of Écurie Bertelli (53 Stilebrook Road, Yardley Road Industrial Estate, Olney, Bucks MK46 5EA, *see* ecuriebertelli.com) for allowing me to visit their premises and take many photos.

From the Owners Club I'd like to thank Jeff Sears, the Area 10 representative for his help and assistance in meeting owners and for running such a friendly branch.

Rob Smith of the AMHT deserves a special thanks for his assistance with the Aston Martin Heritage Trust and for showing me his fine collection of Astons, as well as the AMHT members Sophie Anderson, who facilitated the pictures from the trust, and Tim Cottingham for data on production numbers.

Steve Waddington, the official Aston Martin historian gave a great deal of help during a busy time at Aston Martin, providing answers to my questions and sorting out various photos used in the book.

Finally thanks to my wife Julia and daughter Elizabeth and her husband Simon for putting up with me writing yet another motoring book.

## PICTURE CREDITS

The pictures on the following pages are courtesy of the Aston Martin Heritage Trust: 19, 19, 22 (left), 23, 26, 28, 31, 32 (top left and right), 38, 39 (top), 45, 46, 57 (right), 58, 62, 72, 93 (bottom), 95, 104 (bottom left), 113 (bottom left and right), 116, 122 (all), 123 (left), 126, 146 (bottom), 157 (bottom) and 174.

The pictures on the following pages are courtesy of Aston Martin Lagonda: 177 (bottom left), 179 (bottom), 180, 196 (both), 198 (bottom two) and 203 (both).

# PREFACE

In the automotive world the combination of quality and performance is not cheap and it is a tricky path for a company to pursue and remain solvent. Aston Martin is one company that has followed this path, and suffered mixed fortunes as a result. However, the emphasis on quality and performance meant – and means – that with Aston Martin it is all about the cars. From Lionel Martin's ambition to produce the perfect light car in the formative years of the twentieth century through to today's range, Aston Martin cars always gave great performance underpinned with engineering integrity and style – but it all came with a cost. And of course Aston Martin has always been bedevilled with the classic British industry malaise: not enough money to realize the dream. In over 100 years of its existence, Aston Martin's fortunes have fluctuated from being modestly successful to being on the brink of bankruptcy – indeed, it has gone over the edge on more than one occasion, only to be dragged back from the brink by generous investors who saw the potential in the company.

But despite these vicissitudes throughout the decades, Aston Martin has held a special place in the hearts of the owners and enthusiasts who recognize the marque's almost unique combination of price, performance, quality and style, and are prepared to put their hands in their pockets and pay the premium price that those characteristics demand.

**The V8 Vantage was the Aston Martin of the 1970s and 1980s. A combination of brute force and suave good looks made it the 'poster car' for many a teenage boy of the time.**

CHAPTER 1

# THE HISTORY OF ASTON MARTIN

Aston Martin's history can be traced back to 1913, and since then has been almost continuous – with only a few pauses while new finance was organized – up to the present day, albeit having a rollercoaster ride for much of that time. The fact that the company has survived is in many ways surprising, but the strength of its product and its ethos, along with a certain mystique that has pervaded the brand since its earliest days, have been enough to carry it through wars, depressions and financial calamity.

So what is it that has made the brand so strong and appealing? Is it its strong presence in automotive competition, its successes at Brooklands in the 1920s and 1930s, its record of winning at Le Mans in the 1950s, its racing sports cars dicing with Ferraris throughout the 1950s and 1960s, endurance racing in the 2000s, or its recent return to Formula 1 in 2021? Or is it the Bond effect, which since starting in the 1960s has been a lasting element of the brand since the DB5 first appeared cruising through Europe in pursuit of Goldfinger? Or is it the road cars the company produced – high performance, competitive, lightweight, stripped-down sports cars in the 1920s, more road-oriented and better equipped sports cars for the 1930s 'man about town', followed by sophisticated GT cars in

**The DB2 started the line of 'DB' Aston Martins. This DB2/4 Mark III is a good-looking and high-performance Grand Tourer from the mid-1950s.**

the post World War II era, designed to transport a gentleman and his lady from London to the French Riviera at maximum speed and in maximum comfort?

Perhaps it is the image of the company keeping the lamp burning for the last of the British performance cars during the 1980s, with the plucky V8 Vantage fighting a rearguard action against the massed hoards of foreign mid-engined supercars trying to wrest the performance crown from Aston Martin's increasingly aged hands. Finally, what about the essential elements of hand-built luxury cars built using the highest standards of traditional British metalworking, coach building, trimming and engineering skills – the hand-crafted bodyshells, the state-of-the-art engine with the plaque telling you who built it, and the hand-stitched leather-lined interior?

All these factors make up the DNA of Aston Martin. The cars are more than the sum of their parts: they are an amalgam of exceptional mechanical elements with a dash of nostalgia and magic mixed in, and a big dollop of tradition to make what is a unique product in today's asinine and sanitized world. Any Aston Martin is a car that has character, backed up with an unbroken line of tradition and heritage stretching back to when Lionel Martin was competing at the Aston Clinton hill climb in his modified Singer in those halcyon days before the devastation of World War I.

In many ways it is a miracle that Aston Martin has survived, but its very existence is a result of the strength of the things that make the brand great, and a testimony to the many people who have been prepared to back their faith in the name with their own money. Today Aston Martin appears to be more financially secure than it has been for many years, and has a range of products that make it well placed to weather any future storms. Let us hope that the brand has many more successful years ahead of it, because the world would be a smaller place without it.

The rest of this book tells the story of Aston Martin, the cars and the men who made it all possible. It is a relatively complex story, littered with successes and failures, financial stability and ruin, and many forceful personalities. So it is useful to have a potted history of the company, which will put the rest of the book in context and give the reader an overview of the major events in the company's commercial history.

**By the late 1960s the DB6 was Aston Martin's flagship model. A fine, high-performance, four-seat GT that was capable of extended high-speed continental journeys.**

## COMPANY TIMELINE

**1913–1926:** Bamford and Martin, formed and run by Lionel Martin and Robert Bamford to 1920; Bamford was then replaced by Martin's wife Kate Martin as director.

A number of prototype cars built and competed in various events, but production cars only trickled on to the market from 1923 as Sports and Supersports models. Production cars were mainly powered by a side-valve 1500cc motor.

**1926:** On 12 October Aston Martin Motors was formed. Directors of the new company were Lord Charnwood and his son (John Benson), Bill Renwick and Bert Bertelli. The new Bertelli-designed, overhead-camshaft 1500cc engine was produced.

**1929:** The company was reformed as Aston Martin Ltd: Bertelli stayed, fresh finance came from S.C. Whitehouse, a garage proprietor from Harrow, as well as Nigel Holder and Reginald Straker of Kensington-Moir, and Straker, the then current Aston Martin distributors; then additional finance came from P.C. 'Percy' Kidnet, an old friend of Bertelli and previously joint managing director of Vauxhall before the General Motors takeover of 1925.

**1931:** Aston Martin Ltd acquired new finance from H.J. Aldington of Frazer Nash, then Lance Prideaux-Brune invested capital to buy out Aldington and restore control to Bertelli. Prideaux-Brune gained distribution rights at his Winter Garden Garage in Holborn, London.

**1932:** Late on in the year shipping magnate Sir Arthur Sutherland bought out all the company and put in his son, R. Gordon Sutherland, as joint managing director with Bertelli. In 1936 the 1500cc ohc engine was developed into a 2-litre ohc unit.

**The first Aston Martins, built by Bamford and Martin, had a simple circular badge with the initials 'AM' superimposed on each other.**

**Typical of the early Bamford and Martin-era cars, this is the famous 'Green Pea' racing car, pictured in 1923 just before the Grand Prix de Boulogne.**

During the Bertelli era, Aston Martins had this winged badge.

**1937:** Bertelli left, and Claude Hill was appointed chief engineer. Hill started to look at new designs for Aston Martin cars, moving away from the traditional ladder chassis to more sophisticated designs.

**1938–1945:** Most car production halted for the duration of World War II. The factory turned over to manufacturing parts for the war effort, concentrating mainly on aircraft parts. The Atom prototype continues in development. Hill's new 4-cylinder engine was designed, and the prototype was put into Atom.

**1948:** The Aston Martin and Lagonda companies were bought by David Brown, and Aston Martin Lagonda Ltd was created. Lagonda and Aston Martin relocated to another site on the Hanworth aero park. The first Aston Martin model under David Brown was the 1948–1950 2-litre Sports model. There

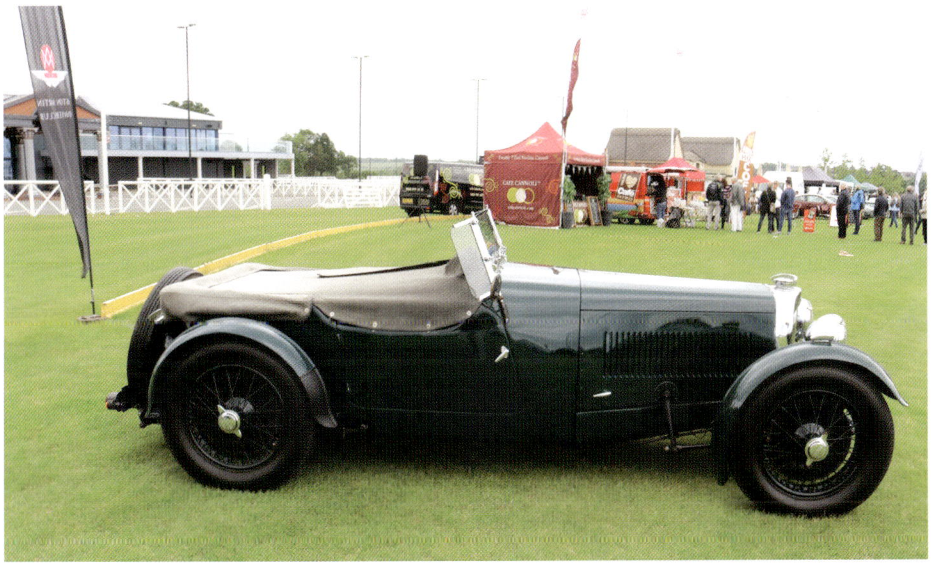

This 1934 1500cc example is typical of cars built by Aston Martin in the 1930s.

The 'modern' Aston Martin badge, seen here on ex-works car 'LM1', was designed by S.C.H. 'Sammy' Davis, the famous racing driver, journalist and team manager who owned LM1 as his daily driver in the 1930s.

**Post war the cars were fitted with the Sammy Davis-designed badge, seen here on the Aston Martin 2-litre Sports, the first model to go into production after World War II.**

**David Brown amended the badge to include his name during the 1950s. This original patinated example is from Chris Bland's DB5.**

was limited Lagonda car production. The Lagonda straight-six, dohc engine was adopted. Claude Hill left the company.

**1950:** DB2 was announced, powered by Lagonda's straight-six 2580cc dohc engine.

**1952:** The DB3 sports racer was developed by Robert Eberan von Eberhorst, to compete at Le Mans.

**1953:** The DB3S was developed by Willie Watson from the DB3. It was lighter and smaller.

**1958:** The definitive 'DB' model was introduced, the DB4, powered by the Tadek Marek-designed, all-new alloy 3670cc dohc straight six.

**1959:** The all-new, space-framed DBR1 won Le Mans and the World Sportscar championship. Aston Martin withdrew from racing.

**1961:** The Lagonda Rapide was introduced – four doors based on the DB chassis, powered by a 3995cc dohc straight six. Production ended in 1966 with just fifty-five cars produced.

**1963:** The DB5 was introduced with a larger 3995cc dohc straight six; it stars in the 1965 James Bond film *Goldfinger*.

**1965:** The DB6 was introduced, still obviously based on the DB4, but longer and with a restyled tail, and more interior room for rear passengers.

**1967:** The William Towns-designed DBS was introduced; it was still powered by the 3995cc straight six.

**1970:** The DBS finally received the all-new Tadek Marek-designed quad cam all-alloy 5340cc V8 engine; it was named the DBS V8.

**1972:** Aston Martin Lagonda was sold by David Brown to Company Developments, chaired by William Willson. The DB initials on cars were dropped.

**The DB4 came to epitomize the David Brown-era cars: smart Italian styling combined with great mechanicals and a strong engine to make a fine GT car.**

**After the DB6 came the DBS. Launched in 1967, the basic shape would be in production until the late 1980s.**

**1974:** The Aston Martin Lagonda Series I was introduced, a four-door derivative of the Towns-designed DBS.

**1974:** The receiver was brought in in December 1974; the production of cars stopped, but the service department continued running.

**1975:** In August, Aston Martin Lagonda (1975) Ltd was set up, with directors Peter Sprague (North American CEO of National Semiconductors), George Minden (Canadian Toronto-based hotelier and car dealer), Alan Curtis (British property developer) and George Flather (retired Sheffield Steel magnate). Production of the Aston Martin V8 resumed.

**1978:** The Lagonda Series II was introduced – the incredibly futuristic wedge-shaped four-door saloon designed by William Towns, which is now indelibly associated with the Lagonda name.

**1980:** Victor Gauntlett bought a 12.5 per cent stake in the company. Tim Hearley of CH Industrials (CHI) also took out a 12.5 per cent stake in 1980.

**1981:** Aston Martin Lagonda was sold to Victor Gauntlett and Tim Hearley, with Gauntlett taking over as executive chairman. Tickford set up as a subsidiary, providing engineering services to the motor industry.

**1983:** Gauntlett sold his share to Greek shipping magnate Peter Livanos; Livanos' share was invested through a joint venture between Livanos and fellow Greeks Nick and John Papanicolaou called 'ALL Inc'. While Gauntlett remain executive chairman, 55 per cent of Aston Martin Lagonda was owned by ALL Inc, with Tickford owned 50/50 by All Inc and CHI. CHI's shares in Aston Martin Lagonda were exchanged for ALL Inc's 50 per cent share of Tickford, and Tickford was separated from Aston Martin Lagonda, although it retained the responsibility for the development of existing models.

**1984:** Livanos' father George bought out ALL Inc's share, and Gauntlett bought a 25 per cent share in Aston Martin Lagonda.

**1986:** The limited edition V8 Zagato model was introduced.

**1987:** Ford took a 75 per cent shareholding in Aston Martin in September, then took over the company in 1991.

**1989:** The new Virage was introduced as a replacement for the V8.

**1991:** The remaining shares in Aston Martin Lagonda were bought by the Ford Motor Company, giving it 100 per cent of the company. Aston Martin Lagonda was placed in Ford's Premium Automotive Group (PAG). Development of the 'base' model DB7 started to give the marque a lower priced model to stimulate demand and give the company the volume of sales it needed to survive.

**1994:** The new DB7 was introduced, the new 'base' model of the Aston Martin range. It was built in the ex-Jaguar/TWR factory at Bloxham. It was priced below the hand-built 'V' cars.

**1999:** The new V12 engine was introduced, initially fitted in the DB7 Vantage. To begin with the engine was assembled by Cosworth.

**2000:** Ford appointed Dr Ulrich Bez as CEO of Aston Martin Lagonda.

**2001:** The Virage range was dropped in favour of the all-new Vanquish with its all-new chassis made from extruded alloy with glue and riveted construction, and new V12 engine. Vanquish slotted into the range above the DB7; it was produced at Newport Pagnell.

The car that arguably saved Aston Martin in the 1990s was the DB7. This is Richard Lovey's Volante example.

The current Aston Martin badge is still the traditional design, and is made in the old-fashioned way, with glass enamel applied over a heavily chromed casting. This is from the author's 2007 DB9.

**2004:** The DB7 was dropped, and the all-new DB9 with VH platform chassis and V12 engine was introduced. DB9 was produced at the all-new factory at Gaydon. An engine manufacturing facility was set up at Ford's Cologne plant, allowing all engines to be built 'in house'. The new V8 engine was unveiled.

**2005:** The second VH platform car was introduced, the V8 Vantage. It was designed as a sports car to compete with the Porsche 911.

**2007:** A consortium headed up by Prodrive chairman David Richards bought Aston Martin Lagonda from Ford for £475,000,000.

**2013:** Daimler AG bought a 5 per cent share in Aston Martin Lagonda with the intention of increasing it up to 20 per cent. Daimler would supply engines and electronics to AM.

**2014:** Andy Palmer was appointed CEO, replacing Dr Bez, and instigated a major development programme.

**2018:** Aston Matin Lagonda Global Holdings IPO was held on the London Stock Exchange Listing, making Aston Martin a publicly listed company.

**2020:** Canadian investor Lawrence Stroll led a consortium – which included Ernesto Bertarelli and Toto Wolff – that bought a 25 per cent share in the company. Tobias Moers from Mercedes AMG took over from Andy Palmer as CEO. Aston Martin re-entered Formula 1 motor racing, renaming Stroll's Racing Point team as Aston Martin. The DBX SUV joined the company's line-up.

**The first of the Gaydon era cars, the DB9. With its 'VH' aluminium chassis and Aston Martin V12 engine, it is every bit an Aston Martin Grand Tourer.**

**The second model to be produced at Gaydon was the two-seat sports car, the Vantage. This is Jeff Sear's V12 S model.**

## PRODUCTION NUMBERS

| Year | Cars Produced |
|---|---|
| 1914 | 1 |
| 1915 | 0 |
| 1916 | 0 |
| 1917 | 0 |
| 1918 | 0 |
| 1919 | 0 |
| 1920 | 2 |
| 1921 | 4 |
| 1922 | 3 |
| 1923 | 8 |
| 1924 | 25 |
| 1925 | 26 |
| 1926 | 0 |
| 1927 | 3 |
| 1928 | 13 |
| 1929 | 13 |
| 1930 | 69 |
| 1931 | 35 |
| 1932 | 30 |
| 1933 | 106 |
| 1934 | 104 |
| 1935 | 69 |
| 1936 | 15 |
| 1937 | 140 |
| 1938 | 14 |
| 1939 | 6 |
| 1940 | 1 |
| 1947 | 0 |
| 1948 | 7 |
| 1949 | 57 |
| 1950 | 191 |
| 1951 | 221 |
| 1952 | 351 |
| 1953 | 242 |
| 1954 | 324 |
| 1955 | 294 |
| 1956 | 199 |
| 1957 | 208 |
| 1958 | 308 |
| 1959 | 221 |
| 1960 | 358 |
| 1961 | 369 |
| 1962 | 245 |
| 1963 | 241 |
| 1964 | 590 |
| 1965 | 487 |
| 1966 | 591 |
| 1967 | 370 |
| 1968 | 488 |
| 1969 | 550 |
| 1970 | 467 |

| Year | Cars Produced |
|---|---|
| 1971 | 317 |
| 1972 | 245 |
| 1973 | 296 |
| 1974 | 256 |
| 1975 | 21 |
| 1976 | 175 |
| 1977 | 257 |
| 1978 | 276 |
| 1979 | 271 |
| 1980 | 193 |
| 1981 | 158 |
| 1982 | 135 |
| 1983 | 196 |
| 1984 | 204 |
| 1985 | 163 |
| 1986 | 193 |
| 1987 | 214 |
| 1988 | 193 |
| 1989 | 208 |
| 1990 | 201 |
| 1991 | 168 |
| 1992 | 46 |
| 1993 | 88 |
| 1994 | 169 |
| 1995 | 719 |
| 1996 | 653 |
| 1997 | 662 |
| 1998 | 625 |
| 1999 | 622 |
| 2000 | 1,029 |
| 2001 | 1,461 |
| 2002 | 1,465 |
| 2003 | 1,511 |
| 2004 | 2,069 |
| 2005 | 4,459 |
| 2006 | 7,052 |
| 2007 | 7,393 |
| 2008 | 6,487 |
| 2009 | 2,649 |
| 2010 | 4,500 |
| 2011 | 6,200 |
| 2012 | 3,500 |
| 2013 | 4,200 |
| 2014 | 3,661 |
| 2015 | 3,615 |
| 2016 | 3,687 |
| 2017 | 5,117 |
| 2018 | 6,441 |
| 2019 | 5,862 |
| 2020 | 4,150 |

## CARS PRODUCED BY ASTON MARTIN ON A YEARLY BASIS

This section gives an overview of the number of cars produced by Aston Martin on a year by year basis. The actual number of Aston Martins built, especially in the times before World War II, is still the subject of research and exploration, and numbers from different sources do vary. However, the object of this section is to give an idea of the relative volumes of cars produced over the company's existence, so the exact numbers are not as important as the overall pattern exhibited by the data. The data are broken up into the significant eras of the company: the Bamford and Martin years, the Bertelli and Sutherland years, the David Brown years, the Company Developments through to Gauntlett years the Ford years, the Ulrich Bez years (2000–2014) and finally the Andy Palmer era (2015–2020). While the graphs speak for themselves, there is some brief text to put the numbers in context.

### The Bamford and Martin Years (1913–1926)

In its early days Bamford and Martin produced only just over sixty cars in total, with a lot of the initial models being prototypes and works racing cars. While the market for cars was obviously smaller than today, the numbers produced were still low, and in some ways it is surprising that the company survived as long as it did – it was reliant on regular injections of cash just to keep going. The company only really got going in 1924 and 1925, with twenty-five and twenty-six cars produced – just before it finally ran out of cash.

### The Bertelli and Sutherland Years (1927–1946)

Rescued from obscurity by Bertelli and his all-new design of light car based on the 'Buzzbox', Aston Martin restarted production in 1927. Based in their new factory in Feltham, the company now had the space and facilities to start to produce cars in serious numbers. However, in their first year of operations (1927) only three cars were produced, and the increase in production was painfully slow, with only thirteen cars produced in 1928 and 1929. But 1930 was a bumper year, with sixty-nine cars produced, and while the next couple of years saw production fall back, 1933 was the company's first year of producing over 100 cars, a feat repeated in 1934 and 1937. Car production then inevitably tailed off as the factory turned its hand to more important war work.

**The DBS is the current flagship of the range. This is a 2019 example.**

**The DB5's Italian styling, GT credentials and of course the 'Bond' effect epitomized Aston Martin in the David Brown era. Here is Chris Bland's beautiful example basking in the sunshine.**

### The David Brown Years (1947–1972)

After World War II, with David Brown at the helm, Aston Martin started off the era slowly, with the 2-litre Sports model selling modestly. However, the introduction of the DB2 in 1950 saw demand and sales soar to unprecedented levels, with yearly production ranging between 199 and 324 up to the introduction of the DB4 in 1958. Production levels peaked at 590 in 1964 after the DB5 was introduced in 1963, and again in 1966 at 591 after the DB6's introduction in 1965. The DBS led to another peak in 1969 – but then production dropped off, with just 245 cars produced in 1972.

### The Company Developments/Curtis/Gauntlett Years (1973–1987)

With the sale of Aston Martin to Company Developments in 1973, production continued at 1972 levels for the first two years; but the company went into receivership in 1975, and production plummeted to a mere twenty-one cars as the factory was closed down. Sales recovered when the company was sold to the Alan Curtis consortium in 1975, with 257 cars sold in 1977. This set the scene for the following decade, during which sales were fairly steady at between 190 and 210 (with a bad year in 1982 with only 135 cars produced); this seems to have been just enough to keep the company afloat.

### The Ford Years (1987–1999)

The purchase of Aston Martin by Ford led to the DB7 – arguably the car that saved Aston Martin by demonstrating there was a market for a luxuriously appointed, well engineered GT car in the Aston Martin tradition. The introduction of the DB7 in 1995 which was produced in the old TWR/Jaguar factory at Bloxham, gave a massive boost to the sales figures of the company: sales of the expensive hand-built Newport Pagnell car slumped to a mere forty-six in 1992, as compared to 719 cars sold in 1995 – mostly DB7s, and the highest ever yearly production figure to date for Aston Martin. Sales of the cars remained over 600 through to 1999, when Dr Ulrich Bez took over.

### The Dr Ulrich Bez Years (2000–2014)

The turn of the century saw great changes at Aston Martin, with Dr Ulrich Bez at the helm and an all-new factory being built to produce a pair of brand new mainstream cars, the DB9 and the Vantage. Production of the DB7 continued at Bloxham until 2003, while the new factory at Gaydon was being built; then in 2004 car production at Gaydon took off with 1,608 DB9s being built, and was further boosted in 2005 as Vantage production started. The hand-built, top-of-the-range Vanquish also made a contribution, with over 500 units being built per year in 2002 and 2003; production dropped to just under 400 cars for 2004 and 2005. In 2006 and 2007 production built up to over 7,000 cars per year, but this was too much for the market, and led to oversupply. From 2008 production was dropped to more sustainable levels, but it was built back up from 2,649 units in 2009 to a steady level of around 3,500–4,000 units between 2010 and 2014.

### The Andy Palmer Years (2016–2020)

From 2015 to date, car production has fluctuated, thanks in part to the global shutdown caused by the Covid 19 pandemic. In the first years of Palmer's leadership production mirrored that of 2010–2014 at just over 3,500 cars, picking up to 5,117 cars in 2017, and peaking at 6,441 in 2018; it then dropped back a little in 2019 at 5,862, and then dropped to 4,150 in 2020 thanks mainly to the pandemic. The introduction of the DBX added another model line to the range for 2020, and hopefully the following years will see a sustainable increase in production numbers.

### Production Numbers: Conclusion

As can be seen from the figures, Aston Martin has never been a mass producer of cars. While this has helped the marque's exclusivity, it has not assisted in the company's liquidity, and most of the financial crises the company has gone through have been caused by failing to build and sell enough cars. It was only when Ford appeared on the scene that Aston Martin received the financial stability and commitment it needed to become the company that we see today – a resurgent Aston Martin with a relatively wide and up-to-date range of models that it is to be hoped will enable the company to trade successfully into the 2020s and onwards.

## BOND AND ASTON MARTIN

When writing about Aston Martin in general, and the David Brown cars in particular, there is no escaping one aspect of the car's life. Never mind Aston Martin winning Le Mans in 1959, it was another event that gave Aston Martin what was probably the company's best advertising ever, which extended from 1964 through to the present day: the appearance of the gadget-laden DB5 in the 1964 Bond film *Goldfinger* alongside

Sean Connery as Bond. While it was probably the first 'product placement' in the film industry that made a lasting impression on viewers, it was not your average 'product placement', as the car with its extras devised by 'Q' was an integral part of the story told by the movie, and made Aston Martin the car of choice for all secret (or not so secret) agents. The author remembers seeing and being inspired by the car in *Goldfinger*, and of course owned (and still owns) the original Corgi model.

The reappearance of the Bond DB5 (or a replica, but it did retain the original *Goldfinger* car's registration number, BMT 216A) in the 2012 Bond film *Skyfall* was a master stroke. When the author watched the film shortly after it was released, the appearance of the car as Bond opened the warehouse doors elicited an auditable gasp from the audience in the cinema – and there were many groans when the 'baddies' shot the car to pieces later on! From the marque's first appearance in *Goldfinger*, Aston Martins have featured in many of the later Bond films, and are now firmly entrenched in the myth that is Bond.

The first Bond movie was 1962's *Dr No*, when Bond had a brief but exciting car chase driving a standard Sunbeam Alpine pursued by an enormous LaSalle hearse, albeit with a lot of studio footage using back projections with Bond see-sawing furiously on the Alpine's wheel! The second film, 1963's *From Russia With Love*, featured Bond in a 1935 Bentley 3.5 drophead coupé fitted with a car phone, albeit only briefly – the action then moved to Turkey, where cars played a subsidiary role to the action. It was in the third Bond film, 1965's *Goldfinger* – still starring Sean Connery – that the first real Bond car made its debut. Fleming's novel, written in 1958 and published in 1959, had placed Bond in the driving seat of an Aston Martin Mark III – assumed now to be a DB2/4 Mark III – so the obvious choice for the film was the then current Aston Martin product, the DB5.

And so was born a cinematic legend, as the iconic Silver Birch DB5, used by Bond to track Auric Goldfinger's Rolls-Royce across Europe, was introduced to the public. It wasn't just the car's looks that caught the public's imagination: the DB5 was fitted with lots of gadgets, including a pair of Browning machine guns in the front wings, the famous ejector seat, telescopic overriders, extendable tyre-chewing rear spinners, a rear bullet-proof screen, rotating number plates, and oil and tack dispensers in the rear lights – a fine collection of nefarious equipment well suited to Bond's role. Of course it all ends in tears at Goldfinger's factory when Bond is dazzled by searchlights and crashes the car, coming round to find himself strapped to the laser table – and of course Goldfinger's classic retort to Bond's question 'Do you expect me to talk?' – 'No Mr Bond, I expect you to die!'

The car was further immortalized by die-cast model car makers Corgi, whose 1:43 scale DB5, with most of the gadgets incorporated, was a massive hit with the fans. There must have been hundreds or thousands of tiny Goldfinger henchmen

**From the front the Bond DB5 shows the telescopic over-riders and the two Browning machine guns concealed behind the indicator lights.**

**This view of the Bond DB5 shows the ejector seat's offset panel in the roof, the extending spinners, the bullet-proof rear screen, telescopic over-riders and the ports in the rear lights to dispense oil, water and tacks.**

scattered and lost in suburban homes after too enthusiastic a use of the model's tiny ejector seat!

After the brief appearance of the DB5 in the starting sequence of 1965's *Thunderball*, where Bond chucks his jet pack into the boot before using more gadgetry – water cannons – to discourage the baddies before roaring off, the next appearance of an Aston Martin in a Bond film came with the 1969 film *On Her Majesty's Secret Service*. In this production Australian actor George Lazenby was in the starring role, along with a largely gadget-free olive green DBS, registration number GKX 8G. The car's appearance started with the lead girl Contessa Teresa 'Tracy' di Vicenzo (played by Diana Rigg) briefly stealing it, and ended with the unforgettable scene on the side of the motorway, bullet holes in the windscreen and Tracy dead beside Bond after their marriage.

The next appearance of an Aston Martin was in 1971's *Diamonds Are Forever*, when there was a brief glimpse of a DBS in Q's workshop. Aston Martin was then absent from the first Roger Moore-era Bond film, as Lotus, that other British sports-car company, provided cars for the next films. The Lotus Esprit that becomes a submarine appeared in the 1977 film, *The Spy Who Loved Me*, starring Roger Moore; Moore had of course starred in the early 1970s ITC television series *The Persuaders* as Lord Brett Sinclair, in which he drove a yellow DBS dressed up to look like a V8, alongside Tony Curtis playing playboy Danny Wilde and driving a Ferrari Dino. The Esprit featured in one other Roger Moore-era Bond film: 1981's *For Your Eyes Only*, although arguably the co-starring Citroen 2CV was given a better role!

The franchise finally returned to Aston Martin after lobbying in 1987 by company executive chairman Victor Gauntlett, with *The Living Daylights*, when Timothy Dalton took over from Moore as Bond and drove a new gadget-laden Aston Martin V8, registration number B549 WUU. Equipped with missiles, side-mounted retractable skis, a jet engine in the rear and laser side cutters – a modern update on the original DB5's extending spinners – along with bulletproof glass, the V8 reverted to the form that most Bond fans loved. The car endured an eventful chase with Communist border guards, which as usual resulted in the unfortunate car being blown up as Bond and the girl escaped by tobogganing over the border into the West in a cello case. There was also a cameo appearance from Gauntlett's personal V8 Volante, which Dalton drove early on in the film.

The next film in the franchise, 1989's *Licence to Kill*, had no Astons in it, and there was then a long hiatus in their appearance in Bond films; this only ended in 1995 with the release of *Goldeneye*, starring Pierce Brosnan. Although the producers had signed up BMW to supply the main cars for the franchise, DB5 BMT 214A made a welcome (if slightly unconvincing) appearance in *Goldeneye*, in a chase sequence where the DB5 outruns a modern Ferrari F355 GTS. In 1999 the DB5 made another brief appearance in *The World is Not Enough*, again starring Pierce Brosnan – but Aston Martin were firmly back in the running in the last Brosnan film, *Die Another Day*. In this 2002 production the brand new Aston Martin Vanquish was the real star – that is, when you could see it, as one of its gadgets was an invisibility cloak. The offensive side of the gadgets was not forgotten, with four missile launchers hidden behind the grille, heavy machine guns in the nose, and a pair of multi-barrelled Gatling gun-style miniguns mounted on swivels on the front wings. All in all a fitting return to the franchise for the new Gaydon era of Aston Martin – even if the Vanquish was build at Newport Pagnell!

In the year 2006 the Bond film returned after a four-year hiatus, with a new lead actor and a grittier, more down-to-earth approach to the story, albeit with the plots placed firmly in the twenty-first century. In *Casino Royale* Daniel Craig played a more flawed but ruthless character rooted in the current geopolitical scene, whilst the storyline stayed quite close to the original plot penned by Ian Fleming in 1953.

The main car that Craig drove in *Casino Royale* was a Gaydon-era DBS, although there is a cameo role for a silver DB5, which Craig wins in a card game in the Bahamas. Aston Martin had not launched the DBS when the film was released, but had supplied two prototypes for filming. Gadgets were limited to a defibrillator and a gun stowed in a sliding draw in the glovebox – the defibrillator maybe being a sensible item that Aston Martin should consider offering as an extra to its older customers? The car's main role in the film was to be sacrificed in a spectacular sequence when Bond wrenches the steering wheel over at speed to avoid running over the female lead, double agent Vesper Lynd (played by Eva Green), who had been dumped in the middle of the road by the villains. The DBS perished in a spectacular sequence of seven complete rolls – a sequence that has been recorded in *The Guinness Book of Records* as a new world record.

The DBS does return briefly in the next film, the 2008 *Quantum of Solace*, participating in a destructive car chase around Lake Garda, with Bond being pursued by a posse of black Alfa Romeo 159s – but otherwise the car is absent. The next Daniel Craig film was 2012's *Skyfall*, in which (as recounted above) the classic silver DB5 makes its appearance, much to the delight of the audience – although it, too, meets its doom.

The next film, *Spectre*, came out in 2015, and again, as in the 2006 *Casino Royale*, featured an Aston Martin that was produced exclusively for the film. The DB10, while obviously a development of the *Casino Royale/Quantum of Solace* DBS, was futuristic and unique. Powered by the V8 engine and designed by Marek Reichman, the DB10's styling was amazing – but the gadgetry was limited to a flame-thrower in the tail, put to use in a duel in Rome with the 'bad guy' in a Jaguar C-X75 concept car – another that never made it into production.

The latest Bond film, *No Time to Die*, was supposed to be released in 2020, but Covid put paid to that, and at the time of writing (February 2021) the film had not been released. There were tasters though – the film features the classic silver DB5, in both the pre-credits scenes filmed in Italy and in the film itself. Eight new DB5s were made for the film, using laser scanning to perfect the carbon-fibre bodywork, with modern underpinnings for the stunt drivers to play with. Gadgets had been brought up to date, with multi-barrelled miniguns replacing the front Brownings to devastating effect, while the ejector seat was primed and ready. The classic V8 last seen in Timothy Dalton's *The Living Daylights* also makes an appearance, along with a right up-to-date DBS Superleggera. All in all the film promises to be a real treat for any Aston Martin aficionado, and hopefully is well worth waiting for!

The Bond franchise has been of immense value to Aston Martin. Obviously from a marketing point of view the cars were popularized virtually every time a Bond film was made or screened, and this exposure has brought the marque into the public eye worldwide. It has also placed it precisely where it needs to be: as an exclusive product that is expensive but not so out of reach that ownership is unattainable. Furthermore it has generated a great deal of goodwill for the brand, which is instantly recognizable to most people thanks to the films – and people are usually genuinely pleased to see an Aston Martin on the road. All in all the placement of that first DB5 in *Goldfinger* was of inestimable value to Aston Martin and the Bond franchise, and long may the relationship endure.

CHAPTER 2

# THE FORMATIVE YEARS: 1913–1925

Aston Martin's early products were very different to those produced by the company after World War II up until the present day, with its product line of large capacity, high performance GT cars. When it was formed, the company was dedicated to extracting the maximum performance from the then current crop of 'light' cars, which featured lightweight bodies and engines of less than 1500cc, eschewing the large capacity behemoths – or 'Chittys' – that had dominated the performance arena at the turn of the century. Aston Martin's founders, Robert Bamford and Lionel Martin, were determined to produce small, light, beautifully engineered cars that could take on and beat their rivals on the road and track, and this was the successful philosophy that would dominate the company for its first decades.

## ESTABLISHMENT OF THE COMPANY

The story of Aston Martin started in 1913 with the establishment of a motor company by engineer Robert Bamford and old Etonian Lionel Martin. The company was called Bamford and Martin Ltd, and was initially based in Callow Street in Fulham, West London. The company was set up not only to sell and tune light cars, such as Singer, Calthorpe and GWK, but also to crystallize and refine Martin's emerging ideas of a perfect lightweight sporting car, and to manufacture it.

The company had arranged a sub-agency for Singer through Percy Lambert, Singer dealer and motor racer, and Martin had personally bought a Singer 10hp from Singer at the London Motor Show at Olympia in 1912, which he had been using in various competitions, including speed trials and hill climbs. The company quickly moved to larger premises in Henniker Place in South Kensington – and this relocation also brought along a new employee, Jack Addis.

The company specialized in buying and selling all light cars, as well as tuning customers' cars and competing in various events with Martin's tuned Singer 10. The origin of the Aston Martin name is obscure, but there are various theories that it was as a result of Martin competing at the Aston Clinton hill climb in his Singer 10-based Special, along with the need to

**Two of the oldest surviving Aston Martins, 'A3' and 'Razor Blade', reunited and pictured on the Brooklands banking in May 2021.**

**Brooklands in 1921 with Aston Martins at the start of the JCC 200-mile race. The Coal Scuttle is no. 20, 'Bunny' is no. 40 and Count Zborowski in the 'track car' is no. 66.**

get the company's name at the top of the alphabetical listings in the press of the day.

In 1914 the company used the name 'Aston Martin' on the first car produced by Bamford and Martin; this car is now known as the 'Hybrid' and was based on an Isotta-Fraschini chassis and a Coventry Simplex motor. It was designed to test Martin's ideas of the perfect light car, and was built while the company waited for a chassis of their own design to be produced. Very little is known about this first product of the infant company, and the car no longer exists.

With the outbreak of war, activity at Bamford and Martin slowed, and the machinery at Henniker Place was eventually sold to the Sopwith Aviation Company for war work. Bamford, who was a member of one of the London cyclist reserve battalions, was commissioned into the Army Service Corps. During the war period extensive testing work was carried out by Martin using the second car the company produced. This car was nicknamed the 'Coal Scuttle' and was based on a new chassis, and powered by an engine based on the Coventry Simplex design used in the Hybrid, but likely to have been built specifically for Bamford and Martin.

In 1918 the company reconvened in the pre-war premises in Henniker Place. During 1919 and 1920 the company's activities concentrated on developing their product, and racing was the medium used to test and advance these developments. The various prototype cars produced were raced extensively, giving the company results that could be channelled back into ever-improving designs. However, development work was expensive, and with little or no money coming in from car sales the company was reliant on Martin's personal wealth. Bamford left the company in 1920 for reasons unknown – perhaps because he considered that any chance of advancement in Bamford and Martin as a producer of cars for actual customers seemed a long way off.

Just after he left, in May 1920 the company moved and set up home in new premises at what was originally No. 51 Abingdon Road (now renumbered No. 53) in Kensington. While the company was not renamed to reflect Bamford's leaving, Bamford himself was replaced on the board by Martin's wife Kate. Kate was not, and never had been, a sleeping partner in the company – she had already thrown herself into the racing programme with some enthusiasm, and was often pictured alongside Martin at various sporting events. She was no mean competitor herself, acting as a passenger for Martin in many of the events he competed in, and she also competed in her own right. As an example, she won the Junior Car Club's Ladies Race at Brooklands in 1920 driving the venerable 'Coal Scuttle' (AM4656) at an average speed of 63mph (101km/h).

In 1922 Count Louis Zborowski invested in the company, financing the construction of two cars to compete in that year's French Grand Prix at Strasburg; he also had a seat on

**A typical Brooklands scene with Kate Martin driving the Coal Scuttle at the JCC Spring Meeting in May 1921.**

the board until his untimely death while racing his Mercedes at the Monza track in Italy in 1924. As a result of his investment of some £10,000, the two cars were fitted with the new dohc 'Gremillion' engine; however, both cars failed to finish.

During this time Martin was cultivating many young and enthusiastic motoring enthusiasts, recognizing that the job of racing Bamford and Martin cars competitively needed more talent than he himself, his wife Kate or works foreman Jack Addis had. Racer and engineer H. Kensington-Moir, a name that would be synonymous with Aston Martin cars during the early 1920s, joined the firm in mid-1921, coming from a post as engineer at Zenith Carburettors after completing his apprenticeship at ABC cars. While much of the success of the company in competition was the result of Kensington-Moir's fine driving, he was destined to move to Bentley, having met with the famous W.O. Bentley himself on the ferry coming back from the abortive trip to compete in the Isle of Man TT race.

Although by 1922 the company had seen a great deal of success in competition, it was still not actually producing any cars. In early 1922 Martin, accompanied by Zborowski, made a trip to Bristol to visit 'an aeroplane firm' to see if they could raise sufficient funds to start producing cars; however, the trip was fruitless, and the company continued to just limp along.

Actual production of road cars for customers eventually started in early 1923, when the first customer car was delivered to a W.G. Barlow. This car was chassis number 1916, and featured front brakes based on the Perrot system. Perrot brakes operating on the front wheels became a fixture on Bamford and Martin production cars from the early 1920s, and were often retrofitted to older cars. The Perrot brake system was devised by Frenchman Henri Perrot while he was working for vehicle manufacturer Argyll in Alexandrea in West Dumbartonshire, Scotland. The system was registered on 18 March 1910 at the British patent office as patent number 6807. It allowed the fitment of mechanically operated brakes to the steered wheels, using a system of universal joints and shafts to connect the movable brake-drum backplate to the chassis-mounted operating cables or rods. The Perrot system eventually led to the formation of the Bendix Corporation by Vincent Bendix in South Bend, Indiana, in 1924. Martin gained a licence to manufacture Perrot-type brakes from the original manufacturers in December 1923.

In fact the 'production' of cars at 51 Abingdon Road was in reality more of an assembly operation, with the twenty or so workers who made up the company payroll assembling bought-in components: chassis frames from Rubery Owen, engine blocks from Rowland Hill and Sons of Coventry, crankshafts from Ambrose Shardlow, and gearboxes from E.G. Wrigley. Other minor components would be bought in as required. Most of the engine components and other parts that needed machining were worked on by Weybridge Engineering at Brooklands and Giusti Patents of Euston Road, so very little actual manufacturing was carried out on site. This is confirmed by the limited amount of machine tools discovered when the premises were inspected by Bert Bertelli after the sale of the company in 1926.

There was no bodyshop at the Abingdon Road premises, so bodies for the racing and production cars were produced by external but relatively nearby coach builders; these included local firms Jarvis of Wimbledon, Compton and Hermon of Thames Ditton, Albany of Hanwell and Moss of the Fulham Road. The cars came in all sorts of body style, including open-topped two- or four-seaters, four-seat saloons, and the then popular 'clover-leaf' three-seaters. Production of the Martin-era Aston Martin cars was small, with just eight cars produced in 1923, twenty-five in 1924 and twenty-seven in 1925; production ceased in November of that year.

John Benson was taken on in May 1924 to perform the role of chief engineer. Benson was the son and heir of the first Lord Charnwood, and like Martin had been at Eton before going up to Oxford to study engineering. Although he left without a degree he was by all accounts a talented engineer, and his appointment was no doubt helped by the prospect of his mother, Lady Charnwood, putting £5,000 into the business.

The Bamford and Martin company of 53 Abingdon Road ran out of money and called in the official receiver on 11 November 1925; Lionel Martin left the company two days later. The family of John Benson, then chief engineer and designer of the Aston Martin engine, purchased the goodwill and assets of Aston Martin, and then approached the Birmingham firm of Renwick and Bertelli with the intention of forming an alliance to rekindle the ashes of Aston Martin.

## BAMFORD AND MARTIN ENGINES

While the Hybrid, Bamford and Martin's first complete car, was powered by a proprietary 4-cylinder side-valve Coventry Simplex engine, all the cars produced after the Hybrid were powered by engines designed and built either for or by Bamford and Martin. All these early engines were 4-cylinder in-line units of varying capacities, but all were just under the 1499cc capacity limit required for the RAC Light Car racing class. Engine configurations reflected the rapid development of engine technology of the time, and Bamford and Martin's thirst for innovation. They ranged from simple side-valve units with combined cylinder head and block, to 4-valve-per-cylinder units, with the valves operated by double overhead camshafts, as well as single overhead camshaft 8-valve and 16-valve units, giving a range that covered most possible combinations

This 1924 car fitted with a 'clover-leaf' three-seater body is typical of the early Bamford and Martin cars.

The oldest surviving Aston Martin, A3, is preserved by the AMHT.

of valve operating gear that could be used on a straight-four engine. Oddly the company in these early days did not produce a simple pushrod-operated overhead valve unit – although this would be in keeping with its sporting profile.

## The Side-Valve 4-Cylinder Engine

Based closely on the Coventry Simplex unit used in the Hybrid, Bamford and Martin's first engine was a 4-cylinder, side-valve, 1486cc unit, with a bore and stoke of 66.5 × 107mm (giving an RAC rating of 11.6hp and still qualifying for the RAC Light Car class limit of 1500cc), a three-bearing crankshaft and a combined cast-iron cylinder block and head – usually described as a 'monobloc'. The combined block and head was used to avoid head-gasket problems, which were common at the time with separate head and block designs. The combined head and cylinder block was bolted on to a light alloy crankcase, which had cast-in 'bearer arms' on each side that were used to mount the engine directly on the chassis. The crankshaft was carried on three main bearings.

The engine was designed with two aims in mind, reliability with power, and to this end a great deal of thought was given to keeping the engine oil clean. This meant that a considerable amount of time and effort was given to the design of the lubrication system, both in terms of the use of the system and the filtration of the oil. The filler was placed in a prominent position on the right-hand side of the crankcase, and when the cap was swung open sideways it also operated a small level tap – when the oil reached the correct level, it would dribble from the tap indicating that the sump was filled to the correct level. A second, larger tap was used to drain the oil from the

**The Aston Martin 1486cc side-valve engine was the first production engine made by Aston. Note the one-piece cylinder block and head, and how the lower crankcase bearer arms are bolted directly into the chassis members.**

sump, and a dipstick was also fitted. Oil was pumped from the sump under pressure to all the engine bearings, and a pressure release valve diverted excess oil to the timing gear in the side of the crankcase.

The oil filtration system comprised three distinct filters. First, a gauze filter was placed in the filler tube to stop debris getting into the engine in the first place; then there was a gauze tray fitted above the sump to catch any large particles from falling from the engine into the sump; and finally there was a patented nest of three gauze filters on the pressure side of the oil pump, through which the oil was forced before it got to the oilways in the crankcase that served the engine bearings.

## The Robb Single-Overhead Camshaft Engine

While the 4-cylinder side valve was producing some relatively high power outputs, the company recognized the advantages of the increased efficiency of overhead-valve designs. So Aston Martin's first overhead-valve engine design was commissioned, with engineer S. Robb, formerly of Coventry Simplex, employed to produce a new engine with the intention of fitting it to at least one of the 'works' race cars. The result was a new unit with a single shaft-driven overhead camshaft operating 16 valves (4 per cylinder) using a complex system of rockers and pushrods.

The camshaft was carried in five bearings and had the rocker shaft mounted above it, which was also carried in five bearings. The rocker shaft carried eight forked rockers, each one operated from the camshaft by a roller, and each of which was connected to two valves using short rods. The valves were all positioned vertically in the casting, and had relatively long bronze guides to allow for the high side thrust generated by the rocker mechanism.

The iron cylinder block and head were cast in one piece, and there were large plates fitted on the sides of the engine to give access to the rocker gear. The water jacket covered the upper part of the cylinders and the head, while the lower half of each cylinder was exposed to the air; there was also an air gap between each cylinder to aid cooling. The cast-alloy crankcase was, like the side-valve unit, a large aluminium casting with cast-in bearer arms or webs to fix it to the chassis frame. The positions of the webs were identical to those seen on the side-valve engine, so making the units interchangeable. The crankshaft was carried on three shell main bearings.

At the front of the engine the camshaft driving shaft was gear-driven from the nose of the crankshaft, and the shaft also drove a horizontal geartrain located in a rectangular alloy casing. This geartrain was used to drive a vertically positioned magneto, the water pump and the oil pump, all mounted on the left-hand side of the engine. With a bore and stroke of 65 × 112mm, the engine displaced 1486cc.

The engine was not particularly successful, mainly because although it was reliable, it showed little if any power increase over the side-valve unit, contemporary reports stating it gave a mere 40bhp. The engine design was therefore recognized as being a dead end from a developmental point of view, so the unit was eventually scrapped.

## The Double-Overhead Camshaft 'Gremillion' Engine

When Bamford and Martin realized that the first Robb-designed 16-valve engine was not particularly powerful, they still recognized the advantages of overhead valves, and so with financial help from Count Zborowski they decided to commission a new racing unit to replace the side-valve engine. The question was how to avoid another dud like the Robb-designed single overhead camshaft unit. Luckily one of the 'works' drivers, Clive Gallop, had served his apprenticeship at Peugeot, and knew talented engine engineer Marcel Gremillion, who had designed the successful straight-eight 3-litre Ballot engine. The company approached him, and apparently for the sum of £50, Gremillion arranged for drawings of a scaled-down version of the Ballot engine's cylinder block and head to be made available to Bamford and Martin.

The company used the new design to modify the original Robb-designed overhead cam engine, replacing the combined head and barrels of the original engine with the new design. The intention was to use the new engine to compete in the 1922 French Grand Prix – the first international event for a factory-entered Aston-Martin car.

The new top end was designed around the bottom end of the rejected single camshaft engine designed by Robb, keeping that engine's bore centres and retaining its bore and stoke of 65 × 112mm, giving a capacity of 1487cc. The 4-valve engine had a pair of separate alloy camshaft carriers that were bolted to an integral head and barrel assembly. Inlet valves of 31mm diameter and exhaust valves of 29mm were fitted, also twin valve springs, and the valve angle was 60 degrees. The valves were operated directly from the cam lobes using bucket tappets, and the two camshafts were carried on three large-diameter roller bearings. As on the previous engine the camshafts were driven from the crank by a vertical shaft. Each camshaft had a gear attached to its end, and these meshed with a central gear, which was driven from the vertical shaft using a bevel gear.

Retaining the existing engine's bore centres meant that the valves were placed asymmetrically, and the valve pockets in the head were relatively large, which constrained the engine's

**The exhaust side of the 1924 1.5-litre dohc engine.**

**The carburettor side of the 1924 Bamford and Martin 1.5-litre dohc engine.**

breathing; but despite this design compromise, the new unit was reported to produce 55bhp and revved up to 4,200rpm, a significant improvement over the 40bhp given by the side-valve unit and the Robb sohc engine. This gave the Strasbourg cars a top speed of around 95mph (153km/h).

While the new top end and barrels endowed the engine with a significant performance boost, the engine's Achilles heel turned out to be the magneto drive. The drive was by a laminated spring coupling, which often failed, the problem causing both the cars in the French race not to finish. The problem reoccurred at a later 200-mile race, but the substitution of a different drive coupling and modifications to the magneto platform solved the problem. Another problem was found to be failure of the exhaust springs, thanks to the pronounced lift and fall of the valves given by the cam profile; luckily in the French Grand Prix the use of double springs meant that this failure was not catastrophic.

Once the magneto drive problems were overcome about six further engines were produced: these were raced by the works for the following two seasons in various works cars, as well as by customer cars with some success. A couple of the engines were also fitted to racing boats, notably Major Johnson-Noad's *Miss Betty*, which had a hull designed by a Mr McCrow and which won the Duke of York's Trophy in the early 1920s.

## The Double Overhead Camshaft Benson Engine

The replacement for the 16-valve 'Gremillion' engine was designed by John Benson during 1924–25, and was a double overhead camshaft 8-valve design. Ultimately Benson wanted to base the engine on a bore and stroke of 74 × 89mm, giving a much shorter stroke with all the advantages that it gave – but a prototype cylinder head was designed to fit on the 65 × 112mm dimensions of the bottom end of the previous Robb-designed 16-valve single overhead cam engine base to avoid producing a completely new unit before the head design was proved. The new engine had a detachable cylinder head, and its overhead cams were driven by a train of gears.

The valve operation was similar to that of the previous 16-valve unit, using bucket tappets to enclose the valve springs and operate the valves directly from the cam lobe. Valves were spaced at 45 degrees to the vertical, giving 90 degrees between the valves, and the inlet and exhaust valves were both 45mm in diameter. The sparkplug was set into an insert between the valves. The new engine gave an exceptional 60bhp when tested.

The first example was installed in a new racing boat for Major Johnson-Noad to succede *Miss Betty*, but the new boat proved to be unstable and incapable of taking the power. However, the head design was considered to be a success, and Martin authorized the production of two further engines, with the originally proposed bore and stroke of 74 × 89mm. In this new guise and with a relatively low compression ratio of 5.6:1 the engine gave a creditable 64–65bhp at 4,500rpm, another significant increase from the previous Aston Martin engines. It appears that only one unit of the proposed two engines was built: this was installed in long chassis car number 1964 and displayed on the Aston Martin stand at the 1925 Motor Show at Olympia.

The car was bought by Benson, who used it as his personal road transport up to 1933 with apparently good reliability, although the increase in power took its toll on the clutch, would twist the propshaft ends and also break the differential mounting bolts. During 1936–37 Benson fitted the engine with a Zoller supercharger and a single-seat body. He sold the car in the late 1930s and it was later broken up.

## The Production Car Engine

Despite the company's experimentation with various configurations of overhead valve and overhead camshaft engines, the production cars produced between 1921 and 1926 were fitted as standard with a side-valve engine. This was similar in design and layout to the unit that powered the early cars, with a monobloc one-piece cast-iron cylinder, and barrels mounted on a cast-alloy crankcase and a cast-alloy sump. At the front and rear of the crankcase casting were extensions that were joined by a fillet, which filled in the space between the chassis members; it was used to bolt the engine in place, with the bolts passing horizontally through the chassis longerons. This arrangement stiffened the crankcase and the front of the chassis.

The aluminium sump bolted directly on to the crankcase, and the three plain main bearings were sandwiched between the crankcase and the sump – there were no separate bearing caps as such, and the crank could be removed when the sump was detached. With a bore and stroke of 66.5 × 107mm and a capacity of 1486cc, and with a standard compression ratio of 5.5:1 (there was an option of an alternative 5.8:1), the unit produced 45bhp and maximum torque of 56.5lb ft at 4,000rpm.

**The Bamford and Martin 1.5-litre side-valve had a combined cylinder and head mounted on an alloy crankcase. The exhaust exits on the left-hand side, and the carburettor is on the right.**

## THE FIRST CARS

Bamford and Martin's first true production cars only appeared in 1923, starting with chassis no. 1917. Prior to this, the company produced a number of cars that were devoted to racing, and were powered by various engines.

Lionel Martin's own car, a Singer 10 bought in 1912 (registered LH3019), was an important element in the start of the company. The car had been completely stripped and rebuilt, and the engine's camshaft re-profiled to increase performance. The car was mainly entered into the popular long-distance trials of the time, including the London to Lands End Trial and the London to Exeter, with some success. All this competition work led to a demand from customers for the nascent company to tune their cars, a task that Martin and Bamford took on enthusiastically.

### The Hybrid and the Coal Scuttle

There is a bit of a mystery surrounding the first two cars produced by Bamford and Martin between 1913 and 1919. While busy tuning cars for customers and competition, and with Martin competing in his company-modified Singer, the first car badged as an Aston-Martin (note the use of the hyphen) was produced by the company in 1913. The car is fairly well documented, and was an amalgam of parts, using an old 1908 vintage Isotta-Fraschini chassis and a newly bought Coventry Simplex motor of 1400cc. It appears that it was road registered locally with the mark LH 7933, 'LH' being the registration code for London.

The car was first used by Martin to compete in the 1914 Motor Cycle Club Brighton Trial, just before World War I intervened and all such motor sport was banned; when Bamford left to join the armed forces, activity at the company was greatly reduced for the duration. However, the company had started to build a second development car, which would be used during the war and after hostilities had ended. This car would be nicknamed the 'Coal Scuttle'.

Once the company of Bamford and Martin reconvened after the war in 1919 they were still using the 'Coal Scuttle', the second car ever to be badged as an Aston-Martin, although the 'Hybrid' had vanished. Martin had registered the 'Coal Scuttle' at the Trowbridge (some sources say Swindon) licensing office in Wiltshire as AM 4656 in March 1915. The 'AM' prefix was issued by that particular licensing office (and the rest of Wiltshire), and it was an obvious marketing ploy for the company to get the car registered at Trowbridge rather than at the company's local office, where it would have been given a London 'LH' prefix. 'AM' prefix registrations were used on a number of the prototypes until the Trowbridge registration office ran out of numbers.

**This picture was taken in 1920, and shows the Coal Scuttle being driven by Lionel Martin.**

AM 4656 was christened the 'Coal Scuttle' by the factory. A two-seater, the car's main feature was the way the scuttle was sloped upwards from the end of the bonnet to the windscreen, which gave the car the appearance of a traditional coal scuttle – hence the nickname. Unlike the first Hybrid, the Coal Scuttle was powered by a 4-cylinder side-valve engine built specifically for Bamford and Martin, and designed by ex-Coventry Simplex designer S. Robb. While the engine was unique to Bamford and Martin, it obviously owed a lot to previous Coventry Simplex designs. The 4-cylinder in-line engine had a split crankcase made in cast-aluminium alloy, a three main bearing crankshaft and a combined block and cylinder head. With a bore and stroke of 66.5 × 107mm, the engine displaced 1486.5cc, close to the 1500cc limit of the Light Car class.

On completion the car was driven extensively during the war years, and then set to work in competition to prove the concept of the sporting light car and provide publicity for the company.

### The Post-World War I Cars: The First Prototype

Following on from the experience gained from building and running the Hybrid and Coal Scuttle, three prototype chassis were bought from Rubery-Owen during 1920. Built to Bamford and Martin's design, the three chassis had a wheelbase of 102in (2,590mm) and were designed to have semi-elliptical rear springs. However, the chassis side rails were only 3in (7.62cm) deep, and this proved to be their undoing. In an article in *Old Motor* Aston Martin employee F.G. Hunt recounts how these chassis were 'rough' when they arrived – presumably meaning they were unfinished. Hunt had to rivet the dumb-irons on to the front of the units using a hand-made dolly, though he does say that they 'never shifted'.

The first chassis was built up as a complete car during 1920 and early 1921; it was written up in the March 1921 edition

## THE FIRST PRODUCTION CARS

| Name | Chassis number | Notes | Registration number (date) |
|---|---|---|---|
| The Hybrid | Not known | Built in 1913, based on a 1908 vintage Isotta-Fraschini chassis and a newly bought Coventry Simplex motor of 1400cc. | LH 7399 |
| 'Coal Scuttle' | A1 | Probably built in 1914/15. Racked up many miles before the company reformed in 1920. | AM 4656 |
| First prototype/'Bunny' | B2 1909B SV | First use of the three initial Rubery-Owen chassis. The chassis was then shortened and strengthened, and it was believed used for 'Bunny' with the new registration number AM273. | XH 2800/AM 273 |
| AM 270 | B2 1909SV | The second Aston-Martin prototype; it originally used the Rubery-Owen chassis, was produced early in 1921 and road registered AM 270; it was fitted with a completely new chassis with the chassis number of 1909. | AM 270 |
| A3: Pre-production car 1, black two-seater | No. 3 / 1918 | The third Aston Martin prototype using the third Rubery Owen chassis. The earliest known surviving Aston Martin. Side-valve two-seater, all black finish, nicknamed N***** in the 1920s. Bought and raced by Capt. J.C. Douglas. Later owned by R.W. Mallabar, with grey body and QD wings painted red. | AM 273 (1921);<br>also used XN 2902 and AM 270 |
| 200-mile car (1 – side-valve) | 1910R | Used the original first or second Rubery-Owen chassis in strengthened form. Long-chassis racing streamlined two-seater. | AM 273 (1922) |
| 200-mile car (2 – 16-valve dohc) | 1910 | Used the original first or second Rubery-Owen chassis in strengthened form. | |
| French (Strasburg) Grand Prix car (1) | 1914 (TT1) | Driven by Zborowski in the French Grand Prix. Re-engined with a side-valve unit, fitted with full road gear and re-registered as XL 3125; it was then sold to R.C. Morgan and named 'Green Pea'. In 1925 it became the 'Thomas Special'. | XL 2445 (1922)<br>XL 3125 (1923)<br>PE 2516 (1925) |
| French (Strasburg) Grand Prix car (2) | 1913 (TT2) | Driven by Gallop in the French Grand Prix. Sold to G.E.T. Elston and re-registered as XL 2445. Then returned to the factory, fitted with a side-valve engine and re-registered as OR 1; it was then sold to R.G. Barlow. Passed on to Major Frank Halford who converted it to the 'Halford Special'. | XL 3125 (1922)<br>XL 2445 (1923)<br>XP 3037 (1923–24) |
| French (Strasburg) Grand Prix car replica (3) | | Assembled by the factory after cars 1 and 2 had been disposed of, and raced by Zborowski at the 1923 GP de Penya Rhin at Barcelona and Gallop at the 1923 Spanish Sitges track. | XP 3037 |
| 'Razor Blade' | 1915 | Special chassis single-seat record breaker and racer. | XO 9958 (1923) |
| 'Green Pea' | | Originally the first Grand Prix car (XL2445). In May 1925 it was re-registered as a 'Thomas Special' as PE 2516. | |
| Pre-production car 2 – 'All-Weather Tourer' | | Long-chassis 'All-Weather Tourer' body. Appeared in Bamford and Martin's catalogue in 1925. | |

**The cockpit of A3, the oldest surviving Aston Martin, dating from 1921. It is a simple layout with form being dictated by function.**

of *The Autocar*. The car was bodied with a simple and basic three-seat 'clover-leaf' body. At the time a clover-leaf body was used to describe the three-seat layout, in which the driver and passenger sat side by side in the full width body, which then tapered towards the rear, giving room for only a single central rear seat for the second passenger.

The car's layout was conventional, following the template set by the Coal Scuttle, with a rigid front axle suspended from two leaf springs, a side-valve 1486cc engine, a four-speed gearbox with a right-hand change, and a bevel-gear differential mounted in a solid rear axle mounted on a pair of semi-elliptical leaf springs. Drum brakes were fitted to the rear wheels only.

The car suffered problems when testing by the factory started. Due to the small size of the side rails (3in in depth) the chassis fractured behind the rear gearbox mounting when the car was run for any length of time on the road. Such a fundamental fault meant that the original Rubery-Owen chassis frames needed a significant amount of work to make them usable, with additional bracing to reinforce the affected area. The last two full-length chassis frames were built up as customer cars – in fact they formed the basis for the two '200-mile race' cars described below. The first chassis also had an extra lease of life, as it was shortened and strengthened and used as the chassis for the famous 'Bunny', also described below.

## The Prototype: AM270 / B2

Thanks to the weaknesses exposed in the original three Rubery-Owen chassis, the second Aston-Martin prototype, produced early in 1921 and road registered AM 270, was fitted with what was described as a completely new chassis, but which was very likely a modified original; it had the chassis number of 1909. While this was developed from the Rubery-Owen design and still featured the parallel side members, these were significantly deeper towards the rear where the original units broke. With a wheelbase of 103.5in (2,630mm), the chassis was of conventional design, with two 'C'-section main longerons with the 'open' side facing inwards towards the centre line. The front suspension was a conventional – for the time – solid axle mounted on a pair of semi-elliptical springs. At the rear the fully floating bevel-driven live axle sat under the main chassis rails and was sprung with a pair of semi-elliptical leaf springs and damped with friction dampers. The car was originally fitted with Rubery-Owen solid wheels and did not have any front brakes, but was later fitted with wire wheels and front brakes.

Importantly the car showed a meticulous attention to detail to ensure that it was as easy to maintain and drive as possible – this being part of Martin's philosophy to design the best car possible.

The engine originally fitted (the car had many changes of engine during its competition life) was a side-valve 4-cylinder unit with a helical gear in the timing case on the front of the engine to drive the camshaft sited on the left-hand side of the block. The head and cylinder block were cast as one unit, and the bore and stroke were 66.5 × 107mm, giving a capacity of 1496cc. The crankshaft was supported on three main bearings, and the oil system was designed to provide a direct feed to all three main bearings.

**The second Bamford and Martin-built Aston Martin, chassis B2, registration number AM270, seen here at the Shelsey Walsh hillclimb in September 1921.**

The clutch was mounted on the flywheel and was a Hele-Shaw multi-plate unit. The output shaft was connected to the separate gearbox via a short driveshaft. The four-speed and reverse gearbox was carried on webs that extended from the chassis side rails and was made from a single casting with removable top cover. The tubular propellor shaft had a single universal joint mounted at the gearbox end, and was fitted to the front UJ carrier and the rear axle with splines. This meant the shaft could float endways, while movement was controlled by a small steel plunger and spring mounted at the front end of the shaft.

Rear drum brakes were fitted, and while the diameter remains obscure, they were described as being of 'considerable diameter', so presumably were larger than the norm on light cars of the time.

Driver comfort was assured because the gear-lever position, pedals, hand-brake lever and the steering-wheel rake and reach were all adjustable to suit the driver. The pedals were mounted and pivoted on a common tube that had a serrated steel pad on each end. These pads mated to a second pair of serrated steel pads mounted in a fixed position on the car's floor. The position of the pedals could be changed by unbolting the pedal pads and moving them fore or aft on the fixed pad.

Under the bonnet the side-valve engine had a large capacity sump along with a sophisticated oil filtration system, while the filler cap and drain tap were designed to be convenient and foolproof to use. Pads were provided on both front and rear axles to take a jack for wheel removal, and the height of both front and rear jacking pads was the same.

The car was used and tested extensively on the road and track, and in May 1921 this car gave Aston-Martin its first win at Brooklands in the Essex Short Handicap race, which it completed at an average speed of 69.75mph (112.23km/h). It also carried out a test run from London to Holyhead in Wales, covering a total distance of 625 miles (1,005km) in two days. The run home was made at an average speed of 33mph (53km/h), covering the 275 miles (442km) in 8hr 20min with a fuel consumption of 31.25mpg (9ltr/100km). The fully road-equipped car also achieved a flying lap at Brooklands of 65.70mph (105.71km/h), and set a best top speed of 72mph (116km/h). It was also awarded Gold Stars when it competed in the 1921 Lands End and London–Edinburgh trials.

The performance and reliability of the car was so good that Martin issued a challenge to the Brescia Bugatti owners to compete against each other. The challenge was taken up but came to nought when the Bugatti, driven by Leon Cushman, broke a propellor shaft while practising and the race did not take place.

While the final prototype car was registered AM270, this number was apparently originally used on the previous prototype tourer with the original Rubery-Owen chassis, and was apparently also used on a later car. As was the way with development cars of the time, the registration number was often swapped between various cars, which leads to considerable confusion when tracing the history of individual cars.

## 'Bunny'

Probably the most famous Aston-Martin of the 1920s, 'Bunny' was created in 1920 and was described in the March 1921 edition of *The Autocar*. The car was originally believed to be all new, but from recent research it appears to have been made using many components from the original prototype, including the original Rubery-Owen chassis used for the

*Photo by kind permission of "The Motor."*

**'Bunny', the first Bamford and Martin prototype, seen here during a world record attempt at Brooklands on 24 May 1922.**

**'Bunny' at Brooklands in 1921; in the driving seat is Bertie (BS) Marshall. The car was photographed before competing in the Coupe des Voiturettes held at Le Mans on 18 September 1921.**

**The third prototype, A3, pictured during the snowy recce of the course for the 1922 Isle of Man TT race. Behind the car are Herbert Kensington-Moir, Lionel Martin, Clive Gallop and Count Louis Zborowski.**

first prototype. In typical Bamford and Martin fashion it also carried two registration marks, XH 2800 and AM273 during the early 1920s.

The car was apparently originally designed to compete in hillclimbs. The weak original chassis was modified extensively both to strengthen it and to shorten it – the wheelbase came down to 90in (2,286mm). It was fitted with a very narrow two-seater body made from light aluminium alloy, and was the first to feature a bulge on the side of the scuttle on the offside to accommodate the driver's right-hand-side gear change, a feature that would appear on a number of later racing Aston Martins.

Powered by a reliable 1487cc side-valve engine and equipped with front-wheel brakes, Bunny was a reliable car with a decent if not outstanding performance, and was run in a large number of races. Probably the most significant was its entry in the September 1921 Grand Prix des Voiturettes in France, which marked Aston Martin's first foray abroad. The race was held at the track that would become famous as the Le Mans 24 Hour course, and the Aston Martin car came in sixth out of nineteen entries – it was the last to actually finish the race. It is believed to have been broken up in Bradford in 1936.

## A3: The Third Prototype

In 1921 the so-called third prototype, now named A3, was produced. It was fitted with a variety of engines, ranging from standard or racing side-valve units to the first of the 16-valve engines. With the engine swaps came a number of different bodies, the car being fitted with either a streamlined racing body or a more conventional two-seat sports body.

**The tell-tale stamping on the dumb iron that identified A3.**

It was originally registered AM273, and had chassis number 'A3' with 'NO.3' stamped on the front of the left-hand-side dumb iron. It was re-registered XN 2902 in 1923, as well as being assigned the conventional chassis number 1918, and was sold. It then had a successful racing career with a Capt. J.C. Douglas as an all-black car nicknamed the 'N' word. This car still exists and is currently looked after by the Aston Martin Heritage Trust.

## The 200-Mile Race Cars: Chassis 1910 and 1912

Produced specifically to compete in the 1921 Junior Car Club 200 Mile race scheduled to be run at Brooklands on 21 October, two racers (one registered AM273) were produced, using as a basis the two remaining Rubery-Owen chassis, which had to be locally strengthened to eradicate the weakness exposed in

**Zborowski standing by the 16-valve single overhead camshaft car, most likely A3, ready for the 1921 JCC 200-mile race at Brooklands on 21 October. Clive Gallop is on the left, Jack Addis is checking the rear wheel, and the man on the right is thought to be Bertie Marshall.**

the rear of the chassis. Both cars were fitted with a narrow, two-seat, high-sided aluminium body made by Kingston-based aircraft manufacturer Hawkers, with staggered seating for the driver and mechanic. The first car (chassis number 1910R) was fitted with a side-valve engine and rear-wheel brakes only. The second car (chassis number 1910) was virtually identical, but was fitted with the Robb-designed 16-valve overhead camshaft engine.

Both cars had only rear-wheel brakes, and were fitted with artillery wheels by Rubery-Owen. The side-valve car made its debut at the BARC Autumn meet where with Kensington Moir driving it won the '90mph Long Handicap' race with a speed of 81.4mph (130.9km/h), and then only weeks before the 200-Mile race, Kensington Moir used the side-valve car to take the Light Car Class one-hour record up to 86.21mph (138.71km/h). In the 200-Mile race, the side-valve car, chassis 1910R, did not finish after its petrol tank was holed by the rear axle after hitting a large bump in the track, while the 16-valve car, driven by Count Zborowski, came in a disappointing tenth behind 'Bunny' driven by B.S. Marshall. However, later on Zborowski, driving the side-valve 200-Mile car, managed to raise the class standing-start mile and kilometre records to 66.82 and 60.09mph respectively.

## TT1 and TT2: The French (Strasburg) Grand Prix Twin Cam Cars

As Bamford and Martin were not making cars for customers, but rather indulging Martin and the other drivers in their racing exploits, a welcome boost in the company's finances was provided when Count Louis Zborowski gave the company a contract worth just over £10,000 to build a pair of cars to compete in the Strasburg Grand Prix. With this extra finance, the company embarked on its second foray into the international competition arena. The two competing Grand Prix cars were made in 1922 and were TT1 and TT2, so named because the first race in which they were intended to compete was the March 1922 Isle of Man Tourist Trophy.

TT1 (chassis number 1913) was registered as XL2445 and was initially fitted with a side-valve engine, although it appeared to have the 'Gremillon' engine fitted for the Strasburg race, and TT2 (chassis number 1914) was registered XL3125 and fitted with the 'Gremillon' engine. A third example, also fitted with the dohc 'Gremillon' engine, was made in 1924 for a Swiss customer.

The cars suffered two major disadvantages: first, the race rule allowed cars of up to 2 litres, and second, there was a minimum weight rule, which meant the Aston Martins had to carry ballast to bring them up to the required weight. Driven by Zborowski (TT1) and Gallop (TT2), by lap 19 out of sixty the cars were running well, with Gallop (TT2) in fifth place and Zborowski close behind in sixth place; but TT1's magneto burnt out, forcing him to retire with no sparks, and Gallop was forced to retire at lap 28, when his magneto drive failed.

Once the issues with the magnetos and magneto drive were fixed, Zborowski entered one of the cars in the Spanish

**Lionel Martin in the pits watches as TT1, driven by Count Zborowski, is refuelled at the French Grand Prix at Strasburg, 15 July 1921.**

The Aston Martin team cars (TT2, race no. 8 on the left, and TT1, race no. 15 on the right) at the 1922 Strasburg Grand Prix.

Grand Prix de Penya held at Barcelona later in 1922 and 1923 where he finished second, both times.

TT1 was sold on where it was nicknamed 'Green Pea', and in May 1925 it was re-registered as a 'Thomas Special' as PE 2516. TT2 was also eventually sold on and became the 'Halford Special'. The car is still extant and is currently displayed at Brooklands Museum.

## 'Razor Blade'

Built between late 1922 and 1923, the 'Razor Blade' or 'The Oyster' were the nicknames for the first single-seat Aston-Martin. This was a rare layout that would not be repeated until 1939 and the modified Speed Series single seater designed to take the 'Cross' sleeve-valve engine, and in the late 1950s with the Aston Martin DBR4 and DBR5 Grand Prix cars, and finally the Formula 1 cars of 2021. First seen at Brooklands in 1923, the car was designed to be the first light car to exceed 100 miles (160km) in one hour. Surprisingly the car was registered for the road with the prefix XO 9958.

The car was unusual in having a chassis that was wider at the front than the rear to facilitate the unusual design, all in the name of streamlining. This chassis allowed for a very narrow rear track, with inboard rear brakes sited close to the rear bevel-gear casing (there was apparently no differential), and had the rear springs also mounted inboard, leaving just the driveshafts and wheels projecting outside the body. The locked rear 'differential' was mounted on a pair of quarter elliptic springs on either side, inboard of the brake drums, and the 'H'-section beam front axle was suspended on a pair of conventionally positioned semi-elliptical leaf springs and faired in with wooden formers to aid streamlining. There were

The Halford Special at Brooklands in 2021. The car started its long and eventful life as TT2.

'Razor Blade' back where she belongs – on the banking at Brooklands when she was reunited with A3 in May 2021.

no front brakes, and the rears were 6in in diameter – with steel-on-steel operation they were apparently not very efficient. The bodyshell was made from lightweight aluminium, and was apparently constructed for Bamford and Martin by the de Havilland aircraft company.

The cockpit was so narrow that the bodywork had to incorporate a bulge to give the driver room to operate the gear lever, which was positioned on his right. The 'Oyster' nickname was coined at Brooklands, and was due to the unusual side-hinged cowl over the driver – this hinged open on the left-hand side to allow the driver access to the cockpit, and when it was closed only the driver's head poked out; this style was later abandoned. Originally the body with the cowl was designed to fit closely around driver Kensington Moir, but while in the factory's hands the car was generally driven by various drivers, including S.C.H. 'Sammy' Davis. The alloy body tapered to a point at the rear, and at 18.5in (470mm) wide at its widest point, was described in the contemporary press as the narrowest single seater to date.

A notable feature of the car was the design of the radiator grille. This had twelve horizontal shutters that were hinged and could be adjusted by the driver to control the flow of cooling air into the body. A vertical vent was formed at the rear of the bodyshell, which allowed the air that had made it through the engine bay to escape. The car originally sat on bolt-on Sankey one-piece wheels, but was later fitted with lighter knock-on Rudge-style wire wheels. The car was initially fitted with a 1500 dohc engine, and later with the engine from one of the cars raced at Strasbourg in 1922.

The car had a narrow rear track, measuring only 36in (91.4cm), and a front track of 48in (122cm). At its widest point the body measured only 18.5in (47cm). Surprisingly it was registered for the road, with the registration number XO 9958. It weighed a mere 18.5cwt (2,072lb, 940kg) and was painted in an eye-catching iridescent green. It exhibited some alarming characteristics when run at speed, with the short and stiff rear quarter elliptic springs making the car difficult to control, while it also had a propensity for shedding the front offside tyre when getting up to about 100mph (160km/h) on the Brooklands banking. This happened several times while trying for the 100 miles in the hour record at Brooklands, and the torque tube connecting the rear bevel box to the gearbox also fractured on more than one occasion.

While the car came very close to meeting its objective, it did not actually achieve it while racing; however, fitted with the 1500cc dohc engine it competed in the 1923 Brooklands midsummer meeting for the 90mph (145km/h) Short Handicap where it averaged 98.04mph (157.75km/h), and at a later Brooklands meeting in the 100mph Short Handicap it won at an average of 99.81mph (160.59km/h). However, the car is said to have completed a lap of Brooklands at

**Razor Blade was a single seater; the narrow cockpit had to have a bulge on the left-hand-side driver's door to make room for the gear change.**

**Razor Blade's handsome front grille was the inspiration for the badge of the British Racing Drivers Club badge.**

103mph (165.7km/h) during 1923. Top speed was said to be around 110mph (177km/h). It was sold by the firm to racers Captain J.C. Douglas and Major Frank Halford and was developed into a moderately successful racing car. It survives today, and at the time of writing was on long-term display at the Brooklands Museum. The shuttered radiator grille is believed to be the inspiration behind L.V. Head's logo designed for the British Racing Drivers Club (BRDC) badge.

## INTO PRODUCTION

There were four models of Aston-Martin car offered by Bamford and Martin between 1921 and 1925. The factory basically offered three different chassis – the long, the short and the sports – and three engine types, all of 1480cc – the side-valve unit, the dohc 16-valve unit and the dohc 8-valve

**While Aston Martin made the rolling chassis, they used external coach builders to produce the car's body. This is a typical offering from 1924 with a three-seat 'clover-leaf' touring body.**

unit. While the overhead cam engines were offered, they seem to have been rarely actually ordered, and so the vast majority of the sixty or so production cars built up to 1925 by Bamford and Martin were powered by the side-valve engine. The actual model combinations were the long chassis with side-valve engine, which was offered from 1921 to 1926; the short chassis with side-valve engine, which was offered from 1923 to 1926; the sports chassis 16-valve engine offered from 1923 to 1926; and the sports chassis with double overhead camshaft 8-valve engine offered from 1925 to 1926.

The first batch of cars made for customers was produced in the winter of 1921, and comprised six side-valve powered chassis. These were offered as chassis only for £500, or with a two- to three-seat tourer body for £650. The cars were fitted with Aston Martin's own design of gearbox, which, like the engine, was fitted into a casing that had two 'wings' incorporated to fix it between the two chassis longerons to stiffen the box and chassis.

The box was fitted separately behind the engine, connected to the clutch via a short shaft, and drive was carried to the worm and gear rear differential by a conventional propshaft.

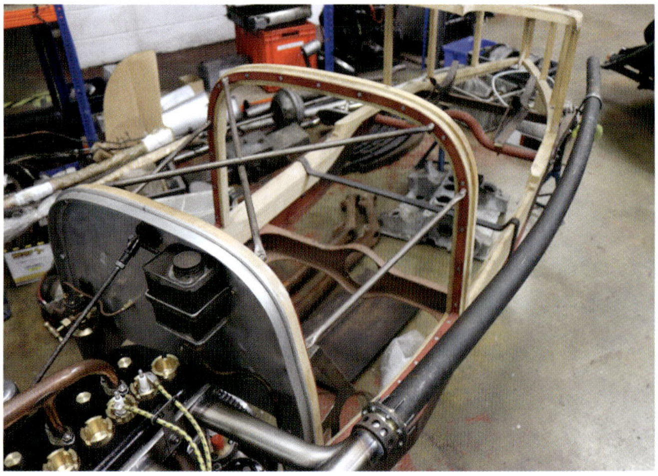

**Pictured at Écurie Bertelli, this bare chassis of a Bamford and Martin-built car shows how the body would be constructed, with wood framing covered in aluminium or fabric.**

Brakes were fitted on all four wheels, using the Perrot system on the front, and were operated by rods.

The first true production cars started to trickle out to the public in 1922, when the Aston-Martin Sports was introduced. Its sporting credentials were underlined by its standard four-wheel brakes, when most cars only had brakes on the rear wheels. The car followed the layout of the many racing cars produced to date, with a front-mounted side-valve 1500cc engine, a simple ladder chassis, and live rear axle suspended on leaf springs. Bodies came from various local coachbuilders, but Aston Martin were particularly fond of the clover-leaf three-seater configuration for their short-chassis cars.

**The Aston Martin always had a handsome grille, which made the 'face' of the car. This 1924 example shows the style that would take the company through to the start of World War II, with only small changes in its proportions.**

The Aston Martin Sports was complemented by the Super Sports, which featured the 4-cylinder 4 overhead-valve per cylinder twin camshaft 'Gremillon' engine. With a lusty (for the time) 55bhp, the engine gave the Aston Martin the power it needed to compete successfully in motor sport. The 16-valve engine had a bore and stroke of 65 × 112mm, slightly different to the side-valve's (and 8-valve's) 66.5 × 107mm, but still providing a capacity of 1480cc. The 16-valve unit had an RAC rating of 10.5hp due to its reduced bore, while the other engines fell into the 11hp RAC category. Before the company closed down in 1925, Bamford and Martin had produced about sixty-two cars in total.

## THE END AND A NEW BEGINNING

With the final descent into financial ruin, the company of Bamford and Martin came to an inglorious end, an end that would reflect the progress of the company to the present day. All too frequently the company would have periods of prosperity followed by a descent into insolvency, followed by a fresh injection of cash, another period of glory, then another financial crash. In the brief space of twelve years, with a significant break of four years for the horror of World War I, Lionel and Kate Martin, along with their band of merry men – drivers, mechanics and engineers – managed to place the name of Aston Martin firmly on the map as a manufacturer of high class, high quality and high performance cars.

The marque's racing successes brought it a profile that was out of all proportion to the size of the company, especially considering that only some sixty-two cars were produced. While it wasn't exactly 'Win on Sunday, sell on Monday', and the money spent on racing might have been more profitably spent on producing cars for sale, the legacy of Bamford and Martin was a name that was strong enough to live on through the rest of the twentieth century and into the twenty-first, surviving wars and economic slumps and that through the sheer strength of the name, would re-emerge time and time again when any normal company would have failed and been consigned to the dustbin of history. Aston Martin was, and is different, and it is the strength of the name and its ethos of producing expensive, high performance and superbly engineered cars which meant the company survived in its many forms through the years to produce the special cars that bear the Aston Martin badge.

**This 1924 long chassis tourer was, at the time of writing, on display at Brooklands.**

## KEY FIGURES

### Lionel Martin

Very much the procreator of Aston Martin, Lionel Walker Birch Martin was born on 15 March 1878. He attended Eton from 1891, leaving after five years, and then went up to Oxford University as an undergraduate at Marcon's Hall; he graduated with a BA in 1902. Martin drew his significant income from the family businesses – Singleton Birch Ltd, which was involved in mining and quarrying, and English China Clays – but his real interest was in designing and developing the best light car in the world.

After his studies were completed Martin moved to Chiswick, West London, and in 1902, having been an enthusiastic member of the Oxford University Cycling Club, he was proposed as a member of the 'Bath Road Club', a cycling organization that would play a large part in his life. His prowess at cycling earned him much acclaim from the club and the cycling community, and he apparently took great care of the mechanical wellbeing of his machines. His thirst for competition was also evident in his cycling activities: one of his finest feats came on Wednesday 27 August 1902, when, leaving Land's End at 07.06am, he set off to beat the Land's End to London cycling record. He arrived at Hyde Park Corner at 05:22.16 on the Thursday morning, and therefore managed to knock 3hr, 9min and 16sec off the previous record. This feat gained him a gold record breaker's button in the club awards at the end of 1902.

The following year, at Easter 1903, Martin and fellow member T.H.B. 'Tadpole' Vade-Walpole attempted to beat the Road Riders Association (RRA) tandem record for the Edinburgh to York run. This they achieved, smashing the existing record by 43min, covering the distance in 12hr 17min, despite meeting snow, headwinds and driving cold rain on the way. These exploits helped him to be voted captain of the club in 1903, only a year after he had joined.

While Martin obviously enjoyed his cycling, he was not blind to the advantages of mechanical propulsion, buying his first motorcycle in 1902, a 2¾hp Humber with the then innovative chain drive. He then progressed to the motor car when in 1903 he joined forces with Montague Napier, forming a partnership with him to buy and sell motor cars. Martin married his first wife, Christine Murray from Auchendinny in Midlothian, in 1909; she died in April 1913, shortly after the birth of their only son John. Martin remarried Katherine (Kate) King in 1917. In 1909 Martin lost his driving licence for two years after contesting a speeding fine, and returned to the Bath Road Club where he met with John Bamford. Their friendship led to the establishment of Bamford and Martin Ltd in 1913, as described above. During World War I Martin worked in various positions while developing Coal Scuttle he returned to Bamford and Martin in 1919.

**Company founder Lionel Martin driving the second prototype, B2 (registration number AM270) at the Essex Motor Club meeting at Brooklands on 7 May 1921.**

Martin left Bamford and Martin when it went into receivership in 1925. Initially he appears to have concentrated on his other business interests at the expense of his motoring activities, but in 1928 he was competing again, this time in a Riley. He rekindled his interest in motor sport, becoming a member of the British Racing Drivers Club (BRDC), and his wife Kate joining the Women's Automobile and Sports Association (WASA) in 1928. He then took an increasingly active role in the administration of the BRDC, while competing in various events throughout the rest of the 1920s and the 1930s.

When war broke out in 1939, Martin went back to his first love, cycling. He rejoined the Bath Road club in 1940, where he continued to ride his bicycle and tricycle, and was re-elected as Vice President. However, in 1943 he was hospitalized when he suffered a serious illness, thought to be linked to his diabetes, from which he suffered all his life. Having recovered and returned to cycling, in 1944 he suffered a broken thigh bone when he was knocked off his bike by a car, resulting a lengthy stay in hospital. Having recovered from this escapade, Lionel Martin died aged sixty-seven on 21 October 1945, from injuries suffered in another accident on 14 October when he was again knocked off his bike by a car.

## Robert Bamford

Robert Bamford was born on 16 June 1883, in Lamarsh in Essex, the eldest son of the Rev. Robert Bamford. A keen

**Lionel Martin sits in AM270 (the second car in) alongside Coal Scuttle (the third car in) on a start line of the Essex Motor Club meeting at Brooklands on 18 July 1921.**

**A portrait of Robert Bamford taken when he was a lieutenant in the Army Service Corps around 1917/18.**

cyclist, by 1910 he had joined the Bath Road Club. He was apprenticed as an engineer to the Thames-based Messrs Hesse and Savory's Teddington Launch works, who built speedboats as well as making some specialist engineering products such as reversing gear for boats. He co-formed Bamford and Martin with Lionel Martin in 1913, where his engineering skills helped to bring Martin's vision of the perfect light car close to fruition. During World War I, Bamford served in the Royal Army Service Corps; he briefly returned to Bamford and Martin after the war, but retired from the business in 1920.

Bamford married fashion designer Matilda Etches in 1919. His daughter, Patricia Bamford, married Robin Jacques, the brother of famous British actress Hattie Jacques. Bamford retired to Sussex in 1939, and died at the age of fifty-nine in 1942.

## Count Louis Zborowski

Louis Zborowski was born in 1895, the son of racing driver William Eliot Morris Zborowski and a wealthy American heiress born Margaret Laura Astor Carey, the granddaughter of William Backhouse Astor Snr. Zborowski's father died in a motor-racing accident in 1903, and on the death of his mother in 1911 Zborowski became the fourth richest under twenty-one-year old in the world. His interest in motor racing led to him designing and building his own racing cars, together with his engineer and co-driver, Captain Clive Gallop, in the stables of Higham Park, his estate in Kent that he inherited from his mother.

In the early part of the twentieth century Zborowski achieved significant fame as a racing driver. He was best known for his three aero-engined monster racers, nicknamed 'Chitty Bang Bang'. The cars were later immortalized by author Ian Fleming in *Chitty Chitty Bang Bang* – and perhaps the Aston Martin link influenced Fleming's choice of car for Bond in *Goldfinger*? The first Chitty was powered by a 23093cc 6-cylinder Maybach aero engine, the second was fitted with an 18825cc Benz aero engine, and the third was based on a Mercedes 28/95 chassis but was fitted with a 14778cc Mercedes aero engine – this was called the 'White Mercedes'. All were raced by Zborowski and Gallop at Brooklands.

The pair produced a final aero-engined car called the 'Higham Special', which was powered by a 27-litre American Liberty aero engine. This car was sold to John Godfrey Parry-Thomas after Zborowski's death; he christened it 'Babs', and used it to take the world speed record at over 170mph (273.5km/h) at Pendine Sands in Wales. Zborowski also raced cars for other teams and marques, and was a great aficionado of Aston Martin, driving the works cars and financing the build of the TT1 and TT2 cars to compete in the Strasburg Grand Prix of 1922. He also drove a Bugatti at the 1923 Indianapolis 500 race, and in the 1923 Italian Grand Prix at Monza drove an 'American Millar 122' single seater designed by American engineer Harry Millar.

**Count Louis Zborowski in TT1 (race no. 15) at the 1921 French Grand Prix at Strasburg. Clive Gallop is driving TT2 (race no. 8).**

On 19 October 1924 Louis Zborowski died when competing in a 2-litre Mercedes in the Italian Grand Prix at Monza: after covering forty-four laps his car left the track at the Lesmo corner and hit a tree.

## Écurie Bertelli, Pre-War Aston Martin Specialists

Écurie Bertelli is run by husband and wife team Robert and Alison Blackmore, along with Andy Bell as technical director. The company is based in Olney, Bucks, and specializes in pre-World War II Aston Martins. Covering the Bamford and Martin, Bertelli, and Sutherland-era cars, the company provides support for owners of early Aston Martins, and specializes in servicing, repairing, restoring and conserving these historic cars, and very importantly, bearing in mind Aston Martin's pre-war competition history, also prepares cars for historic racing and rallying.

The company's main premises are on an unassuming industrial estate in Olney, and the exterior gives few indications of the magic that goes on behind the shutters. When the author visited in September 2021 the spacious workshop was crammed full with pre-war Aston Martins with all sorts of work being carried out on them. One car in particular stood out: a dark green 1920s Sports model that had been the subject of a full-blown conservation project.

Conservation is an area of the company work that is receiving a great deal of attention at present. People are starting to realize that a car is only original once, and it can be important in some cases to preserve a car's original condition rather than do a bare-metal restoration. As an example, the Aston Martin Sports registration number MY 1720 is the twenty-fifth made, and after being used through the 1930s, 1940s and 1950s the car was laid up in the 1960s. After sitting for some fifty years in a dry shed stored underneath a sailing dingy, of all things, Écurie Bertelli carried out a conservation exercise on the car to get it back on the road after its long incarceration. Today the vast majority of the car is as it was found.

While the car was subjected to a complete nut and bolt, body-off mechanical renovation, wherever possible the existing finish was conserved and original parts repaired and reused. Paint was touched up, rather than sanded down and replaced, the leather interior was gently cleaned and fed, and repairs made where needed. Some of the car's suspension components still show signs of its original factory-applied light blue paint under the conserved dark green paint that it had received sometime after its manufacture but before it was placed into storage. As an example of the conserver's art, the car's original wooden dashboard had deteriorated too far to be reused, so a new replacement was built for it – but the instruments and switches are original, and the new dash has been sympathetically aged to remain in keeping with the rest of the beautifully patinated but tidy interior.

As Robert observed, the car's unveiling for the owner (who lives in the USA) was rather an anti-climax as it really appeared that nothing had been done to it – but that was the whole point, and the owner was delighted. The car looks just as it did before it was laid up, bearing the signs of a busy pre-war decade of use, and a lot more activity in the post-war years.

Mechanically the car has been thoroughly overhauled so runs and drives perfectly. It is firmly in the 2020s, with every

**Écurie Bertelli specialized in inter-war Aston Martins. Here an early Bamford and Martin car is being restored and fitted with a period supercharger.**

**This Bertelli-era Aston Martin Sports has been carefully conserved by Écurie Bertelli. With its perfect mechanicals and patinated but mainly original paint and fittings, the car is a rare survivor from the era.**

wearing part in the engine, gearbox and rear axle, along with the suspension and brakes, restored to as-new condition, while the finish charmingly evokes the car's condition as it was in the 1960s – used but not abused, with slightly tatty and patinated paintwork from an earlier respray, but no rot, rust or decay: a car that has been loved but used to the full. It looks as if it has just been parked up after a quick jaunt through the picturesque Surrey lanes to visit a sadly derelict 1960s Brooklands in order to relive some of the pre-war Aston Martin's competition triumphs at the track.

This is just one aspect of Écurie Bertelli's expertise – alongside the Sports model in the workshop when the author visited was a wide range of early Aston Martins, with Bertelli-made cars rubbing shoulders with Bamford and Martin cars and Sutherland-era cars. From gentle refreshes, through rebuilds and race preparation to nut-and-bolt restorations, the company is working hard to keep the pre-war cars both on the road and track and in fine fettle. Their ability to service and restore the pre-war Aston Martins is a major benefit to present and future owners, who can use their cars secure in the knowledge that should any mechanical mayhem occur, Écurie Bertelli has the skills and expertise to set them right. To assist with this aim the company has a large stock of spares, made up of parts manufactured in house, as well as other parts produced by outside contractors to Écurie Bertelli's strict quality control; furthermore they employ a staff with an extensive knowledge of the cars.

The company's mechanical expertise and the range of cars they work on means that they are well aware of what is needed to keep the cars on the road and to restore them. Their experience in working on the cars also identifies when parts are getting rare, and they can commission batches of new stocks when needed, producing them in house where possible. This expertise is backed up with an extensive archive of material that includes original drawings, factory technical information and marketing material for the pre-war cars.

What is interesting today is the increasing interest in the early Aston Martins. With Aston Martin production now reaching unprecedented levels there are many Gaydon-era Aston Martin owners who are knowledgeable about the marque's recent history, and usually conversant with the last fifty years of Aston Martin history, mainly thanks to the David Brown and of course the James Bond effect. However, many have little or no knowledge of Aston Martin's pre-World War II history. It seems that for many owners of newer cars, the Aston Martin story started with David Brown, and they have no knowledge of the company's pre-war history. Écurie Bertelli takes part in and exhibits cars at many classic car events, and Robert has often been asked by modern-day owners at various Aston Martin shows and events 'What are these MGs (or "funny old cars") doing at an Aston Martin event?' Écurie Bertelli are only too happy to educate these owners on Aston Martin's early history – and to give them their due, the owners are happy to be informed of Aston Martin's pre-war history.

**A gearbox for a Bamford and Martin car. Note the wide webs on each side of the main case allowing the box to be bolted in between the chassis fore and aft members.**

So in their own small way Écurie Bertelli are spreading the word about the illustrious history of Aston Martin, and this can only help to embellish the brand and widen the knowledge of Aston Martin aficionados.

In conclusion, Écurie Bertelli doesn't just 'talk the talk' on pre-war Aston Martins, they 'walk the walk': with their wealth of experience in the marque, they have the skills and expertise to keep these historic cars on the road and track where they belong. Long may they continue!

## THE OLDEST ASTON: 'A3'

The third prototype Aston-Martin, built on one of the three chassis originally supplied to Bamford and Martin in 1919, is the oldest known Aston-Martin car in existence. Currently the car is owned by the Aston Martin Heritage Trust Collection, based in Drayton St Leonard in Oxfordshire, UK, and housed in a barn that dates back to AD1349.

A3 is typical of the early Bamford and Martin Aston Martins in that it is relatively lightly built, with a minimal chassis and bodywork and a 1500cc side-valve engine. While it has had a long and involved history, there is no dispute that it is the third Aston Martin built and is the oldest remaining. Recently treated to an engine rebuild after a piston had picked up and come near to seizing, A3 is, at the time of writing, in rude health, running well and looking good. The simple bodywork, with its two seats and beetle-back tail, is finished in black, as are the mudguards. At the front the flowing front guards merge into wooden running boards, a characteristic not shared with later cars into the 1930s, when Aston Martins always had cycle-style guards. The cabin is small, narrow and cramped, with the passenger seat set back from the driver's to give more elbow room to manipulate the large diameter, leather-bound steering wheel.

The car is equipped with rear brakes only, and carries the cast-steel Sankey 'artillery' wheels popular at the time as being stronger but heavier than equivalent wire wheels. Still visible on the left-hand-side front dumb iron is the all-important 'A3' stamp – the main way of identifying the car as such an important survivor. In its centenary year, 2021, A3 had been doing the rounds, with appearances alongside its contemporary 'Razor Blade' at Brooklands circuit, and as the star at the AMHT Festival. The visit to Brooklands was especially important as it was probably the car's first outing on the historic banking since its heyday in the early 1920s. A3 as a car in its own right is impressive, and is a great survivor from the early days of motoring – and as the earliest extant Aston Martin it holds a unique place in our motoring heritage.

**A3 is the oldest surviving Aston Martin car. Now owned by the AMHT, it is exhibited around the country. Here it is in its spiritual home, Brooklands, in May 2021. Note how the passenger sits slightly behind the driver to make enough room for both in the narrow cockpit.**

**It is hard to believe that A3 was 100 years old at the time of writing. It has been beautifully restored and is an important and historic car.**

## TECHNICAL DESCRIPTION: BAMFORD AND MARTIN SIDE-VALVE 1.5 LITRE

The first production Aston Martin models made by Bamford and Martin were front-engined, rear-wheel-drive models powered by a 1.5-litre side-valve four-stroke engine. The cars were made in long (standard) or short (sports) chassis form. They had a four-speed manual gearbox and a spiral bevel rear axle. The solid front and rear axles were sprung with semi-elliptical leaf springs and were originally fitted with rear drum brakes only – front brakes operating on the Perrot system were fitted from 1923. The brakes were rod operated, the rears from the brake pedal and the fronts from the hand lever. The cars were fitted with a body to the customer's specification, and were usually one of a two-seat sports, three-seat touring or four-seat touring type.

## SPECIFICATION TABLE: BAMFORD AND MARTIN SIDE-VALVE 1.5 LITRE

| | |
|---|---|
| **Layout and chassis** | Front-engined, rear drive, two-, three- or four-seat sports or touring car. Ladder-style chassis |
| **Engine** | |
| Type | Aston Martin side-valve, monobloc head and barrels |
| Block and head material | Cast iron |
| Crankcase material | Aluminium alloy |
| Cylinders | 4 in line |
| Bore and stroke | 66.5 × 107mm |
| Capacity | 1486cc |
| Valves | 2 valves per cylinder, operated directly from camshaft in crankcase |
| Compression ratio | 5.5:1 (alternative 5.8:1) |
| Carburettor | Single carburettor, SU, Solex or Zenith |
| Max. power | 45bhp |
| RAC rating | 11hp |
| Max. torque | 56.25lb ft at 4,000rpm |

| | | |
|---|---|---|
| **Transmission** | | |
| Gearbox | 4 speed manual | |
| Clutch | Hele Shaw multiplate unit 15 plate (8 bronze, 7 steel) | |
| Overall ratios | 1st | 14:1 (optional 10.5:1) |
| | 2nd | 7.2:1 (optional 6.2:1) |
| | 3rd | 5.1:1 (optional 4.5:1) |
| | 4th | 4:1 (optional 3.5:1) |
| Reverse | 14:1 (optional 10.5:1) | |
| Final drive | Spiral bevel, 4:1 (options: 3.7:1, 3.5:1) | |

| | |
|---|---|
| **Suspension and Steering** | |
| Front | Beam axle, leaf springs |
| Rear | Live axle, semi-elliptic leaf springs |
| Steering | Marles steering box |
| Wheels | Sankey Pressed Steel (1921–22)<br>Rudge Whitworth Wire (1923–25) |
| Tyres | 710 × 90 |
| **Brakes** | |
| Type | Drums, cable operated<br>Rear only 1921–22<br>Front Perrot system 1923–25 |
| **Capacities** | |
| Fuel capacity | 8gal (36.4ltr) |
| Oil capacity | 9 pints (5.11ltr) |
| **Dimensions** | |
| Track | Front and rear 48in (1,220mm) |
| Wheelbase | Standard: 105in (2,670mm)<br>Sports 96in (2,440mm) |
| Overall length | Standard: 145in (3,680mm)<br>Sports: 132in (3,350mm) |
| Weight | 1,792lb (813kg) |
| **Performance** | |
| Top speed | 77mph (124km/h) in three-seat touring trim |
| 0–60 | Not known |

CHAPTER 3

# RESCUE AND THE BERTELLI YEARS: 1925–1946

In 1925 Bamford and Martin fell into liquidation, and Lionel Martin and his wife Kate left the company; however, subsequent to this a new company was created sited at new premises, with Augustus 'Bert' Bertelli appointed as chief engineer – and the Aston Martin car took on a new lease of life. Aston Martin Motors Ltd was sited in Feltham, and the new company took up residence in three sheds built during World War I and later used by Citroén as their UK manufacturing base. In these works the influence of Bertelli would be felt with the introduction of an all-new model that would lead on the famous Aston Martin inter-war icons: the Ulster and the international models.

A minor but notable change with the new company was the dropping of the hyphen in the Aston Martin name. However, the hyphen continued to pop up from time to time in company literature and badges through the 1920s and 1930s.

With the departure of Bertelli in 1935, the company was then run with Claude Hill as chief engineer. As the country quickly headed on to a war footing, the production of cars rapidly became secondary to supporting the war effort. Britain's major expansion of the Royal Air Force resulted in a massive expansion of the aeronautical industry, and small, competent engineering companies such as Aston Martin were quickly utilized by the major aircraft manufacturers as sub-contractors to produce components and sub-assemblies to support the production of aircraft for the RAF and the Fleet Air Arm. To support this lucrative line of business Aston Martin largely ceased car production in 1939 and devoted all its energies to supporting the war effort.

After the war, even though Aston Martin was solvent, it lacked the funds it needed to develop a new car, so was put up for sale in 1946.

## THE COMPANY

In late 1925 the remains of Bamford and Martin were bought by a consortium of investors, including Dorothea, Lady Charnwood (the mother of Chief Engineer John Benson),

**The 1934 'Ulster', owned by the Aston Martin Heritage Trust, is typical of the sporting cars produced by Aston Martin in the 1930s.**

with Baron Charnwood (Godfrey Rathbone), Bill Renwick, Augustus Bertelli and John Benson appointed as directors. The company was renamed Aston Martin Motors Ltd and was moved from the Kensington address to a factory in Feltham, Middlesex, West London.

The new factory comprised three large units, originally built on the edge of the Hanworth Air Park by the Whitehead Aircraft Company, and latterly used by Citroën as their UK manufacturing plant before their move to Slough. The three units were divided up into three functions: service, manufacture and body shop, this latter unit being under the control of Bertelli's brother Enrico.

The first product of the new company was based on a prototype built by Bertelli and Renwick when they ran their own business. This light car was nicknamed 'Buzzbox' and was of a type similar to the previous Aston Martins as it was a 1500cc 'light' car. However, the car was powered by an all-new overhead camshaft engine, so was much more up to date than the side-valve models produced by Bamford and Martin. Renwick and Bertelli also brought skilled draughtsman and engineer Claude Hill to work for them at the new company.

These changes were installed in the Feltham factory during 1926, and the car was enhanced and made ready for production during the rest of the year. Originally it was intended that the new engine would be offered to other manufacturers, but they did not appear to sell any. Oddly the original Renwick and Bertelli company was not disbanded until 1937, perhaps because the presence of Enrico Bertelli and his bodyshop gave Aston Martin access to their own body manufacturer instead of having to rely on external companies. Car production started in earnest in 1927, with a range of cars with both open and closed touring bodies and open sports bodies.

One major issue with the company almost led to its demise. When Bertelli had visited Aston Martin after it had gone into liquidation, he was surprised at the lack of machine tools, and also by how much of the car was made from bought-in components. This offended his engineering principles, and he wanted to make as much of the new Aston Martin in house as possible. However, admirable as this aim might have been, it flew in the face of economic sense. Bertelli and Renwick were engineers first and businessmen second, and by making so much of the cars in house, the Aston Martin cars Bertelli made between 1927 and 1931 were very expensive. The cost of a new Aston Martin was high when compared to the competition, and this obviously meant that there were fewer sales than there might have been had the cars been cheaper. While it was a selling point that many of the elements of the car were custom made by the company, this also meant that as well as being expensive, the cars were slow to produce.

With Aston Martin by then producing their own engines, gearboxes and rear axles in house, there was little they could do to reduce the costs of the car, and even Bertelli was quoted as saying they never managed to produce a good rear axle! Sales of the cars were slow, with only some thirty cars produced in 1928 and 1929, although sixty-four were sold in 1930. Sales then dropped to thirty in 1931 and only twenty-five in 1932. In 1931 the company underwent a number of upheavals: Renwick left, and the owners of the London Aston Martin London agents (Kensington-Moir and Straker Ltd), Nigel Holder and Reginald Straker, were both given seats on the board. Later there was a further shake-up when Lancelot Prideaux-Brune joined the company as a director, and Holder and Straker both left.

**General view of the Feltham works in June 1934, with the cars entered at Le Mans lined up. No. 22 is LM11, no. 23 is LM12, no. 20 is LM10, LM14 is no. 21, and no. 24 is a 1.5-litre Second Series Le Mans.**

All this changed in 1932 when the in-house rear axle was replaced with a proprietary unit. However, the company did keep its own engine, which obviously made sense as this item would be seen (and hopefully admired) by the owner, and helped to maintain the exclusivity of the Aston Martin name. These major changes were accompanied by a number of less significant engineering alterations, ranging from updating the previously rod-operated brakes to cable operation, changing the radiator to a simple separate type mounted in the chromed shell, as well as modifying the engine by replacing the dry-sump oil system with a simpler wet-sump system, replacing the camshaft drive's expensive inverted tooth chain with a simple roller type, and relocating the dynamo. The changes meant that the list price of the International model dropped some £120 to £475, well under the emotionally significant £500 mark, which stimulated sales and probably saved the company.

In 1933 another bailout occurred, when Newcastle-based shipping magnate Sir Arthur Munro Sutherland bought out Prideaux-Brune for around £10,000 and set up a new board with just three directors: himself as chairman, and his son Robert Gordon Sutherland and Bert Bertelli as joint managing directors. Sutherland senior was responsible for the finance of the company, his son for the business side (mainly sales and advertising), and Bertelli for engineering and development and racing. At last, with adequate finances in place, Sutherland put in place a proper production line and bought in enough components to produce 100 new cars based on the Le Mans model.

In 1934 the production of cars stabilized and the company entered a period of relative stability; it even had the finances to run a works team of cars. The famous 'LM' series of works cars continued to be built, based on the production cars, with some sold and competing in races as private entries, and with Bertelli managing the racing effort. After a disastrous showing in the 1934 Le Mans 24 Hour race, when the cars either crashed or suffered mechanical failure, the company had a triumphant 1935 with class wins in both the Mille Migla and the Le Mans 24 Hour race. In 1936 the company developed a 2-litre engine (based on the 1500cc unit and described below.).

Bertelli eventually left Aston Martin in February 1937, bringing to an end the 'Bertelli' era of Aston Martin production, an era in which as usual the company relied on regular injections of cash to keep it afloat but produced some of the most famous and successful sports cars of the age.

With the departure of Bertelli in 1936, Sutherland promoted Claude Hill to be chief designer and engineer. One of his first jobs was to work on the road-going version of the 2-litre racing engine, which resulted in the production of the 13/98 series of cars. As the 1930s progressed the need for a new car was becoming more and more obvious, and Hill was responsible for designing two. The first was based on a 13/98 steel chassis but with a tubular steel frame mounted on it to provide strength, rigidity, and a structure on which an unstressed body could be mounted – this car was nicknamed 'Donald Duck'. Then, utilizing what he had learned from this exercise, Hill went on to design the space-frame car known as 'The Atom' – so called because, to quote Hill, 'it had lots of performance in a small package'. At the same time, before the war, Hill started to design a new engine to replace the venerable 2-litre unit, whose roots could be traced back to Bertelli and Renwick's original engine from the 1920s.

In 1939 the company moved from making cars to war work, and by all accounts had a good and profitable war, the steady work putting the company into the black and resulting in a run of reasonable profits. During the war the company was kept busy making numerous components, mainly for the aeronautical industry, which included components for the de Havilland Mosquito and wing brackets for the Vickers Wellington. Claude Hill described how he found the designing of tooling and jigs for the many parts the company made to be satisfying work, and that he found designing and producing all the tooling for the production of Spitfire control columns to be particularly rewarding.

**View of the Aston Martin Service Department at Feltham in 1934.**

In between the war work, the company continued to develop the 'Atom' prototype and Claude Hill's new 4-cylinder engine, along with running up an impressive number of test miles on the Atom. During the hostilities the factory escaped any major damage until it had a near miss by a V1 flying bomb in 1944, which caused severe damage to the old Service Department building. Post-war hopes were pinned on the Aston Martin Atom. This had a space-frame chassis, a Cotal electrically operated four-speed gearbox, independent front suspension, and a new 4-cylinder 1970cc pushrod engine.

At the end of the war the Victoria road premises were very dilapidated. Not only had maintenance on the buildings been a low priority, but they had also suffered from the V1 near miss and as such were approaching a time when some major work would be needed if they were to remain habitable. In early 1946 the company bought a replacement for the wrecked service department, Friary Motors Ltd, a modern garage and showroom in Old Windsor. The intention was also to use these premises as the company's experimental and racing department, but these plans never came to fruition. It was in these premises that a small number of the new 2-litre Hill-designed engines were fitted to various pre-war 2-litre cars, both for use as works development cars and to give private owners a more up-to-date unit.

Despite the relative commercial success of the company during the war, it soon became apparent that there was not enough money to develop the completely new car, based on the Atom, that the market demanded. Drastic measures were needed, and the result was an advertisement in the personal column of *The Times* newspaper in 1946 placed by Sutherland offering a 'sports car company' for sale.

An important aspect of the company history was the setting up of the Aston Martin Owners Club. The AMOC was founded in 1935 by Mortimer Morris-Goodall, an enthusiast

**The Ulster model usually came with two-seat bodywork with the spare wheel stored horizontally in the tail, giving the car a sleek, streamlined look.**

and racer who, having purchased LM7, competed 'under works control' at Le Mans in 1933. Having agreed with Sammy Davis, who was sports editor of *The Autocar,* that a club was a good idea, Morris and Davis placed an advert in the magazine calling for interested parties to attend a meeting at the Grafton Hotel on 25 May 1935. At the meeting, which was attended by twenty-five to thirty people, a committee was set up and Charles Jarrott was appointed President with Sammy Davis as Vice President. Leslie Keevil was appointed Honorary Treasurer, and Mortimer Morris-Goodhall was Honorary Secretary.

The club's Memorandum of Association stated that the club was intended to 'develop interest in the Aston Martin car, promote the sport and pastime of motoring, and encourage social intercourse between members'. To this end the club was mainly social, with annual dinner dances at the Park Lane Hotel. World War II curtailed the club's activities, and the club was reconvened by Dick Stallebrass at a meeting at the Royal Automobile Club on 5 March 1948. Unfortunately Stallebrass was killed at the Spa 24 Hour race some four months later driving a pre-war Aston Martin 2-litre Speed Model, and the running of the club was taken over by Dudley Coran, with Eric Cutlet as chairman.

In 1998 the club purchased a new headquarters building, an old barn dating back to the fifteenth century, in Drayton St Leonard, Oxfordshire; at the same time it set up a charitable incorporated organization, the Aston Martin Heritage Trust (AMHT). Now managed by the AMHT, the barn was refurbished, and opened in 2002: as well as housing the headquarters of the AMOC, it is also used to store and exhibit the AMOC and AMHT's extensive collection of Aston Martin artefacts – these include the archives of the club and the company, as well as various historic Aston Martin cars, in particular the oldest extant Aston Martin, the A3.

## THE ENGINES

### The Bertelli 4-Cylinder Overhead Camshaft Unit

Developed from the unit that powered the Renwick and Bertelli 'Buzzbox', the new Aston Martin engine was a 4-cylinder 1488cc chain-driven overhead camshaft unit and featured a new wedge-shaped combustion chamber design proved in the 'Buzzbox' unit. The unit would be relatively long lived and would power the new generation of Bertelli-designed Aston Martins through to the middle of the 1930s when the 2-litre engine took over.

With a bore and stroke of 69.25 × 99mm, the 1488cc engine adopted the state-of-the-art practice (still followed today) of

**The standard engine for the 1930s Aston Martin was the 1.5-litre overhead cam unit. This is the carburettor side of the engine from Richard Lovey's 1933 long-chassis tourer.**

casting the iron engine block and cylinders in one piece. The cast-iron crankshaft was carried on three main bearings, and the connecting rods were light alloy, as were the pistons. The detachable cast-iron head carried the camshaft in a bolt-on light alloy cradle, which carried three plain bearings with oil feeds to all three. The head was a cross-flow design, with the valves sited in the head in pairs, the inlet on the right and exhaust on the left, and each valve was fitted vertically into the head. The combustion chambers were oval, and each valve was operated from a rocker sited on each side of the camshaft. A handsome polished alloy cam cover was fitted on the top of the engine, and the engine breather through a single SU-type carburettor.

On the crankshaft nose there was a gear that drove a large diameter composite 'Fabroil' secondary gear pinion, which turned a countershaft at half engine speed. The Fabroil gear was used to keep the geartrain to the countershaft quiet, and the whole mechanism was encased in the front of the crankcases. The camshaft itself was driven by an inverted tooth chain fitted on this countershaft, and the chain was tensioned using a 'Weller'-type blade spring. The design allowed for the camshaft sprocket to be unbolted from the camshaft and fixed to a vertical bracket bolted to the block when removing the head, to avoid disturbing the valve timing. The cooling system was quite sophisticated, as the water in the head was circulated directly from the water pump mounted in the front of the crankcase, while the water around the cylinders relied on thermo-syphoning to promote circulation.

**The 1931 1.5 ohc engine was a clean and neat design. The trademark twin exhaust pipes are shown here.**

In 1928 the engine was fitted with a dry-sump lubrication system for fitment to the sports models. The original plunger-type oil pump of the wet-sump engine was replaced with a pair of gear-type pumps fitted to the front of the engine. One pump sent oil from the tank into the engine under pressure, while the second scavenged the 'used' oil from a small sump in the base of the engine back to the tank; this pump had twice the capacity of the pressure pump. The oil pump was mounted in the front of the car between the front dumb irons below the radiator, and was usually covered by a louvred cowl.

The engine did not escape the cost-cutting measures introduced in 1932. The inverted tooth cam chain was changed for a roller version, as not only was the roller chain cheaper, but the sprockets that carried the chain on the intermediate shaft and the camshaft were cheaper and easier to make. By the time of the modifications, some engines had suffered failure of the Fabroil pinion, with consequent disaster for the engine as the camshaft stopped turning and the pistons met various valves. So the countershaft's Fabroil secondary

**This long-chassis International model shows how the 1.5-litre engine was mounted between the chassis longerons.**

gear was replaced with a steel item; while no cheaper and noisier, this was done to protect against the failure of the Fabroil gear.

The cylinder head was redesigned, with modified porting that enabled the fitting of properly designed inlet and exhaust manifolds. The valves gained triple springs, retained with threaded collars that were fixed in place with threaded caps. Separate cast-iron manifolds could also be fitted, although engines with magnetos retained the original design of exhaust manifold with a rear exit to avoid overheating the magneto that was mounted low on the side of the engine. The starter was moved from the right-hand side to the left, where it was fitted into the new bell housing designed to accept the new proprietary gearbox, which was now in unit with the engine.

The engine was reworked for 1934, with a new block casting that incorporated a revised oil-filtration system, along with a new block breathing system with a wider front timing case. The wider timing case held wider timing gears and a triple blade 'Weller'-type spring tensioner for the timing chain. The new engine breathing system had an alloy casting mounted on the rocker cover, which was connected to a steel convoluted hose to vent the engine gases. The dry-sump 'Le Mans' unit also had modified oil pumps fitted.

**The 1936 2-litre overhead camshaft engine was a redesign of the previous 1500cc unit. With a capacity of 1949cc, the main new feature was that the inlet and exhaust had swapped sides, putting the carbs on the left and the exhaust on the right.**

## The 2-Litre Overhead Cam Engine

In June 1936 Aston Martin unveiled a new engine, which broke tradition by displacing 2 litres rather than the 1500cc that the company had previously specialized in. Designed by Claude Hill but still based on the Bertelli and Renwick 1500cc unit, the new engine was destined to carry the company forwards to the start of World War II.

While it retained the overall layout of the previous 1.5-litre engine, the 2-litre engine had a bore and stroke of 78 × 102mm, which gave a capacity of 1949cc. In keeping with the constraints placed on engine dimensions by the RAC car-tax formula, the engine was under-square, or long-stroke, with all the engineering disadvantages this gave – but the under-square dimensions meant that the engine fell into the 15hp taxation class.

The engine had a cast-iron block and head, and a bolt-on alloy sump, and the layout was virtually identical to the preceding engine. The cylinder head was a cross-flow design, with the inlet ports on the left-hand side and the exhaust ports on the right, the opposite way to the 1.5-litre engine – and somewhat oddly the change was claimed to produce more power. The camshaft ran in three bearings and operated the valves via rockers. The valves were operated by finger tappets, and these were pivoted on eccentric pins, allowing the clearances to be set by rotating the pins and then locking them in place. The inlet valves were of larger diameter than the exhaust.

While the normal road-car models had a conventional wet-sump oil system, the super sports cars had a dry-sump oil system, with the oil tank in the traditional Aston Martin position between the front dumb irons where the oil could be cooled by the airflow. The dry-sump oil system utilized two oil pumps, both mounted externally on the front of the engine. The smaller pump picked up oil from the oil tank and supplied oil under pressure to the engine bearings via the oil filter and the cylinder head, while the larger pump scavenged the oil back from the small sump and into the oil tank. The dry-sump system also used a scraper-type oil filter, which had to be cleaned by turning a lever on its top – an operation which it was recommended was done every morning the engine was started, and the whole filter cleaned out when the oil was changed every 2,500 miles (4,000km). In service the 2-litre engine proved to be a reasonably reliable unit with a small performance boost over the venerable 1.5-litre engine.

## The 2-Litre ohv 4-Cylinder

At the end of the 1930s, Aston Martin had their 2-litre ohc engine, but the company recognized that, thanks to the use of the 1500cc unit as a basis, the 'new' 2-litre unit had very little development potential, and that an all-new engine was needed. The company had experimented in the years before the war with rotary valve engines, but the engine that would emerge as the company's post-war powerplant would be a

4-cylinder unit with pushrod-operated overhead valves and an unusual but very efficient combustion chamber design. Designed by Claude Hill, the all-new 2-litre unit was to power the Atom prototype, and was also designed in conjunction with a 3-litre straight six, which shared the new engine's architecture. Thoughts were also turned to a high-powered, flat twin air-cooled engine with rotary valves to power a smaller, lightweight sports car – but again these plans did not come to fruition.

The all-new 4-cylinder Aston Martin unit had a bore and stroke of 82.55 × 92mm, giving a capacity of 1970cc, and a prototype unit was fitted into the Atom prototype during World War II. The bore and stroke dimensions, while still over-square, were moving in the right direction of shorter stroke and larger bore, showing that the company was at last breaking away from the old 'RAC' tax formula that so compromised engine development in the UK during the inter-war years. The unit had a cast-iron head and block, and, unusually for Aston Martin, had pushrod-operated overhead valves. This made the unit the first Aston Martin engine so equipped – the earliest engines had side valves, while the rest of the pre-war units had overhead camshafts.

When compared to the pre-war engines, reverting to pushrods appears to have been a retrograde step, but Aston Martin justified the move on the grounds that while the power output was barely affected, the 'cylinder head became much easier to handle' – whether this meant easier to make or easier to maintain, or indeed both, is unclear. However, it is undeniable that it was easier to work on the unit, especially if setting the valve clearances or removing the head, than it was on some overhead camshaft units.

The head had wedge-shaped combustion chambers, with the inlet valves positioned vertically in a line along the fore and aft axis of the head in the lowest part of the wedge, and positioned slightly off centre (towards the inlet side of the engine) to the centre line of the cylinder. When closed at top dead centre there was very limited clearance between the inlet valve heads and the pistons, positioning the combustion chamber under the exhaust valve heads. The exhaust valves were placed in the higher part of the combustion chamber wedge: they were inclined at around 15 degrees to the vertical, and the exhaust ports were angled directly upwards to give the exhaust gases an unfettered exit from the cylinder. The result of this unusual route for the exhaust ports meant that the exhaust manifold was bolted on to the top of the head rather than the side, giving the engine an unusual appearance when viewed in the engine bay.

The spark plugs were bolted horizontally into the side of the head below the exhaust valve, and a water jacket was bolted on the side of the head to provide adequate cooling of the exhaust valve seat and the combustion chamber through cast-in water passages in the head. The valves were opened using rockers, which were equal length for inlet and exhaust as the tops of the valves were all at the same level despite the different alignment of inlet and exhaust valves. The rockers were carried on a single shaft mounted on the head on

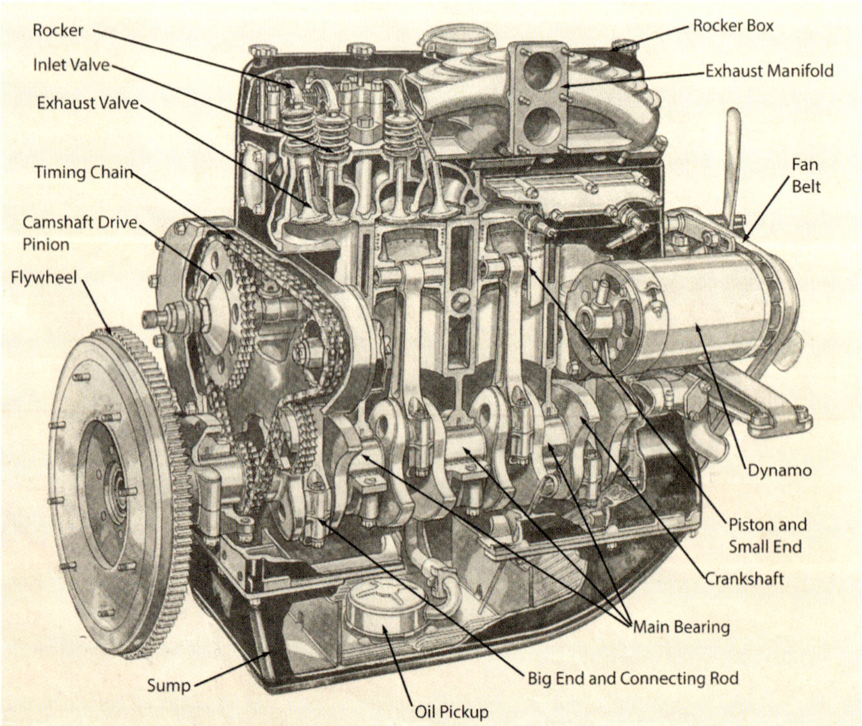


**Claude Hill's 2-litre overhead valve engine from the early 1940s was a solid and worthy unit, but ground breaking it was not. The raised exhaust manifold was an easy recognition point.**

five mounts. The shaft was hollow and was pressure-fed oil through a metering valve. The short pushrods were operated by tappets mounted on the block on the inlet side directly above the high-mounted camshaft.

The camshaft was carried in plain bearings and ran in an oil trough. It was driven by a duplex roller chain positioned in the rear of the engine; the chain also drove the water pump, an engine-speed water pump positioned on the exhaust side. The camshaft was fitted with a skew gear, which powered a shaft that ran diagonally across the engine between cylinders 2 and 3. The top of this shaft emerged on the exhaust side of the engine and drove the distributor, while the lower end emerged on the inlet side and drove the oil pump.

The oil pump was a gear type, which, after picking up oil from a floating filtered pick-up in the sump, passed it through an externally mounted 'Auto-Klean' full-flow filter before distributing it at pressure to the crankshaft via the main bearing, the camshaft and the rocker shaft. Pressure feed to the big-end bearings was via drillings in the crankshaft, while the piston sides and small-end bearings were lubricated by splash. Oil pressure was 90psi, oil capacity was a generous 12 pints (6.8ltr), and all oilways were internal.

The cast-iron crankshaft was carried in the crankcases in five plain split main bearings. Three of these bearings – numbers 1, 3 and 5 – were wide, while bearings 2 and 4 were narrower and were described as acting more as locating or steadying bearings. There were three compression rings and one oil scraper ring fitted to the light alloy pistons, which were carried on light aluminium alloy connecting rods with split shell big-end bearings and floating gudgeon pins. The water pump was positioned on the rear of the engine on the exhaust side, and was driven directly from the timing chain at engine speed.

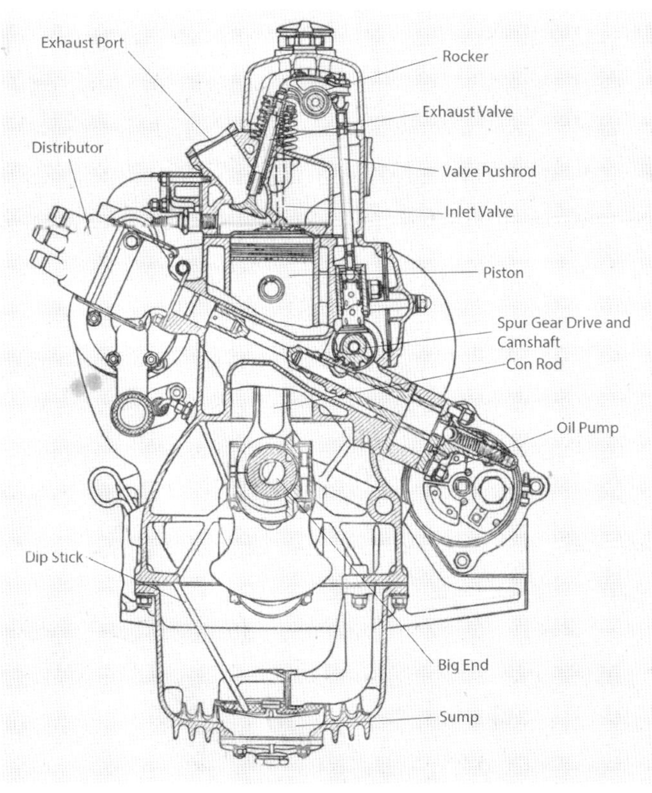


**In cross-section the Hill 2-litre engine displays its vertical inlet valves and the angled exhaust valves.**

The cooling system was designed to actively circulate water through the head, with special emphasis on cooling around the exhaust valves, as shown by the separate water manifold bolted to the head below the exhaust manifold. The total capacity of the system was about 3.5gal (16ltr), and the water in the block relied on thermosyphon action to provide limited circulation. This system was introduced as early tests showed the cylinder block was overcooled if the water was circulated through it as well as the head. When combined with the cooling properties of the extensively finned alloy sump, the alloy water manifold bolted to the exhaust side of the head and the finned alloy exhaust manifold, the unit had a reputation for cool running.

The exhaust manifold had two ports incorporated into it, one for cylinders 1 and 4, the other for cylinders 2 and 3, which gave a small amount of negative pressure to help scavenging. The inlet ports were paired in the head, and were fed by a pair of SU constant velocity carburettors.

The light alloy sump was bolted on to the base of the crankcase, and was finned both internally and externally to help cool the oil. Internal baffles were fitted in front of and behind the oil pick-up float. At the front of the engine a fan and dynamo were driven by a belt from the front of the crank.

The 4-cylinder engine was developed during World War II, and was introduced to the public in late 1946 after being extensively tested in the Atom. With a compression ratio of 7.25:1 it produced a healthy 90bhp at 4,750rpm. The engines were produced for Aston Martin and Lagonda at the David Brown Tractors Group factory at Meltham Mills, near Huddersfield in North Yorkshire.

## THE CARS

The new Aston Martin model, named the 1.5-litre model, was introduced in 1926. Available in both short and long chassis form, the new cars lead to the development of the International and Le Mans models. In 1934 the 'Ulster' model was introduced.

### The Aston Martin Series 1 'T'-Type Cars

The first fruits of the reformed company, and the first cars to be produced at the new Feltham works, were the Aston

Martin 'T'-type cars, which are generally referred to today as the 'First Series' cars. These cars were originally available in one chassis size and were fitted with three types of body – a four-seater saloon, a four-seat, four-door open tourer and a two-seat open tourer. The only part carried over from the Bamford and Martin era was the design of the radiator grille. These First Series models were launched at the 1927 London Motor Show at Olympia, where Aston Martin described them as 'The car that is built for the owner's pleasure'. Also displayed at the show was a mock-up of a short-wheelbase 'sports three-seater'. This had an underslung rear chassis, giving the car extremely low lines, and was the forerunner of the famous 'International' model; however, it did not make it into production, although a new Standard Sports model did appear in 1928, which shared the show car's short chassis and general lines.

The first Series I 'T'-type model had a wheelbase of 114in (2,896mm) with a front and rear track of 52in (1,320mm) and an overall length of 150in (3,810mm). The chassis had seven cross-members – five tubular and two 'U'-section – joining the two pressed-steel main longerons, making it quite rigid. In the sports model the chassis longerons were swept up over the front and rear axles. This gave the car a low mounted body, which in turn meant the car had a low centre of gravity, which helped the handling, and sporty looks.

The tourer was powered by Aston Martin's new 4-cylinder engine designed by Renwick and Bertelli (described above), and all the tourer models incorporated a wet-sump oil system. The gearbox was Aston Martin's own design, and was a four-speed unit with straight-cut gears; it was mounted behind the engine and clutch rather than being in unit, with the explanation that like this, the gear lever was more conveniently positioned. The rear axle was made by Aston Martin, and was an underslung worm type, with a central alloy casing and steel tubes carrying the halfshafts to the hubs. Brakes were 14in diameter drums all round, mechanically operated with the fronts being operated via the Perrot system seen on the earlier cars.

While the car was available in bare chassis form, it was also offered with two types of body – a closed saloon, and an open four-seat tourer. Both types of body were produced by Enrico Bertelli's bodyshop for Aston Martin. The four-seat tourer was typical of the time, with a long folding roof and a simple four-door body. The saloon was a neat and attractive four-door design, with a 'V' windscreen and fabric-covered roof and rear quarters. A distinguishing feature of the 'T'-type saloon's bodywork was that the earlier cars had the chassis frame exposed between the bottom of the doors and running boards, while later models had the chassis hidden behind the bodywork.

The 'T'-type steering was unique to the model and comprised a Marles-type steering box mounted high on the front of the cast-aluminium alloy bulkhead, with a vertical drop arm and linkage to move the right-hand-side wheel, which was connected to the left wheel by a further linkage.

Four-wheel brakes were fitted as standard, along with Rudge Whitworth wire wheels and Hartford shock absorbers. There were two body styles offered: an open four-seat four-door tourer, or an enclosed four-seat four-door saloon.

**LM1, a 1928 works car based on the first series Standard Sports car. It was the first works racer.**

## The Aston Martin Sports 11.9hp/1.5-litre

Following on from the mock-up Sports model shown at the 1927 show, in 1928 Aston Martin produced a new model to run alongside the 'T' type. This was the Standard Sports model, which had a 138in- (3,505mm-) long chassis with a 102in (2,590mm) wheelbase and an underslung rear axle, but retained the 'T' model's 52in (1,320mm) track.

The Standard Sports model was more than just a lightly souped-up version of the tourer. Aston Martin put a lot of thought into the model, and this resulted in a significantly different car to the tourer, and more than justified the 'Sports' name. However, the major difference to the 'T' was that the 'S' chassis was 'underslung', with the rear axle sitting above the chassis. While the 'S' model's overall chassis layout was similar to the 'T', the 'S' had six tubular cross-members, one replacing the 'T's channel-section cross-member above the rear axle, and an additional tubular cross-member fitted between the front dumb irons that was pierced to accept a bearing for the starting handle.

A dry-sump lubrication system was fitted, with the oil tank fitted in the front of the car below the radiator and extending forwards between the front dumb irons. The car was fitted with a conventional steering box rather than the bulkhead-mounted one seen on the 'T' type. The engine was the same basic 4-cylinder unit as fitted to the 'T' type, but had a higher compression ratio, a twin carburettor, and some examples were fitted with a dual ignition system, with two spark plugs per cylinder.

Fitted with a three- or two-seater bodywork, the cars had a new, lower radiator design and 'helmet'-type front wings that turned with the front wheels, a feature that would be synonymous with sporting Aston Martins of the Bertelli era. The Standard Sports was lower, lighter and shorter than the Tourer, and had a significantly better performance than the 'T' type. Two versions were produced – a three-seater with a single seat positioned centrally behind the two front seats, and a true two-seater.

The car was an immediate success, and in 1929 the company received more orders for the Standard Sports model than for the 'T'-type cars: this was the Aston Martin that would prove to be the template for sporting Astons up to the start of World War II.

## The Aston Martin International

The International is one of Aston Martin's iconic models. Introduced in 1928, it was an evolution of the Sports model, and was initially somewhat clumsily named the 'Four-Seater International Sports' model; however, it soon adopted the simple 'International' name. The car's chassis was similar in layout to the Standard Sports, but its length fell between the 'T' type and the Sports model at 138in (3,505mm), and it had a 103in (2,616mm) wheelbase. One of the definitive features of the International models was the retention of the dry-sump lubrication system first seen on the Sports model, along with a 'wet' radiator shell, where the complete radiator was used to contain the cooling water without any outer shell.

With other small modifications from the Sports model, such as a new design of the braking system and a repositioned gearbox, the car was built to the highest standards and was generally accepted by the press and customers of the day to be a very high quality product. However, this came at a price: because virtually all the mechanical components were built in house, the cars were very expensive.

In 1932 the four-seater International Sports was complemented in the range by the four-seat Open Tourer, which although fitted with a slightly shorter and lighter chassis at 118in (2,997mm), weighed more than the previous model – and performance suffered as a result of the additional weight. The shorter chassis range was further extended by a pair of saloon-bodied cars in two- and four-door form, but they were still too heavy and were generally considered to be the slowest of all the pre-war Aston Martins; they were not good sellers, and only one two-door saloon was built. On the up side the cars were very well built, with apparently very nicely trimmed interiors.

The performance image was revived with the introduction of the International 'Le Mans' two-seat sports model in 1931. These were replicas of the 1930 team cars – LM5, LM6 and LM7, which ran at Le Mans in 1931 – fitted with two-door open bodies with a fold-down windscreen and the lower radiator profile of the works cars. These cars should not be confused with the later 1932 two- to four-seat Le Mans cars, which had a completely new design of chassis, gearbox and final drive. The exhaust made its exit from the body via two pipes, and was connected to a large exhaust box fitted on the bonnet

**The 1930 International was a development of the Sports model, and is now an iconic Aston Martin model.**

side, while the lowered radiator gave the cars a distinctive sporting look. Five were built in total.

In 1931 a drop-head coupé version based on the short chassis was produced for Lance Prideaux-Brune, owner of the Automobile Service Company (and who would buy into Aston Martin in the 1930s) to compete in the 1932 RAC Rally, while another similar car was produced for a second customer. At least two further cars with similar bodies were produced by outside coachbuilders on chassis supplied by Aston Martin. A one-off fixed-head coupé bodied by Bertelli was supplied to ship owner W.S. Headlam, again based on the short-chassis International. Bertelli also produced six two-seater International Sports models with two-door short-tail bodywork with the spare wheel mounted on the rear.

From 1930 the factory offered a tuned engine named the 'Ulster'. The 1.5 litre engine was modified with a new stronger crankshaft, high-compression pistons, revised combustion chambers, larger valves, cleaned-up ports and a pair of 1¾in aluminium-bodied SU carburettors. This gave a claimed output of 56bhp at 4,500rpm, and boosted the top speed of the cars to around 90mph (145km/h).

**A 1934 1.5-litre Mark II short-chassis sports car. The vertical radiator louvres are typical of the Mark II.**

## The Second Series Cars: 1931–1933

The Second Series cars were produced from 1931. Their main distinguishing feature was the all-new chassis, but they also benefited from some major changes to the engine (see above), and a proprietary rear axle sourced from ENV. The new chassis – as before, a simple ladder affair with two side members or longerons joined by cross-members – had an underslung rear end, and retained the existing track and wheelbase measurements of the long and short Series 1 cars. The engine mounts were revised to make the engine a semi-stressed part of the chassis, which significantly stiffened the front end of the car.

The braking system was revised, with mainly cable operation, which meant the Perrot-type operation of the front brakes was no longer necessary, and thumbscrews on each drum meant adjustment could be done quickly and easily. The drums were still relatively large 14in-diameter items, but the width of the shoes was increased to 1½in. This meant that there were more bought-in components than before, but the quality of the cars was still high, even though the prices were dropped. Short-chassis models were fitted with a chassis of 102in (2,590mm), while the long-chassis models had an 118in (2,997mm) wheelbase.

The base model of the range was, as previously, the 1.5-litre model, and was called the 12/50; it came with the longer chassis and could be supplied with either the tourer or the saloon bodies from the factory, or could be supplied as a rolling chassis for the customer to choose their own coachbuilder. The cars were fitted with the old-style cylinder head, and only some twenty-seven were built.

The cars' heavy weight and low performance engine meant that they were not very sporty, and so sales were slow. They were fitted with the two-door touring or four-door saloon bodies, along with the new dry radiator. A single two-door fixed-head coupé was also built.

The Second Series New International was only produced for a short while during 1932, with only six cars completed, and was quickly superseded by the Second Series Le Mans as the sports model in the range. This was very much the Series 1 International body fitted to the new Series 2 chassis, with minor modifications to accommodate the new mechanical fixings. The wet radiator was replaced with a dry outer shell holding the actual radiator. The chassis was the short version with the 102in (2,590mm) wheelbase.

### *The Second Series 12/50*

Essentially the 12/50 was a four-seat long-chassis version of the New International, with the sporting model's mechanical elements mounted on a long chassis. The 12/50 was built in small numbers and had four-seater coachwork, either in open tourer or saloon configurations. The fuel tank was enclosed in the rear of the body, and the spare wheel was mounted externally on the back of the body. The saloon version was fitted with four doors, which were all hinged on the 'B' pillar. Generally considered to be slow and somewhat ponderous, the 12/50 did not fit with Aston Martin's sporting image and sales were slow, with only twenty-seven examples being sold over two years.

**The 1934 car's ladder-type chassis was simple and robust, with plenty of cross-members to give it strength and rigidity. Note the rear leaf springs and friction dampers.**

### *The Second Series Le Mans*

The most successful model of the Second Series was without doubt the 'Le Mans'. Fitted with the short chassis, the sporting Le Mans took over from the New International and was by far the most popular model in the range, sealing Aston Martin's reputation for producing lightweight sporting cars that were a cut above the opposition. The first version was the 'Competition two-seater', which when compared with the earlier cars had a lower radiator with a more pronounced 'V' shape, cooling louvres stamped into the top of the bonnet halves, and a fold-flat windscreen. The snug two-seater cabin was accessed through two doors, was neat and workmanlike, and the rear body tapered neatly into a rounded point at the back. A two/four seater version was also produced, still utilizing the 102in (2,590mm) wheelbase chassis but fitted with an external rear fuel tank to make room for the extra rear seats.

The final version of the Le Mans was the 'Le Mans special four-seater', which used the longer chassis to give the rear passengers more room. Mechanically identical to the standard Le Mans, the four-seater was virtually as fast and was a popular choice for the man looking for a roomy family car with a sparkling performance.

## The Third Series Cars: 1934–1935

The Third Series cars were produced between 1934 and 1935 and were known as the Mark II models. They were equipped with a new chassis that retained the overall layout and the 102in (2,590mm) wheelbase of the previous cars, but had significantly deeper channels for the longerons, which were made from thicker section steel, and having more bracing around the front and rear of the engine bay, and larger and thicker alloy bulkhead plates, were used to secure the alloy bulkhead to the chassis. A new 'U'-section cross-member was fitted below the rear of the engine, which was no longer used to brace the chassis. As usual the new chassis came in either a long – 120in (3,048mm) – or a short – 103in (2,616mm) – wheelbase.

The Third Series Mark II had the modified engine with wet sump, and the new strengthened chassis. It was available as a 2/4 tourer with the 103in (2,616mm) wheelbase chassis or as the four-seat tourer with the 120in (3,048mm) wheelbase chassis. The Sports Saloon Mark II was built on the 120in (3,048mm) wheelbase chassis and was fitted with the very neat two-door four-seater saloon body, with a sliding sunroof and no running boards, giving the car very smooth lines. Only seven Mark II drop-head coupés were built on the long chassis, as a special order for Lance Prideaux-Brune for his Winter Garden Garage; these were fitted with a fixed windscreen and wind-up windows in the two doors. Finally around four Mark II two-seaters were built, though these were never listed as actual models.

The Ulster was the seminal pre-World War II sporting Aston Martin, and was so named after the works cars' success in the 1934 Ulster Tourist Trophy (TT) race held at the Ards circuit in Northern Ireland. With a lower radiator line than the Mark II, the Ulster's main distinguishing feature was the rear of the bodywork, where the spare wheel was stored horizontally in the lower half of the body, resulting in the distinctive 'boat-tail' lines of the car. Eleven works cars (LM11–LM21) and seventeen production cars were built. While the chassis was standard Mark II specification, the engines were uprated, with a stronger bottom end featuring a new, stronger crankshaft, lowered combustion chamber roof, and domed pistons used to give a higher compression ratio. A higher lift camshaft was fitted, and to aid breathing a pair of

**With its large steering wheel and unergonomic sprinkling of instruments and switches, the charming cockpit of the AMHT's 'Ulster' is typical of the era.**

specially made, all alloy 1⅛in SUs sat on the inlet side, and the exhaust was a four-into-one system. The engine modifications gave a healthy 85bhp, 15bhp more than the standard Mark II.

## The Aston Martin 2-Litre (15/98): 1936–1940

The new Aston Martin 2-litre not only introduced the new larger engine, but was also equipped with a new chassis. The 2-litre car's ladder chassis was all new, and designed from the outset to use hydraulic brakes and so did not have to carry the heavy and strong mounts for the rods, cross-shafts and linkages needed on the previous generations of cars. This simplified the design of the chassis significantly, and so the unit had the usual pair of 'U'-section longerons that were joined by five cross-members – four pressed-steel 'U' section and one fabricated from sheet steel. The chassis was underslung at the rear, and was fitted with a propriatory front axle from Alford and Alder. The chassis was, as usual for Aston Martin, built in two lengths: the long version had a wheelbase of 116in (2,946mm), while the short version was 102in (2,590mm).

The brakes were 14in alloy drums with steel liners all round, and were operated hydraulically by Lockheed master and slave cylinders.

As well as the new engine, the Aston Martin-designed gearbox was comprehensively revised and strengthened. While many manufacturers were introducing synchromesh in their gearboxes, Aston Martins retained the strong, straight-cut gears as a nod to their racing heritage and the driving skills of their owners.

In the 1930s many cars were named after the combination of their RAC horsepower rating and the car's actual rating – hence the new 2-litre Aston Martin was named the 15/98: 15 for the RAC horsepower rating, and 98 for the claimed actual engine output. The 15/98 was introduced in 1936; initially it came in the longer of the chassis lengths made by Aston Martin and was fitted with either the two-door four-seater Sports bodywork, or the four-door saloon bodywork, but in 1937 it was also supplied with the short chassis as a 2/4 seater Sports or a two-seater drop-head coupé.

The 2-litre Speed model was the successor to the Ulster as the sports car in the range. Fitted with the short chassis and the dry-sump engine, the Speed model was built in small numbers so there was no 'standard' bodywork, with most cars having lightweight two-seater bodywork from various suppliers. Enrico Bertelli built five cars with 2/4 tourer-style bodies, and these are generally known as Type 'A' cars, while Abbey Coachworks of Farnham built a pair of two-seater road cars with bulbous front wings – these are known as Type 'B'.

**The 2-litre model can be identified by the exhaust system exiting on the right-hand side. This is a 1939 2-litre model.**

## The Type 'C'

In an attempt to make the then current 2-litre more up to date, the Type 'C' with Claude Hill-designed streamlined bodywork was produced. The style can be summed up as a halfway house between the pre-war narrow bodywork with cycle-type mudguards or running boards as seen on the previous Aston Martin models, and the all-enveloping designs that were starting to appear – notably the BMW 328 of the late 1930s.

Introduced at the Earls Court Motor Show in October 1938, the Type 'C' Speed model Aston Martin was basically a rebodied 2-litre Speed model – and by all accounts people either loved the styling or they loathed it. The show car was also painted in a somewhat garish green and yellow scheme,

**The Type C 2-litre was a not unsuccessful attempt to update the traditional Aston Martin styling into the streamline age.**

**'Donald Duck' – this was a modified 1939 saloon used to explore Claude Hill's initial thoughts on space-frame design.**

with the green on the central bodywork and the bulbous wings in yellow – and was unkindly but unsurprisingly nicknamed the 'Flying Banana'. With only around eight actually built, the sales figures indicate that the public's attitude towards the car tended towards disliking it, although the price of £775, some £225 more than the most expensive current model, may have had something to do with it; the 15/98 may also have played a part in the model's poor sales. Not only was the price high, but the performance was also only equal to, if not bettered by the 15/98, so it was hard to see what the customer got for the extra cost.

Nonetheless the model remains rare and quite desirable today; the excursion into 'modern' styling is today seen as an interesting but abortive design path that Aston Martin did not, or was unable to pursue to a logical conclusion. The company was experimenting with the styling as the cars were built – the first two cars had the headlamps mounted in the wings, while subsequent cars had the lamps placed in front of the radiator behind the stone-guard grille, giving a much cleaner look.

## 'Donald Duck'

Towards the end of the 1930s, Aston Martin was exploring ways of modernizing their cars and moving away from the traditional and expensive bodybuilding techniques of hanging a hand-made bodyshell on ashwood frames. The factory took a standard 15/98 saloon chassis (number 703/4S, registered EML132), and produced an all-new, four-door closed bodyshell, the steel panels of which were supported on a framework of steel tubing. The framework was made from readily available and cheap electrical conduit, other higher quality steel tubing being in demand from the burgeoning rearmament industry. The unusual choice of material for the frame dictated to some extent the body profile, but the end result was, despite its somewhat unkind nickname, not unattractive, with a long tapering bonnet line, split front windscreen and a nicely integrated tail, although it did have a disproportionately high roofline. Separate front and rear wings joined by vestigial running boards betrayed the conventional underpinnings, but the car was modern in appearance and probably more attractive than the 'Atom' that followed it.

Under the radical body, the mechanicals were updated: while the standard Lockheed brakes came from the saloon, the 2-litre engine was equipped with twin Zenith carburettors, while the ignition timing was fitted with a vacuum advance mechanism rather than the standard manual type.

## The Atom

In the late 1930s, while concentrating on the production of the sporting International and the Ulsters, Aston Martin was also looking towards the future. The company recognized that the gathering pace of engineering developments, which were being fed by the prospect of war, would soon render their current range of cars mechanically obsolete.

One of the most important developments in car construction in the late 1930s was the use of monocoque construction, where a separate chassis and body were combined into a single structure made from a number of usually steel pressings welded together. While this method was undeniably superior to the separate chassis and body, giving a rigid, strong and relatively light structure, the downside was the cost of the tooling to create the pressings, and the need for heavy and expensive presses to produce the pressings. While the cost of this emerging technology was not out of the reach of mass manufacturers, Aston Martin recognized it was prohibitively expensive for small-volume car makers – but they also realized they had to find a new way of producing their cars, as the construction of hand-made bodies over ash frames sitting on a separate chassis was also expensive and seen as old-fashioned. Engineering developments included the adoption of independent suspension, which would improve handling and, possibly more important from a social perspective, the ride comfort.

Engine technology was also advancing, thanks in part to better understanding of the combustion process, resulting in more power from smaller engines, and greater refinement and economy. The development of new alloys that were stronger and lighter than those seen previously meant that structures could be built more efficiently, while the creation of new plastics and other man-made materials also meant that many components could be made both better and more cheaply. Another element of these new plastic materials meant that interiors could be upholstered in cheaper and more resilient materials than before, and could also incorporate innovative and modern designs.

On top of these ever-changing technologies, changing social conditions and a general increase in economic activity was leading to unprecedented prosperity and a burgeoning middle class that could afford to own their own car. This social revolution was starting to create a new and large market for practical, economical and most importantly modern cars, which Aston Martin's current sporting range was not well placed to address. The social developments called for streamlined, clean and all-enclosing bodywork, a smooth and comfortable ride with minimal noise, vibration and harshness, and easy-to-use controls. These factors would increase the accessibility, desirability and ease of use of the car to the general public, and move the car into the mainstream.

**The Atom followed Donald Duck. The car was a four-door saloon with unstressed body panels fitted to a space-frame chassis.**

**While the styling was not to everyone's taste, the Atom was innovative in its design and led directly to the 2-litre Sports.**

If Aston Martin did not address this new market not only would their current range of sporting cars be relegated into a small niche market, it would also be seen to be utilizing increasingly obsolete engineering, and would potentially not have the performance to compete with their rivals who were using modern technology to build their cars. However, Aston Martin also recognized that they would not be able to afford to construct a pure monocoque body, so were forced to look for an alternative method of constructing their cars, a method that would be seen to be innovative and modern, while avoiding the costs of pure monocoque construction.

So in the late 1930s Aston Martin started to develop a prototype car to explore how it could exploit these technological and social changes to produce an all-new and advanced car, with engineer Claude Hill leading a small development team. The car built on their experience of building the 15/98-based 'Donald Duck', and featured a completely new chassis and body construction method. The car was named 'Atom', and was completed soon after the start of the war. The Atom was registered for road use in 1940 with the registration number LMF 386, and was described in *The Autocar* of 4 October 1940. Road tests came later, in the 18 July 1941 issue of *The Autocar* and the *Motor* of 22 July 1942, and the June 1942 issue of *Motor Sport*.

Ultimately the Atom was, to use modern parlance, more of a 'technology demonstrator' than an actual prototype, being used by the factory to explore the new design and technology of the semi space-frame chassis, the new engine, and the use of the cotal gearbox; in this role it apparently clocked up in excess of 100,000 miles (160,000km) during the war, often being driven by Gordon Sutherland. The car was driven by David Brown when he was looking to buy the company, and the overall design of the lower half of the chassis contributed much to the design of the first of the DB-era cars.

The Atom was virtually the last Aston to try to meet Lionel Martin's ideal light car philosophy, and although it had a major influence on the first two Aston Martin models produced after World War II, in reality it was a dead end, both in terms of technology and the overall concept. Technologically the space-frame chassis was superseded by the platform chassis seen on the first DB4, which was stiffer, and cheaper and quicker to produce. The concept of the expensive 'light car' with a small capacity engine and relatively high performance thanks to lack of mass had largely died by the end of World War II. Not only were the mass manufacturers producing efficient, well engineered cars that were much cheaper than Aston Martin could ever hope to match, the customers who could afford to buy Aston Martins wanted a GT car with trans-continental performance.

The only Atom car spent many years in a French museum, until it was brought back to the UK by Dr Tom Rollason, who had this important piece of Aston Martin's heritage fully restored. It is now in Ireland.

## Competition: The Works Cars – The 'LM' series Aston Martins

As seen in the Bamford and Martin days, competition was still seen as a valuable development and marketing tool by Aston Martin and Bertelli. During the 'Bertelli' period the chassis numbers of the works Aston Martins were prefixed with 'LM'. The first works car, chassis number LM1, was produced in late 1927, and was based on the Le Mans team cars, and ran in Le Mans with LM2 in 1928. Basically it was the prototype for the new production International model, and was used as the works demonstrator on its return from Le Mans and with the fitment of road gear such as new cycle-type mudguards. The car was later bought by S.C.H. 'Sammy' Davies, who ran it as his 'daily driver' through the 1920s and 1930s.

LM2 was prepared and run at Le Mans in 1928 alongside LM1, and with a newly prepared LM3, these formed the works cars for 1929. The pair of cars competed in the JCC Double Twelve race at Brooklands; LM2 failed to finish with engine failure, but LM3 came fifth and so became the first of the Bertelli-era cars to finish a major event.

LM4 was another completely new car, and was built for the 1930 season, where it was one of the two works cars, the second being a rebodied LM3. LM4's body was similar to the International, but had no doors. Its best result was finishing fourth in that year's JCC Double Twelve race at Brooklands.

LM5, 6 and 7 were made for the 1931 season and were built for H.J. Aldington of Fraser Nash cars, who financed the building of the three cars as well as running the team. Based on the production International, the three works cars had new bodies with a lowered radiator line and rear end, and cowls on the scuttle in front of the driver and passenger. This style would be reflected in the later 1931 production International. LM5's rear axle was fitted with a worm gear assembly supplied by David Brown & Sons (Huddersfield) Ltd, a company that would assume great significance for Aston Martin after World War II. LM6 was experimented on when it was fitted with a supercharger during late 1931.

LM8, 9 and 10 were the 1932 season cars based on the new chassis. These were low radiator cars and competed at Le Mans, with LM8 finishing in seventh place. All three cars were sold off after Le Mans. The privately owned LM9 was lent to the works and entered in Le Mans for 1933, along with the works cars LM7 and LM10, which the works had bought back after its sale in 1932. Success was achieved with LM9 coming

**Quite a few of the 1930s competition cars survive – this is LM2.**

fifth overall and first in class, and LM10 seventh overall and second in class. LM11 through to LM21 were ten Ulster models supplied to the works team and private entrants, which raced from 1934 through to the late 1930s with varying success.

## Feature Car: The First Bertelli-Era Works Car – LM1

Some cars are so much more than a collection of steel, alloy, wood, cloth and leather – some are special in that they are the personifications of an age or a marque, or they hold memories of times and people long gone. The first of the Bertelli-era works Aston Martins, LM1 is just such a car: not only is it a historically significant car that is firmly embedded in the marque's history, it was owned by the famous racing driver Sammy Davis, and is now owned by the sons of the man who owned and raced the car in the 1980s and 1990s. James Beven and his brother David currently own LM1, the first of the Bertelli-era works cars. The car has led a chequered life, but for the first decade of its life it was at the heart of the British racing scene, until finally coming into the Beven family ownership when James's father bought the car in 1988.

The story behind LM1 is interesting and not untypical of works cars in the early years of Aston Martin and other small manufacturers. The car was built as the first Aston Martin (as opposed to the previous Bamford and Martin Astons) 'works' racing car, and competed alongside the second works car LM2 at the 1928 Le Mans 24 Hours. After competing, the car was displayed on the Aston Martin stand at the Olympia show, and then, with a few modifications, was pressed into service as the works demonstrator, giving prospective customers road tests of the new International model. After this spell of duty it was sold to famous racer S.C.H. 'Sammy' Davis, who used it as his daily driver. It is believed that the car was rebodied to meet Davis's requirements, and that the original body may have been reused on LM2.

Davis owned LM1 from late 1928 through to 1939, during which time the car was often taken back to the factory for updates and modifications. Two stand out: first was the use of the lever from a loo being repurposed as the gear lever knob, as Davis liked the shape and feel. The second was rather more radical – the handbrake lever was extended so it could be used as the main braking control. It is believed that Davis had this modification made after he broke his leg in a crash at the 1931 Brooklands Easter Meeting when he was driving a friend's Invicta. With the quirky pedal layout of 1930s Astons – with the throttle pedal sited between the brake and the clutch – having only one working leg meant Davis could only brake or push the clutch in at one time, so the extended hand brake lever meant he could exert enough pressure on the cable-operated brakes to use it to stop the car without needing additional pressure from the foot lever and while operating the clutch.

As war clouds loomed, Davis sold LM1, then during the war the car was bought and sold on a couple of times, seeing little use. After the war it was bought by Hubert Pickup, who intended to take it racing; however, he ended up using it as his 'go to the pub' car. He then moved to Canada, and the car passed through a couple more owners, before it was bought by Dr Robert Follows, who exchanged another Aston and some cash for the car. Follows dismantled the car and rebuilt it as far as possible to the specification that it would have been in when Davis was using it – and judging from the car's condition today he did a sterling job.

Follows exhibited the car at the Pebble Beach concourse, where it won Class G – European Sports and Racing Cars 1925–1939 – in 1985. The car only returned to the UK in 1988 when it was sold through Coys, when James's father bought it.

When he bought the car James's father meant to race it, but after a few outings he felt that the 1500cc engine meant

**LM1 is now owned by the Beven family, and is taken to shows regularly. Here it is at the AMHT 100 Years celebration.**

With its traditional wooden dash and previous AMOC event badges and RAC scrutineering labels, LM1 wears its past with pride.

that he was not competitive, especially when racing against 2-litre Ulsters and the like. So he took it to Bill Elwell-Smith, the legendary specialist in pre-war Aston Martins, to sort it out and hopefully gain the performance boost that he felt the car needed.

James's father didn't just use the car for classic racing, he also used it on the road. James remembers one anecdote from this time. The family were going on holiday to France, with James's mother driving him and his brother in the family car, while his father was to follow on later after sorting out some paperwork for his business. Having done this he had to post it, so having loaded up the Aston and started on the road to the ferry he stopped at a postbox. As he posted the letters, the car started to move of its own accord – he had left the engine running but hadn't set the handbrake! He had to chase after the car, throw himself into the vehicle from the passenger side – there are no doors on this former racer – and get the brake on. He succeeded in regaining control of the runaway, but not before the car had run over his foot. Driving on to the ferry and through rural France to his holiday destination must have been agony, and he needed quite a bit of (somewhat late) first aid when he arrived at the holiday destination and hobbled in! A couple of crushed toes necessitated a trip to hospital, and the holiday was rather more sedate than normal, with his father laid up for the duration.

The front grille carries the Sammy Davis-designed badge that would become the Aston Martin standard from the 1930s onwards. Note also the oil tank positioned between the front dumb irons, with its offset filler cap.

Sadly in 1994, while the car was being sorted by Elwell-Smith, James's father died. After his mother retrieved the car from Elwell-Smith (who died soon after) it was put in store, where it stayed until James's mother passed away. Now James and his brother have decided to get the car back on the road, and while they are not going to go racing in it, they want the car to be seen. Taking it out of storage was relatively painless, but even though the car was complete, it still needed some fettling to get it back up and running. As can be seen from the accompanying photos it is in excellent condition, and is in fine condition mechanically. It is now back on the road, running nicely, and is being given the public exposure it deserves – it was at the AMHT Festival in June 2021, lined up and reunited with fellow works cars LM2 and LM3, and this was followed by a period of being on display at the AMHT barn, as well as a visit to Brooklands in August 2021. It is great to see that its owners are prepared to allow the car to be seen by a wide range of enthusiasts, rather than just leaving it in storage. As such, the car is a living memorial to James and David's father, as well as being an irreplaceable part of Aston Martin's history.

## KEY FIGURES

### 'Bert' Bertelli

Augustus Cesare Bertelli was an Italian engineer who had been brought up in England, but served his early working years in Italy; he was the mechanic to Italian motor-racing hero Felice Nazzaro while winning in a Fiat in the 1908 'Circuito di Bologna', and later worked at Fiat in Turin. He returned to England in 1918, where he took up the post as general manager of the newly formed Enfield and Alldays car company. There he oversaw the introduction of a 5-cylinder radial-engined light car, which was swiftly replaced with a car of his own design. This was a conventional light car, powered by a 10hp (RAC Formula) side-valve engine of 1488cc, with a cone clutch and three-speed gearbox. Bertelli was a firm advocate of racing improving a car, and Enfield and Alldays cars regularly competed against the Bamford and Martin cars at Brooklands in the early 1920s, running in events such as the JCC 200-mile race and the RAC 1500cc Tourist Trophy races.

In 1923 Bertelli, along with Captain J.C. Douglas, designed a track racing car for Woolf Barnato, and three were built at Barnato's private garage in Lingfield, Surrey, about 10 miles south of London. The three cars used a unique 4-cylinder sleeve-valve engine, and ran unsuccessfully in that year's JCC 200-mile race, driven by Woolf, Bertelli and Douglas. In 1924 Bertelli went into partnership with his former colleague and works manager at Enfield and Alldays, W.S. Renwick; they set up a workshop in Birmingham with the intention of designing and manufacturing their own design of light car. The firm, Renwick and Bertelli Ltd, Engineers, was registered on 8 December.

The first year of activity centred round the development of an engine, with the intention of combining the characteristics of an efficient wedge-shaped combustion chamber as championed by Ricardo, along with overhead valves. This resulted in a cylinder-head design in which the inlet valves were positioned in a line on one side of the head and the exhaust valves in a second line on the other side, making the unit a 'cross-flow'. This meant that the inlet manifold was positioned on the right-hand side of the unit and the exhaust on the left. The valve and head layout was patented in February 1926, and featured in an all-new engine designed by Bertelli and Renwick. The prototype engine used a 1488cc (bore and stroke was 63.5 × 117mm) Enfield bottom end to validate the head design. Bertelli and Renwick then built a second engine that was entirely their own design, although it retained the Enfield unit's bore and stroke measurements. This new engine gave 50bhp at 4,500rpm and was fitted into a modified Alldays and Enfield chassis fitted with a two-seater body.

Nicknamed 'The Buzzbox', it was registered as a Renwick & Bertelli car and was assigned the registration number ON6638 – it still exists at the time of writing, although the UK registration authorities call it a 'Renwick & Bartelli'. This was the only car made by Renwick and Bertelli. In 1926 they, along with the Carnwoods, formed the firm of Aston Martin Motors Ltd, and set up the new company in Feltham. However, Bertelli and Renwick's engine design would live on in the cars produced by Aston Martin.

**To the left is 'Bert' Bertelli standing next to engine designer Louis Coatelen at Le Mans practice, 1935. The car is thought to be LM20 driven by Martin and Brackenbury, which came third overall in the race.**

## TECHNICAL DESCRIPTION: BERTELLI-ERA ASTON MARTIN ULSTER

The 1.5-litre Aston Martin models produced by Aston Martin at Feltham from 1929 were typical sports cars of the 1930s. They were front-engined, rear-wheel-drive models powered by an overhead camshaft, 1.5-litre, in-line 4-cylinder motor. They were made in long (standard) or short (sports) chassis form, and were fitted with a four-speed manual gearbox and a spiral bevel rear axle. The solid front and rear axles were sprung with semi-elliptical leaf springs, and they were fitted with drum brakes. The brakes were cable-operated from the foot pedal, and additional effort could be exerted using the hand lever. The cars were usually fitted with an in-house body, but outside coach builders were used if a customer required their own specification. In-house bodies included closed saloons, open four-seat tourers, 'short' two or four-seat tourers or strict two-seaters, and in the case of the Ulster, a specially lightened two-seater was used. The Ulster was the 'super sports' model of the mid-1930s, and the distinguishing feature of its body was the spare wheel, which was stored horizontally in the rear of the bodywork.

## SPECIFICATION TABLE: ASTON MARTIN 'ULSTER' MODEL

| | | |
|---|---|---|
| **Layout and chassis** | Front-engined, rear-drive, two- or four-seat sports or touring car. Ladder-style chassis | |
| **Engine** | | |
| Type | Aston Martin single overhead camshaft | |
| Block and head material | Cast iron | |
| Cylinders | 4 in line | |
| Bore and stroke | 69.3 × 99mm | |
| Capacity | 1495cc | |
| RAC rating | 11.9hp | |
| Valves | 2 valves per cylinder, operated by rocker arms from a chain-driven camshaft in the head | |
| Compression ratio | 9.5:1 | |
| Carburettor | Twin carburettor, SU CV type | |
| Max. power | 80bhp at 5,250rpm | |
| Max. torque | 56.25lb ft at 4,000rpm | |
| **Transmission** | | |
| Gearbox | 4-speed manual | |
| Clutch | Multiplate unit | |
| Overall ratios | 1st | 11.5:1 |
| | 2nd | 7.15:1 |
| | 3rd | 5.22:1 |
| | 4th | 4.11:1 |
| Reverse | 11.5:1 | |
| Final drive | Crown wheel and bevel | |

| | |
|---|---|
| **Suspension and steering** | |
| Front | Beam axle, leaf springs |
| Rear | Live axle, semi-elliptic leaf springs |
| Steering | Marles steering box |
| Wheels | Rudge Whitworth wire |
| Tyres | 18 × 5.25in |
| **Brakes** | |
| Type | Drums, cable-operated |
| **Capacities** | |
| Fuel capacity | 15gal (68.2ltr) |
| Oil capacity | Dry sump 2.9gal (13.2ltr) |
| **Dimensions** | |
| Track | Front and rear 52in (1,320mm) |
| Wheelbase | Standard: 120in (3,050mm) |
| | Sports: 103in (2,620mm) |
| Overall length | Standard: 173in (4,390mm) |
| | Sports: 166in (4,220mm) |
| Weight | 2,128lb (965kg) |
| **Performance** | |
| Top speed | 102mph (164km/h) |
| 0–60 | Not known |

From 1926 through to 1937 Bertelli was Aston Martin Motors Ltd's technical director and was responsible for designing all new Aston Martins: these are now generally referred to as 'the Bertelli cars'. Bertelli left Aston Martin in February 1937 due to the 'culmination of of an ever worsening relationship with the Sutherlands', to quote Inman Hunter's book *Aston Martin 1913–1947*. Bertelli continued to work as a consultant, mainly with Coventry Simplex, and maintained contact with his brother, who still ran his coach works at Feltham. In this time he designed and produced a small fire pump, with the pump and Climax engine mounted on a two-wheeled trailer that could be towed by a saloon car. Just before the war he was employed by High Duty Alloys where he set up and ran a factory, Templewood Engineering Company, in Slough.

Bertelli retired in 1955, and died in 1979.

## Claude Hill

Born in 1907, Claude Hill was a talented engineer and draughtsman. He joined Renwick and Bertelli in 1924 after showing a flair for engineering – and as well as winning third prize in a Midlands competition for engineering drawing, he was also an accomplished mathematician. He was employed initially as a draughtsman, but quickly displayed a talent for interpreting Bertelli and Renwick's ideas and converting them into reality.

He moved with Bertelli and Renwick to Feltham in 1927, where he was apparently an indispensable member of the Aston Martin design team. He was able to take outline designs and translate them into properly engineered working drawings that could be put into production. His first job on joining Aston Martin was on the International, when he took Bertelli and Renwick's designs and made them production ready.

Hill's time at Aston Martin was interrupted by two brief periods when Aston Martin's usual precarious financial situation meant he had to be 'let go'. In 1929 he went to Morris Motors, where he worked in the drawing office, and in 1932 he was employed in Vauxhall's chassis design office. Apart from these brief interludes he would stay at Aston Martin until well after the departure of Bertelli in 1937, when he was appointed chief designer. His tenure under Gordon Sutherland resulted in him working on the new 2-litre, or 15/98 model, as well as experimenting with body-building techniques, exemplified by the semi space-frame saloon 'Donald Duck' and of course the 'Atom' projects. He was also responsible for the design of the Type C cars, the aerodynamic but somewhat inelegant line of cars produced just before World War II.

Probably his greatest work at Aston Martin was the design of the 4-cylinder overhead-valve engine, which powered the first post-World War II Aston Martin, the 2-litre Sports. He resigned from Aston Martin in 1949, after his proposal for a 6-cylinder engine based on his 4-cylinder design was rejected in favour of the Lagonda dohc straight six, which subsequently powered the DB2. Hill joined Harry Ferguson Research, where he remained working on the application of four-wheel-drive systems on road cars until he retired in 1972.

CHAPTER 4

# THE START OF THE DAVID BROWN YEARS: 1946–1956

The 1940s, 1950s and 1960s were to redefine the public's image of Aston Martin, a perception that would carry the company through the turbulent times of the 1970s and 1980s, and which would be invaluable to the ultimate rescue of the company by Ford in the 1990s. The post-war Aston Martin was to move away from the pre-war philosophy of producing the best light car for the sporting enthusiast towards an altogether more ambitious goal: to produce the best GT car. This would mean several major changes from the characteristics of the pre-war cars: the post-war Aston Martin would eschew the lightweight, stripped-out, hairy-chested high-performance pre-war models, replacing them with cars still giving class-leading performance, but which would be delivered in a package that would also provide excellent comfort, along with great handling and roadholding. The new Aston Martin would be the type of car that you could jump into on Monday morning in London, and be playing the tables in Monte Carlo the same evening.

To achieve this the cars would need to be bigger, more refined and heavier, and so would need more power to propel them along; they would also need sophisticated suspension to allow for the greater weight due to the increase in size and the creature comforts provided for the driver and passenger. That this ambitious aim was achieved is all down to one person: northern industrialist David Brown. It was his vision and money that enabled Aston Martin to become the iconic brand that it still is today.

## THE COMPANY

The next phase in Aston Martin's tumultuous life was triggered by a pair of events. The first was an advertisement published in late 1946 in *The Times* newspaper. Hidden away in the adverts section was the following:

> *High Class Motor Business, Established 30 years. £30,000 Net Profit last year £4,000. Write Box V. 1362, The Times, EC4.*

**The DB2 was the epitome of the 1950s Aston Martin. This is the last of the line, Tim Slow's 1958 DB2/4 Mark III.**

**The 2-litre Sports was Aston Martin's first post-World War II model, and was powered by a 4-cylinder ohv engine.**

This terse advertisement intrigued northern industrialist David Brown, and resulted in him buying Aston Martin for the grand sum of £20,000 in 1947.

The second event was the acquisition of the ailing Lagonda concern by David Brown, which included the rights to a new engine designed by W.O. Bentley. With David Brown's purchase of Staines-based Lagonda (albeit without any premises), there was also a need for more space, and a new home was found close to Aston Martin's existing factory on the adjoining Hanworth air park. So the company decamped from its dilapidated wartime site in Victoria Road to the new hangers, along with the Lagonda personnel, parts, machine tools and prototype cars from Lagonda's Staines factory.

Brown's vision for his new acquisition was for a company producing a range of upmarket cars – stylish Lagonda saloons, and high performance Aston Martin GT cars, which would sit a class above the pre-war Aston Martin market of small-engined sports cars. These new cars would have to have enough power to have a performance significantly better than the pre-war cars, and be refined enough to compete with the

**Lagonda produced their own range of four-door saloon car under David Brown's stewardship. The $2\frac{1}{2}$-litre name reflected the use of the new 2.5-litre 6-cylinder Lagonda dohc engine.**

crop of modern cars starting to appear at the top end of the market. The chief driver of the market in the UK was Jaguar, with their brand new XK engine with its 6 cylinders, double overhead camshafts and 3.4-litre capacity, as it appeared in the XK120 at the 1948 Earls Court Motor Show. With superb styling, unrivalled performance, captivating looks and incredible value for money, the XK120 was an instant success, and led the Jaguar range of four-door saloons that were also powered by the unit. In the early post-war period the XK unit had rapidly become the benchmark for a sporting engine, and Brown knew that if Aston Martin were to retain their pre-eminent position in the industry they had to have a creditable alternative.

The only real 'product' that Aston Martin had was the Atom, a wartime take on what a low-volume, up-market car should be. However, while the structure of the car was intriguing, innovative and modern, the styling was utilitarian, and the engine was the Hill-designed 4-cylinder pushrod-operated overhead valve unit, which, while new, was not exactly sophisticated, refined or powerful, and was no rival for the Jaguar unit. When he drove the Atom David Brown was impressed with the car's ingenious design and the roadholding and handling, but was not so enamoured with the car's speed and acceleration, despite Claude Hill's claim that it 'had a lot of performance in a small package'.

The solution was found in the recently purchased Lagonda company, which had already announced its new post-war car, the W.O. Bentley-designed, Frank Feeley-styled Lagonda 2.5 Saloon, but was struggling to find the finance to get the car into production. The heart of the new Lagonda was a new 6-cylinder dohc engine designed by Willie Watson, which had both the design sophistication and pedigree to be a creditable rival to the new Jaguar unit. The first post-war Aston Martin was the 2-litre Sports, retrospectively called the DB1, which was more in line with the Lagonda products, and was more of a relaxed open-topped tourer powered by Hill's 2-litre 4-cylinder engine. The first true DB-era road car, the DB2 was released in 1950, and was the first Aston Martin powered by the W.O. Bentley-designed engine.

The DB2 marked Aston Martin's resurgence in the world market, but also marked its move from producing 'light' 4-cylinder cars to its penetration of the larger, exotic Grand Touring coupé market, which would carry it through the following decades. DB2/4 followed in 1953, marketed alongside the Lagonda 3-litre of Duke of Edinburgh fame.

The company was sited in its 'new' premises in Hanworth aero park, having moved from the dilapidated building nearby, and production of the DB1, DB2 and Lagonda models was undertaken on the site, although the chassis were manufactured by David Brown's Huddersfield factory from 1953, alongside the engines, which were produced by David Brown from the start. The low numbers of the 2-litre Sports model could be catered for on site, and while the company had produced the prototype bodies for the DB2 in house, they did not have the capacity to produce the numbers required when production started. Combine this with a spate of industrial action at the factory, and the DB2 bodies were initially produced by Mulliners in Birmingham. Then in 1955 David Brown bought Tickfords in Newport Pagnell, and the fate of the Feltham site was sealed.

DB2 body production was transferred from Mulliners to Tickfords in Newport Pagnell. DB2 Tickford bodies are easily recognizable as the bonnet shut-line ran from the top of the front wheel arch back to the bulkhead, rather than along the sill line. All Aston Martin's production operation started to be moved from Feltham to Newport Pagnell in the early 1950s, but the process was not fully completed until 1963, when the service department was finally moved and the Feltham site closed.

**The replacement for the 2-litre Sports was the DB2. This sleek coupé had up-to-date styling and was powered by the Lagonda dohc engine.**

## THE ENGINES

During this period in Aston Martin's existence, the company used two brand new engine designs in their cars: the 4-cylinder unit designed by Claude Hill (described in full in Chapter 3), which harked back to the company's pre-war years, and the state-of-the-art 6-cylinder unit designed by Willie Watson (under the oversight of W.O. Bentley) for Lagonda, which would define the company's direction in the post-World War II era. Both units were designed during World War II, and while the 4-cylinder unit was first seen in the Atom, and only powered the short-lived and low-production 2-litre Sports model, the Lagonda straight six would power both the Aston Martin DB2 and various post-war Lagonda models.

The Lagonda engine was designed by Willie Watson while working under W.O. Bentley at Lagonda. The dohc unit had an iron block and head, and initially produced just over 100bhp.

### The Lagonda 6-Cylinder dohc Engine

The Lagonda unit was the first 6-cylinder engine to be used by Aston Martin, and would prove to be the foundation and keystone of the dynasty of 'DB' cars produced by the company for the next decade.

The new engine, designated LB6, had a capacity of 2580cc with a bore and stroke of 78 × 90mm, and with a compression ratio of 6.5:1 produced a healthy 105bhp at 5,000rpm and maximum torque of 125lb ft at 3,100rpm. Later versions were stretched to 2922cc with an increase in bore to 83mm; in this configuration and with an 8.2:1 compression ratio the unit produced 140bhp at 5,000rpm.

The LB6 engine was made in several variants, all of which shared the same layout as described below, but which incorporated improvements to increase both performance and reliability. The variants are summarized in the table opposite:

The Lagonda engine was a snug fit under the DB2's bonnet – this is a Mark III. The alloy cam covers give the engine an attractive appearance.

The Lagonda engine was at the heart of the range of DB2 Aston Martins. It was a state-of-the-art design and provided power and smoothness for the marque.

The new engine had a cast-iron crankcase and cylinder head, and was fitted with wet, replaceable liners. The design of the engine had one unique feature: it had a barrel-type crank, with the rear three of the four main bearings carried in a two-piece alloy 'cheese' or sandwich with the crankshaft; its main bearing cheeses had to be threaded into the crankcases from the rear. The front main bearing was fitted with a conventional bolt-on cap, and also served to align the crankshaft in the cases.

The crankshaft was cast iron, and had four plain main bearing journals; the big ends were also plain bearings. The carriers

## LB6 ENGINE VARIANTS

| *Engine series* | *Tune* | *Capacity* | *Fitted to* | *Approx dates* |
|---|---|---|---|---|
| LB6B | Standard | 2580cc | DB2 | 1950 |
| LB6E | Standard | 2580cc | DB2 | Believed 1952 |
| VB6B | Vantage | 2580cc | DB2 | 1951 |
| VB6E | Vantage | 2580cc | DB2 and DB 2/4 Mark I | 1952 |
| VB6J | n/a | 2922cc | DB2/4 Mark I and II | September 1953 |
| DB/A | n/a | 2922cc | DB Mark III | 1957 |
| DB/B | Competition | 2922cc | DB Mark III | 1959 |

were located in position in the crankcase by a combination of dowels and oil-transfer bolts, which allowed for the oil to be fed from the crankcase into each main bearing. The main advantage of this system was that the crankcase was very strong and rigid, but the downside was that it was difficult for the design to cater for the difference in expansion of the various metals used in the construction. With the oil feed to the main bearings and big ends having to travel through the sandwich, it was an obvious source of oil leaks, which could result in a loss of oil pressure in the crankshaft, resulting in bearing failure.

**Initially in the DB2, the Lagonda engine breathed through a pair of SU carburettors.**

**The first DB2s had two doors that also gave access to the luggage area behind the seats. The small hatch at the rear gave access to the spare wheel.**

There were three oval openings in the top of the crankcase, each receiving two wet cylinder liners. The cylinder liners were seated on their base, and were compressed into place when the head was torqued down, with the bottom joint seals available in multiple sizes to ensure a correct fit. This construction left the top of the crankcase between each pair of liners open to the water jacket, and the head gasket was relied on to form a seal between the water jacket, the outside of the engine, the cylinder liner, and the head.

The water pump was incorporated into the front timing cover and driven from the timing chain, and the cooling water in the crankcases was in direct contact with the cylinder liners. There were coolant passages cast into the cylinder head, and these were designed to have a good flow around the exhaust valve seats to ensure good cooling.

The design meant that the crankcase was very strong and rigid, as it basically formed a box around the crank, with two central braces along with the front and rear faces of the box. The sides of the crankcase extended downwards to fully enclose the crankshaft and the main bearing carriers, making the crankcase very stiff and strong.

The cylinder head was state of the art (for the time), with the valves inclined at 60 degrees to each other (30 degrees from vertical), which allowed for the perfect hemispherical combustion chamber. The spark plugs were 10mm in diameter, rather than the more common 13mm diameter, to allow more room for water passages in the head casting to ensure good cooling; this also gave more room for the valves, which at 1.515in for the inlet and 1.365in in diameter for the exhaust, were as big as possible to promote good breathing. The plugs were placed in the well between the two camshafts.

Separate cast-alloy cam covers gave the top end of the engine a handsome appearance and emphasized the presence of the state-of-the-art dohc mechanism when the bonnet was lifted. The inlet valve cover had a secondary alloy lid that covered the HT leads and kept them tidy. A pair of camshafts were mounted in the head, and were driven by a two-stage duplex chain drive from the crankshaft. Each camshaft had a bearing on each side of each cam lobe, so ran in twelve individual bearing surfaces, and each lobe had a dual bearing cap held on to the head with four bolts, two each side of the lobe to locate the camshaft. No bearing shells were fitted: the camshaft ran directly in the head.

The valves were operated directly from the camshafts using cast-iron bucket tappets under each camshaft lobe. There were no shims in the system, and tappet clearance was originally set at the factory. Further adjustment was achieved either by grinding the top of the valve stem if the gap had closed up and needed to be widened, by replacing the valve, which also required grinding, or fitting a new tappet. The tappets were available in four different various thicknesses, and each thickness was made with 30-thou oversize diameters to allow for wear in the socket in the head. There were pressed-in valve seats, and the centre of the outer stem of each valve guide was exposed to the water jacket and had to be properly sealed when replaced.

A short duplex chain drove a sprocket on the intermediate shaft at half engine speed, and a second sprocket on the intermediate shaft drove both camshafts via a second duplex chain. While the prototype had blade-type chain tensioners, these caused problems in prototype engines and led to the production engines being fitted with a pair of automatic hydraulically operated jockey-wheel tensioners, one for each chain, which used the engine's oil pressure to operate them.

A second duplex chain drive was taken off the nose of the crank, behind the camshaft driving sprocket, to drive a short shaft positioned on the inlet side of the engine running parallel to the crankshaft. The shaft had a skew gear on it, which was used to drive a vertical shaft, the top of which drove the distributor, and the bottom the oil pump. The sump was a large light alloy casting that was ribbed to aid cooling the oil. On the original Lagonda design the cooling fan was driven from a separate shaft driven from the timing chain. However, the DB2's bonnet line was much lower than the Lagonda applications, so for the DB2 the timing cover was adapted to have a separate shaft to carry the fan, which was belt driven (along with the dynamo) from the nose of the crankshaft. On early engines the original shaft was left in place but with no function, and it was later deleted from the design.

**The ultimate incarnation of the Lagonda engine, the DBA could be fitted with triple Weber carburettors for maximum power. This is Phil Taylor's racing DB2 Mark III.**

The oil system incorporated a gear-type oil pump that took its feed from the sump, and then passed the pressurized oil through a Purolator (Auto Klean on early cars) oil filter and into an annular supply duct around the front main bearing, and also into an oil gallery that ran the length of the block.

The LB6 engine was a cross-flow design, with the inlet on the left and the exhaust on the right. The inlet manifold was connected to the water passages in the engine block to keep it cool, and the water pump itself was incorporated in the timing case on the front of the engine; it was driven directly from the intermediate shaft, cutting down the risk of leaks that bolt-on water pumps with exterior belt drives could be prone to, and of course there is no overheating if the fan belt breaks.

The VB6J was a rework of the LB/VB engine to increase the capacity to just under 3 litres. The major obstacle to increasing the size of the standard 2.5-litre engine was that the bores were siamesed in pairs, with each pair too close together to allow for a significant increase in the bore. However, by increasing the bore of the cylinders asymmetrically – that is, moving the bore centres of each pair of cylinders apart and encroaching into the 'gap' between each pair of cylinders – the bore could be increased; in this way the capacity of the unit was raised to 2922cc for the 1953 racing season. In order for this to work without changing the crankshaft, the small end bearings in the connecting rods had to be offset from the centre line of the big end to provide the extra distance between the cylinders. This modification was carried into the production engines, resulting in the VB6J being fitted to the DB2/4 Marks I and II in the summer of 1954.

Alongside the introduction of the DB2/4 Mark III in 1957, the 6-cylinder engine was subjected to a significant amount of redesign, including a new crankcase and head along with a new designation of DBA. Carried out by Tadek Marek, the redesign was comprehensive, with a new, stiffer crankcase design, and top-sealing cylinder liners. With the new cylinder liners the method of sealing the bottom of the cylinder liners to the block was changed from the original 'figure-of-eight' gasket to 'O' rings. The bottom of each liner was fitted with a pair of 'O' rings, the lower one to seal the liner from the sump, the upper one to seal the liner from the water jacket. So if an 'O' ring failed, water would not contaminate the oil, and vice versa. There were holes drilled in the side of the block, which vented the gap between the 'O' rings to the atmosphere, so

**The exhaust side of Phil Taylor's Lagonda DBA engine in his racing DB2 Mark III.**

if an 'O' ring had failed, either water or oil would leak out, exposing the problem. This feature was carried forwards to the Marek-designed straight-six and V8 engines.

The engine also had revised timing gear, with manually adjustable timing-chain tensioners and a new worm drive for the repositioned oil pump. There was also a new sump, a new cylinder head with larger valves and improved porting, and 14mm spark plugs, along with new inlet and exhaust manifolds. As with the 2-litre 4-cylinder Aston Martin engines described above, the 6-cylinder engines were produced for Aston Martin and Lagonda at the David Brown Tractors Group factory at Meltham Mills, near Huddersfield in North Yorkshire.

## THE CARS

### The Aston Martin 2-litre Sports, or 'DB1'

The first new production car produced by Aston Martin after the war was the Aston Martin 2-litre Sports, which has been retrospectively referred to as the 'DB1'. Introduced to the public in October 1948, the 2-litre Sports was preceded by a development mule that was an open-top two-door four-seater touring car, and was used to test the proposed 2-litre Sports's mechanical underpinnings.

With a wheelbase of 108in (2,743mm), the mule's chassis, like that of the Atom, was in effect a space frame constructed from square- and rectangular-section steel tube. As there was no roof, the structure was significantly strengthened below the door apertures, when compared to the Atom, to maintain rigidity, and was the same as the production unit fitted to the production Aston Martin 2-litre Sports of 1949. The mule was road tested by *Autocar* in May 1948, when the ride and road-holding were praised. While the mule was being tested, the first of the production-standard 2-litre Sportss was produced, with an open two-/three-seater body designed by Lagonda's Frank Feeley. Christened somewhat unimaginatively 'The Blue Car' due to its light blue colour, and registered THX 231, the new two-/three-seat roadster was first shown to the press in October 1948, and appeared at that year's Earls Court Motor Show.

A third prototype, road registered as EML 127, was also produced with the intention of competing in the forthcoming Spa 24 Hour race in Belgium in July 1948. This car was fitted with a modified chassis, which, while retaining the overall length of the other two cars, had the rear end of the chassis cut about to accommodate a large fuel tank. To allow for the only available rear axle ratio of 3.9:1, the car's gearing was raised by fitting 18in-diameter rear wheels, which gave it an unusual appearance, thanks to the standard 16in units. The engine was the new 4-cylinder 2-litre unit, but was lightly tuned, having a skimmed head to raise the compression ratio to around 10:1 and a pair of larger SU carburettors. Unfortunately the race organizers could only provide low-octane 'pool' petrol, so the skimmed head had to be replaced with a standard head with less meat skimmed off to give a compression ratio of around 8.5:1.

**The Aston Martin 2-litre Sports of 1948 was similar in appearance to the contemporary Lagonda and was a four-seat touring car rather than a sports car. With its sleek but slightly bulbous lines, the 2-litre Sports was an attractive car but did not sell particularly well.**

The car was fitted with a special one-off body designed by Claude Hill, and went on to win its class in the 1948 Spa 24 Hour race (held on 11 July), driven by Jack Horsfall and Leslie Johnson. Of note was that the future Aston Martin race manager and technical manager John Wyer was also at the race, working for Monaco Motors owner Dudley Folland, who was driving his pre-war 2-litre Aston Martin in the event.

Rebodied and painted red, the Spa car (EML 127) was shown as the 'Spa Special' alongside the new 2-litre Sports at the 1948 Earls Court Motor Show on the Aston Martin Lagonda stand. While it was offered as a model in its own right alongside the standard 2-litre Sports, it did not generate enough orders to put it into production, and was quietly dropped from the range. EML 127 went on to compete in the 1949 Le Mans 24 Hour race alongside the DB2s.

The 2-litre Sports's semi space-frame chassis was a relatively massive affair. It was built using lengths of square- and rectangular-section steel tubing, the square-section tube being of 1¼in (3cm), while the rectangular tube was 1¼in wide but the depth varied up to 3in (7.5cm). The use of square and rectangular tube made the various elements easier to cut and weld than if round tubing were used, as well as presenting a flat surface for fitting the body and other components to the chassis.

The car was open, so to maintain strength the sill structure was beefed up. On the Atom there was a single rectangular beam on each side; on the new car the beam was doubled up by placing a second beam alongside the existing one. While this increased the strength of the structure in the horizontal plane and gave plenty of room for the door opening, unfortunately it wasn't as strong as it should have been in the vertical plane, and right from the start the car suffered from door-fitting issues, as the chassis allowed the front and rear of the car to flex up and down independently. The issue was not fixed for the 2-litre Sports, but it was for the following DB2.

Other than this issue the chassis provided more than adequate strength and rigidity to allow for softly sprung and relatively long travel suspension to be fitted.

The 2-litre Sports's bodywork was an attractive and modern design, with smooth lines, two doors and a folding soft-top roof. It was designed by Lagonda's Frank Feeley, and was the first Aston Martin with 'full width' design, with no separate wings, but with nods to the past in the shape of a distinct front-wing line at the front, which ran back over the door, and a somewhat bulbous pair of vestigial rear wings shrouding the rear wheels. It did bear a family resemblance to the new Lagonda, also designed by Feeley.

Constructed in lightweight aluminium, and supported on the space-frame chassis, the body was open-topped with a large manually operated hood. When opened the hood was stored under a tonneau cover, giving a clean and smooth appearance with no extraneous cloth or hoops breaking into the smooth lines. While the prototype had a 'V'-shaped windscreen, production versions had a flat screen that could be folded flat on to the bonnet of the car; it incorporated non-opening quarter lights that were fixed to the bodyshell. Wind-up windows retracted fully into the doors and mated to channels in the quarter lights to give a good weather-proof and windproof seal.

The interior was quite luxurious rather than sporting, as befitted the car's character. With a full-width front bench seat that could seat three at a squeeze, and a very small seat behind the bench, the car was arguably a four-seater, but at least one occupant would need to be fairly small, and the other three well acquainted with each other – and if they weren't at the start of a journey, they would be by the end!

**The chassis of the 2-litre Sports was based on that of the Atom, and was built up using square-section tubing. The sills had additional bracing to make up for not having a roof.**

**The family resemblance of the 2-litre Sports to the Lagonda is more apparent in the drop-head Lagonda. Frank Feeley penned both cars.**

**The 2-litre Sports cabin was well appointed and a nice place to be.**

While a fair proportion of the production cars came with a column-mounted gear shift, many have now been converted to floor-mounted shift, which tends to limit the car to having a single front passenger. However, the car did make a spacious two-seater, with plenty of room for luggage in the separate boot as well as behind the bench seat.

The instrument panel was a simple slab affair, with a large diameter circular speedometer and rev counter in front of the driver, and four small circular minor instruments surrounding a matching clock in the middle of the dash. There was a decent-sized open cubby hole in front of the passenger, and the minor switches are scattered in a non-ergonomic but balanced way across the dash.

The front of the body, comprising the bonnet and wings from the scuttle forwards, was a one-piece design that could be completely removed from the chassis to give unfettered

**From the side, the 2-litre Sports displays some fussy styling features that detract from the car's smooth lines.**

**There was a big hatch on the top of each of the 2-litre Sports's front wings, which gave access to lockers carrying the spare wheel and battery.**

access to the engine and the front suspension. This meant removing the front bumper and then drawing the complete panel forwards to clear the bumper brackets before lifting it off. There was a conventional hinged bonnet in the centre of the unit to give engine access for regular servicing, as well as a hatch on the top rear of both wings to provide access to the battery on the left and the spare wheel on the right.

The front grille was chrome plated and was built up in three elements, so looked rather messy and unfinished. On the top of the central grille was the 'Aston Martin' winged enamel badge across the fold. On each side at the base of the central grille was a smaller grille, chromed with vertical slats, which, while separate from the main grille, formed the shape that would become the traditional Aston Martin grille. While the styling of the car was pleasant, the pre-war roots were still visible in the well defined front and rear wing lines, and the design was actually quite typical of early post-war semi-sporting coupés, such as the Alvis TB14 and TB21 and the Lagonda 2.5-litre, all of which had lines that were elegant and sweeping but were not exactly what you would call sporting.

The 2-litre Sports was fitted with independent front suspension and had a live rear axle. The front suspension was of the twin trailing arm type, with the lever-arm shock absorber forming the top link. The main lower link was pivoted in on a large diameter shaft, which was carried in a substantial cast-alloy unit that spanned the front of the car. This was bolted to the front of the chassis and was filled with oil to provide the shaft with lubrication, and also contained a torsion bar that acted as an anti-roll bar. This torsion bar was enclosed in the housing, and was splined into the front end of the lower link of both sides. When one side moved, the torsion bar would twist and impart some movement to the other link, which helped to reduce the car's roll rate. Each side's single coil spring was mounted directly on the end of the lower link in line with the axle, and the top of the spring was located in a large alloy casting that was bolted to the cross-member. The design would be carried over to the DB2.

At the rear, the live rear axle was sprung using coil springs, and was located using a pair of parallel radius arms on each side; these were mounted on the outer end of the axle, and fitted inboard on the chassis on the third of the central cross-members. There was an arm mounted transversely to counteract

**From the front, the 2-litre Sports was an imposing car. While the car's style is moving towards the modern full-width look, the front wings hark back to pre-war styling.**

**The vertical main grille flanked by a pair of lower side grilles on the 2-litre Sports was the first step towards what would become the traditional Aston Martin grille shape.**

the side loads on the axle while cornering, a configuration generally known as a 'panhard rod'. The bottom of the coil springs was located on the lower trailing arm just in front of the axle, and the top was located in a socket in the chassis side rails, which swept up over the axle at that point. The dampers were lever-arm type and were mounted on the rear axle, with their arms connected to the chassis using drop links.

The 2-litre Sports steering column led to a bracket-mounted steering box on one side of the chassis, with the column on the outer side and a drop arm mounted on the engine side. Movement of the steering column was translated into fore and aft movement of the drop arm, which was linked to an arm mounted on a vertical spindle mounted centrally on the alloy cross-member. This spindle pivoted on needle roller bearings lubricated from the oil contained in the central cross-member. A second arm ran back from this spindle, and carried the two tie-rods on a 'T'-shaped end, designed to provide the correct steering geometry. The tie-rods ran to the rear of the swivels on the front suspension hubs.

As befitted the car's relatively sporting character, the 2-litre Sports was equipped with relatively large drum brakes. Both front and rear were 12in-diameter cast-iron drums, and the fronts were twin leading shoe. The brakes were hydraulically operated from the foot pedal, and the cable-operated handbrake operated on the rear drums. The handbrake lever was fitted between the driver and his door to allow for unobstructed three-abreast seating.

The 2-litre Sports showed that with intelligent suspension and chassis design a sporting car could be comfortable as well as have good roadholding and handling.

The 2-litre Sports was fitted with the all-new 4-cylinder 2-litre overhead valve unit described above. The four-speed all-synchromesh David Brown gearbox was fitted in unit with the engine with a single-plate clutch. Drive was taken to the live rear axle by a conventional propellor shaft.

The 2-litre Sports proved to the buying public that Aston Martin was back in the running and could produce an all-new car for the early post-war market. But the 2-litre Sports was not exactly what David Brown had in mind for his new company. While the car had reasonably attractive styling, it was undeniably old-fashioned with its nods to pre-war styling cues, and in many ways in both appearance, performance and market positioning was too similar to the Lagonda 2.5. Compound this with its rather underwhelming performance, a result of the small 2-litre engine and excessive weight, and it quickly becomes apparent that the car was really only a stopgap. The company only produced fifteen cars before production was ended, and the car was replaced with the altogether more modern and more sporting DB2, powered by the new 6-cylinder engine: this placed Aston Martin at the forefront of the market niche it needed to be in – that of the Sports GT car.

## The Aston Martin DB2, DB2/4 and DB Mark III

The car that followed the short-lived 2-litre Sports was the DB2. This car, the first to receive the 'DB' prefix, was described as a 'sports saloon' by Aston Martin, and would set the mould for Aston Martin's products for the following decades: large capacity, 6-cylinder engined, Grand Touring cars with a performance that placed them at the pinnacle of their market, overlaid with an unmistakably British veneer of luxury and class.

The origin of the DB2 was obvious: it was a derivation of the 1949 Le Mans works cars. The genesis of the DB2 came with the creation of three works cars to run in the 1949 Le Mans 24 Hour race, an event that would soon dominate the racing calendar and be particularly important to manufacturers of sports/GT cars as the event to showcase their wares. The DB2 was announced to the market in April 1950, appearing in public for the first time at the New York Motor Show, and giving a foretaste of how important the US market would become to Aston Martin. The open-topped variant would become available later in 1950.

While still related to the unit used on the Atom and 2-litre Sports models, the DB2's chassis not only had 9in (228mm) taken out of its wheelbase when compared to the 2-litre Sports, it also had a completely new design for the sill structure around the sides of the cabin area, to counteract the 2-litre Sports chassis' predilection to bend round its centre. The side-by-side girder structure of the 2-litre Sports, which

**The DB2 moved forwards to full-width styling. This early DB2 (the fifty-ninth made) has the later one-piece grille design that defined the 'trademark' shape of the Aston Martin grille.**

**The DB2 chassis was, like the 2-litre Sports, built from square-section tubing. It had considerably more reinforcement in the sills.**

**From the rear, the early DB2 shows its small rear hatch covering the spare wheel, and the large rear window.**

joined the bottom of the 'A' and 'B' pillars, was replaced with a pair of square-section tubes, with one placed approximately 5in (12.7cm) above the other, making the structure much stiffer in the vertical plane and better joining the front and rear of the structure together. Rather than using the 2-litre Sports's three transverse cross-members, on the DB2 the two sides of the centre of the chassis were tied together with an 'X'-shaped cross-brace, the front of which was fixed to the bottom of the side members at the bulkhead 'A' pillar, and at the rear at the 'B' pillars.

While the new central reinforcement to the chassis gave a slightly higher sill than the 2-litre Sports, the combination of the revised sill structure and the reduction in wheelbase, and hence the distance between the front and rear chassis superstructures, meant that the revised chassis was a lot stiffer than that fitted to the 2-litre Sports. At the front and the rear the chassis was broadly similar to the 2-litre Sports unit, with local changes to accommodate features such as the bonnet hinges and the rear storage for the spare wheel.

Designed by Frank Feeley, and constructed initially in house at Feltham but quickly farmed out to specialist coachbuilders Mulliners of Birmingham, the DB2's body was a two-door closed coupé unit and had full-width styling with particularly clean and smooth lines; it was described by the factory as a Sports Saloon. With the exception of the grille, there were no pre-war styling references, or indeed any resemblance to the 2-litre Sports. Described by the press of the time as an 'envelope' design, the new car had no residual wing lines, a fully enclosed cabin, and just a small hatch on the rear of the car to access the spare wheel well. The shape of the car was an outstandingly modern design, and its modern, purposeful appearance gained a lot of praise in the press of the day.

The DB2 body was a semi-stressed skin construction, its lightweight alloy outer panels being affixed to a lightweight

**A factory photo of a DB2 Coupé from 1952.**

**An early DB2 showing the large drum brakes and painted wire wheels.**

steel frame that followed the contours of the body, and which was made up of 'Z'-section steel channels with localized, welded-on steel-tubing reinforcement. The edges of the alloy skin were wrapped round the edges of the 'Z'-section channels to give strength to the structure. An important element of the body were the steel rear-wheel inner arches, which had the alloy body panels wrapped round its edges. There was a sheet-steel bulkhead fitted between the steel rear-wheel arches, which gave additional strength and rigidity to the body structure. The windscreen was a 'V'-shaped unit, made from two flat panes of glass with a slender centre join.

At the front of the body the bulkhead area was sheathed in two layers of sheet steel to provide reinforcement, and the space between the sheets was filled with glass-fibre insulation for soundproofing. On each side of the car there were compartments on the outside of the footwells that were covered by the bonnet assembly when it was closed. The battery was located on the passenger side, while the same space on the driver's side accommodated the wheel-changing tools, including the bottle jack. A set of smaller tools was fitted into a tailored compartment between the driver and passenger seats. The complete body was bolted to the chassis with four silentbloc rubber bushes to provide insulation from both the mechanical elements of the car and the road surface; it was surprisingly light and strong.

The DB2 took the removable one-piece front body concept seen on the 2-litre Sports a step further, and while keeping the one-piece front end, hinged the whole assembly at the front. This gave excellent access to the engine bay, front suspension and the chassis itself with the front panel open, and the complete panel could be removed relatively easily thanks to the provision of removable pivot pins. The inner wheel arches were incorporated into the bonnet structure, and the main body's structure was extended forwards of the bulkhead; this included a fixed splashguard running forwards from the bulkhead to just behind the front wheels to help keep the under-bonnet area free from road spray. The concept was similar to that seen by the later Triumph Herald/Spitfire family of cars, and of course the Jaguar E-Type.

On the bonnet's nose the grille initially mimicked that of the 2-litre Sports, with vertical slats and a pair of small secondary openings to provide cooling air to the brakes on each side of a larger central grille that fed the radiator; all three grilles had a separate chromed surround and vertical slats.

**All DB2s had forward-hinged bonnets. Later ones had fixed panels running from the front wheel to the bulkhead, as seen on the Mark III.**

This arrangement was fairly quickly replaced in early 1951 with a one-piece opening with the now classic Aston Martin shape. There was no chrome surround to the new grille, and horizontal slats filled the space. Early cars also had a large square extractor grille placed on the side of the bonnet behind the wheel to aid engine bay and brake cooling. When the new front grille was adopted the side grille disappeared.

The headlamps were 7in-diameter units and were fully integrated into the front wing; below them was a small round parking light. Thin alloy bumpers, which were really no more than rubbing strips, adorned the bonnet under the grille and wrapped around the back of the car, running from the back of the rear wheel arch. On early cars the strips also ran along the side of the car just below the door opening.

The DB2's interior was quite luxurious, as befitted the car's GT market position, with leather seats, a floor-mounted gear lever, a reach adjustable, sprung three-spoke steering wheel, and a fully trimmed cabin. The doors were relatively long, and opened wide enough to give comfortable access to the cabin, although the sills were quite wide. There were separate driver and passenger seats, the passenger seat being wider than the driver's, and the pair of seats gave room for three to sit abreast – although space was tight and the three incumbents would need to be good friends, and the optional floor-mounted gear lever could give rise to some embarrassing moments.

The instruments were centrally set into a full-width dashboard, which had cubby holes on each extremity. The instrument panel spanned the centre of the dash, and had a pair of circular full-sized instruments, the speedometer and

**The DB2/4 and Mark III had occasional rear seats.**

tachometer nearest to the driver, a third circular unit that incorporated four minor instruments (fuel level, engine temperature, oil pressure and amps), and a circular switch panel furthest away from the driver. A row of warning lights and other minor switches were arranged in a line under the central two instruments.

As on the 2-litre Sports, the handbrake lever was on the outside of the driver's seat, but was positioned under the dashboard rather than on the sill. There was space behind the seats, which extended back to the rear window; while it could be fitted with cushions to accommodate passengers, the space was narrow and had limited leg and headroom. An adult (or large child) would have to squeeze in sideways to fit, and once in would not have much room for manoeuvre. However, when the space behind the seats wasn't occupied by a passenger it did provide a usefully sized luggage platform, and then the car's interior was perfectly adequate for two people and the luggage needed for an extended European tour. Access to the area was only available from the front via the doors; however, access was facilitated by each front seat having a folding rear squab.

There was no conventional boot as such; at the rear of the car there was a small hatch that gave access to a narrow compartment designed to accommodate the spare wheel. The spare wheel was fixed in place with a built-in over-centre locking mechanism, and to get it out it slid out of the compartment. Under the spare wheel compartment was the fuel tank. Two fillers were provided, one on each side; these were concealed under flaps on the rear wings and were remotely controlled from inside the car.

In late 1950 a drop-head version of the DB2 was added to the range. While this was mechanically identical to the saloon version, it featured a revised bodyshell with a folding roof and flat rear deck. There was a small area behind the

**Early DB2s had their instruments mounted in the centre of the dashboard. Overall the interior of the DB2 was well trimmed and the cars well equipped for the time.**

**Later DB2 interiors had the instruments mounted in a binnacle opposite the driver. This is a drop-head coupé with the hood down.**

seats adequate to carry a child, or a small adult in some discomfort. The hood was manual and the perspex rear window gave limited rearward visibility, but the rear three-quarter view was limited. When folded down the hood was flush with the bodyline, giving a neat and tidy aspect; to some, this was more attractive than the fixed-head coupé. The drop-head continued in the range through to the DB Mark III.

After its introduction in 1955 a fixed-head coupé – or 'notchback' version of the DB2/4 Mark II – was introduced; this was effectively a fixed hardtop version of the drop-head coupé.

The DB2 shared its suspension design with that previously used on the 2-litre Sports. This meant that at the front there was an independent system with trailing links, with the top link doubling up as a damper; this was mounted on a bolt-on alloy casting on the front chassis cross-member. The live rear axle was located with a pair of parallel trailing arms on each side, one above the other, and a separate panhard link to provide lateral location; the axle was sprung with coils fitted in front of the axle, with its lower mount on the lower trailing arm and the upper mount on the chassis. Lever-arm hydraulic dampers were also fitted to the rear. The front suspension had a total travel of 5in (12.7cm), with a 3in (7.6cm) rise and 2in (5cm) of rebound. At the rear there were 4in (10.2cm) of rise and 3in (7.6cm) of rebound, giving a total travel of 7in (17.8cm).

The DB2's steering followed the example set by the 2-litre Sports, with the steering box mounted on one side of the chassis, with the column on the outer side and a drop arm mounted on the engine side.

Again like the 2-litre Sports, the DB2 was equipped with hydraulically operated 12in-diameter drum brakes, with twin leading shoe operation on the front. The cable-operated

**Factory publicity material showing three views of the convertible DB2.**

**A contemporary picture of a 1952 drop-head coupé.**

**Press picture of a 1952 DB2 drop-head coupé.**

**Detail shot of the DB2 front end, showing the hefty alloy spring mounts, the trailing arm suspension, and the transverse alloy torsion bar housing casting.**

**Another shot of the DB front end. The square chassis tubes are obvious, as is the space for the engine and gearbox and the front suspension.**

handbrake operated on the rear drums, and the handbrake lever was fitted under the dash to give room for three-abreast seating.

The suspension and brakes of the DB2, while not really advanced from the 2-litre Sports, were still modern and endowed the DB2 with above-average roadholding and handling.

The DB2 was fitted with the Lagonda-derived 6-cylinder double-overhead camshaft engine (see the section above 'The Lagonda-Cylinder dohc Engine – LB6/VB6' for more details), making the car the first Aston Martin to be produced with a 6-cylinder engine. In the DB2 the engine gave a healthy but unstressed 105bhp at 5,000rpm, which gave the car a sparkling performance for the time. The engine also gave the marque considerable kudos – among UK manufacturers only Jaguar had a similar state-of-the-art unit, while most other

**A DB Mark III engine from the carburettor side. The DB2 engine bay has good access thanks to the front-hinged bonnet.**

**From the exhaust side the DB Mark III's standard three-into-one manifolds are obvious.**

6-cylinder engines relied on pushrods to operate their valves. Double overhead camshafts were usually reserved for racing exotica, but in Aston Martin (and, to be fair, Jaguar) their mechanical robustness meant that the engines needed little extra attention between service intervals – and this meant that, unlike some exotic and more highly strung units, cars so equipped did not turn into mechanical nightmares for their drivers. Rather they provided more than adequate performance, along with bar-room bragging rights that less sophisticated units could not offer.

The DB2 was originally offered with either a column or a floor-mounted gear lever, but the option reverted to floor only fairly soon after production got going. Two types of David Brown gearbox were fitted: the DBR or DBC, both of which could be had with close (DBRC or DBCC) or wide (DBRW or DBCW) ratios. The hypoid rear axle was manufactured by Salisbury.

The DB2 was subject to ongoing development throughout its life. The first significant set of changes occurred in early 1951, when a number of alterations were made that appear to have been done primarily (and not unreasonably) to cut down manufacturing costs. This was despite the price of the car being raised some 20 per cent as well. The changes included the removal of the rectangular side grilles on the front wings, the simplification of the radiator grille itself, the under-door rubbing strip becoming an optional (costed) extra, the removal of one of the two fuel fillers, as well as a general downgrading and simplifying of the interior trim.

On the mechanical front there were few modifications made, apart from increasing the width (and hence the braking area) of the front-brake drums from 2in to 2½in to improve braking performance.

The first major change to the DB2 came in 1954, with the introduction of the DB2/4 – sometimes referred to as the DB2 Mark II – at the Earls Court (London) Motor Show in October. This car was mechanically similar to the DB2, but had a number of modifications to the bodywork that made it capable of actually carrying four people in some comfort; production of the bodywork had by then been moved to Mulliners of Birmingham, rather than remaining in-house at

**In the foreground is a 1958 DB Mark III with its hatchback rear window, and behind it is a 1954 DB2/4 drop-head coupé.**

**With doors and rear hatch opened, the versatility and practicality of the DB2/4 and this DB Mark III can be appreciated.**

Feltham. While the wheelbase and other basic dimensions of the car remained the same as the DB2, there was considerable reworking of the rear of the chassis and the bodyshell to make more interior room. Behind the front seats a pair of seats were formed in the bodywork, with thin cushions for the seat and backrest. Behind the rear seats was a flat luggage area, accessed either via the seats or through an opening hatch – making the DB2/4 one of the first hatchback cars.

The rear seat squabs could fold open to give an increased luggage area. The most obvious visual clue was the raised rear roofline and the incorporation of the hatchback with a much larger rear screen, but the car also had a curved one-piece windscreen replacing the flat 'V'-shaped unit fitted to previous models, and significantly longer rear side windows. At the rear of the car the hatch's rear screen was larger than the DB2's, and the hatch for the spare wheel at the lower end of the rear panel was deleted. Under the skin the sill and 'A' pillar were made in cast aluminium.

At the front the nose remained largely unchanged, although larger chromed steel bumpers with overriders replaced the thin wrap-round items seen on the DB2. Under the skin the positions of the fuel tank and spare wheel were reversed, with the spare now sitting under the tank in a cradle; also the rear chassis structure was redesigned, and the steel bulkhead between the rear wheel arches was changed. These not insignificant changes provided a significant increase in the space available for two rear-seat passengers to sit, if not in luxury then at least in tolerable conditions, as well as making the luggage space larger and easier to access.

The DB2/4 was a significant improvement on the DB2, being a much more practical car that appealed to a larger range of customers.

The advent of the DB2/4 Mark II in October 1955 marked a major change for Aston Martin, as the body was restyled and produced by Tickford in Newport Pagnell, now owned by David Brown. The Mark II was a refinement of the previous car, with a raised roofline to increase headroom for rear seat passengers, a pair of vestigial rear fins, on which were perched the rear lights, and the bonnet was comprehensively altered. The biggest change was to remove the panels behind the rear wheels from the bonnet assembly, and incorporate them into the main body. This gave a new horizontal shut line for the bonnet sides, which ran from the top of the wheel arch back to the scuttle, and was emphasized by a chrome marker strip. The modification made the bonnet lighter and more rigid. The front of the car retained the 2/4's grille, but the front wing headlamp line was raised, placing the 7in (18cm) diameter headlamps a couple of inches (5cm) higher than the DB2/4.

The DB Mark III was introduced in March 1957, and featured a major tidying-up of the design, with alterations both inside and out. The most noticeable change to the exterior was a new design for the front end, which was based on the racing DB3S. As with the previous DB2 models, the DB2 Mark III was available in fastback and soft-top form, but could also be specified as a coupé, with a fixed hardtop that mirrored the soft-top's lines. There was also a de-cluttering exercise carried out on the exterior, one result of which was the car

**The evolution of the front end of the DB2: to the right is an early DB2 with its channel alloy bumpers and low headlamps; to the left is a mid-1950s DB2 dhc with higher headlamps, revised grille and steel bumpers; and in the middle is the last of the line, a Mark III with its last grille design and sculpted bonnet top.**

**The last of the line: the DB Mark III has clean flowing lines and is a classic GT car.**

losing the fussy chrome trim along the bonnet shut line, and a second being the adoption of larger rear-light clusters on the back of the vestigial fins.

The light clusters were standard Lucas units originally fitted to the Humber Hawk Mark IV of 1954, also seen on the Alvis TD21 through to the TF21, and also used subsequently on the DB4; they were tall and slim and had a red combined tail- and stop-light sitting below an amber indicator lens, with a chrome surround that included a separating strip between the two lenses. The shape caused them to be nicknamed 'cathedral' lights, because their outline resembled a gothic window.

The interior aquired a completely redesigned dash, with the instruments sitting in a cluster directly in front of the driver; it was shaped like the Aston's grille, a design feature that would be carried forwards through to the DB6.

Mechanically, early on in production the car was offered with front disc brakes as an option, and these were standardized from chassis number 1401. Most significantly the DBA engine, which was an extensive revision of DB2's VB6 unit, was fitted from the start. With its revised block and many other modifications (see the section above 'The Lagonda 6-Cylinder dohc Engine – DBA Series' for more details), the new LBA unit produced a healthy 162bhp, which was an extra 22bhp over the Mark II's 140bhp, and this gave the DB Mark III a significant performance boost.

## The DB2 Works Racers

The first DB2 racers were built for the 1949 Le Mans, and the three cars were very close to standard in production specification. Of the three cars entered, two (chassis LMA/49/1 and LMA/49/2) were powered by Hill's 1970cc 4-cylinder engine, while the third (LMA/49/3) was powered by the 6-cylinder 2.5-litre Lagonda unit. LMA/49/1 unfortunately crashed at the event, and sadly the driver, Pierre Marechal, was killed. The second (LMA/49/2) came seventh in class, while the Lagonda-powered car did not finish due to a water pump failure.

The following year, John Wyer took over the works team, and three DB2s were used, again in close to production trim. That year at Le Mans two out of the three cars entered finished: LML/49/3 suffered a broken crank, but LML/50/7 came in fifth overall, and LML/50/8 came fifth overall. However, the cars came first and second in the 3-litre class, and first and third in the Index of Efficiency.

The 1951 works DB2 cars were subjected to a comprehensive programme of lightening and careful preparation under Wyer's supervision. A pair of these lightweight cars was prepared, which weighed some some 350lb (19kg) less than the 1950 Le Mans DB2 cars, and around 450lb (204kg) less than the standard car. The weight loss was achieved by substituting magnesium castings for alloy where possible, and extensively drilling the chassis. Lighter and thinner alloy sheet – 18-gauge instead of 16-gauge – was used to construct the body, plexiglass windows were substituted for glass, and all the exterior trim was removed. The standard seats were replaced with lightweight racing units – each standard seat weighed some 40lb (18kg). The cars were also a little more powerful than the 1950s cars, with the engines producing around 138bhp by fitting triple Weber 35DCO carburettors.

At the 1951 Le Mans, three cars were fielded by the works: the two lightweight cars, registered XMC 76 and XMC 77 (chassis numbers LML/50/50 and LML/50/55), and the previous year's DB2, registered VMF 64 (chassis number LML/50/8) – this car was not a true lightweight but had undergone a weight loss programme for the season, which left it some 150lb (68kg) heavier than the true lightweights.

**A contemporary show of the classic works DB2: VMF 64 competing on the track.**

The three works cars had a good race: XMC 77, number 25 in the race, driven by George Abecassis and Brian Shaw-Taylor, finished third overall; XMC 76, number 26, driven by Lance Macklin and Eric Thompson, came in fifth overall; and VMF 64, number 24, driven by Reg Parnell and Duncan Hamilton, came seventh overall. Importantly these placings meant that the three works Astons were placed first, second and third in the 3-litre class. A further two privately entered cars finished: number 28 driven by Nigel Mann and Mortimer Morris-Goodall came tenth overall and fifth in the 3-litre class, and number 27 driven by Peter Clark and James Scott-Douglas came in thirteenth overall and sixth in the 3-litre class. The positions of the works and private cars in the 3-litre class were split by the Ferrari 212 coupé of Norbert Jean Mahé and Jacques Péron with a fourth place in the class. However, the overall result gave Aston Martin a fine finish of five starters and five finishers, and total domination of the 3-litre class.

With the DB3 sports racing cars coming along for the 1952 season, the works DB2s saw limited use, but privately owned DB2s continued to be used in racing and rallying for several years, and saw a revival in historic racing, especially in the AMOC 'Feltham Cars' class.

### *Conclusion: The DB2 Legacy*

With the business knowledge of David Brown and the engineering resources of the David Brown group of companies, at long last Aston Martin had the capability to produce a class-leading car in the notoriously competitive Grand Tourer class, which could go head to head with its mainly continental competitors.

Trading on its pre-war reputation and the company's post-war competition successes, Aston Martin presented the DB2 as a high performance GT car with a sprinkling of traditional British automotive character – although it held back from the whole 'walnut veneer everywhere' formula that some other up-market British manufacturers indulged in. With the production of the DB2, Aston Martin went from being a small, quirky company producing niche sports cars for enthusiasts, to a successful company producing Grand Touring cars with a Le Mans-winning pedigree and great engineering integrity that would provide the owner with excellent performance, comfort and reliability.

**The DB2 attracted a lot of British and European private owners, who used the cars in competition. This is Walter Lambert finishing the 1956 Ollan Villiars Hill Climb in Switzerland.**

**Typical of race-prepared DB2s in the 1990s, this is Phil Taylor's DB Mark III.**

**With its lowered stance and purposeful looks, Phil's DB Mark III looks ready to return to the track.**

**The DB2 dhc works demonstrator, pictured in 1951.**

**The last of the DB2s was the Mark III. This is Edward Holloway's fine example.**

Essentially the DB2 set the mould for the company's products for the following three decades, carrying the company's reputation up to the 1990s. Production of the DB2 finished in August 1959, while its replacement, the DB4, was announced to the public in November 1958.

## THE RACERS: DB3 AND DB3S

In the late 1940s and early 1950s Aston Martin had returned to the racetracks of Europe with a vengeance. With the DB2 they had a saloon car that could compete successfully in its class at events such as Le Mans, but as racing developed it quickly became apparent that specialist cars were needed to win the prestigious sports-car events outright. The first manifestation of this was the development of the DB3. Similar in concept to Jaguar's 'C' type, the DB3 was designed by Austrian Robert Eberan-Eberhorst under the direction of Aston Martin's competitions manager John Wyer; while sharing some of the DB2's mechanical underpinnings, the DB3 had a completely new chassis and a beautifully styled, open-topped, two-seat aluminium-alloy body. The DB3 was too heavy and large to be competitive, and was replaced by the DB3S designed by Willie Watson, which, while retaining much of the DB3's running gear, had a shorter and narrower chassis and performed significantly better than the DB3.

### Introduction to the DB3

The DB3 was produced between 1952 and 1954 when it was superseded by the DB3S, which, while retaining many of the features of the DB3, was extensively modified, making it a much more competitive car. While the DB3 and DB3S were the main force in racing, with factory support the DB2 continued to compete and then was active in historic racing in later years.

*The DB3 Chassis*

The DB3's chassis bore no relation to the DB2's semi space frame, but was in its own right an interesting if not innovative structure – it was in essence a rectangle made from large diameter, circular cross-section tubing with three crossmembers, also made from circular section tubing, bisecting the centre of the structure. The two side tubes were 4in (10cm) in diameter and made from 16-gauge steel, and the cross-members were also fabricated from 16-gauge steel but were 5in (13cm) in diameter. The complete structure formed a strong, reasonably stiff chassis, but in a lot of ways was simply a reinterpretation of a pre-war ladder chassis using tubes rather than 'U'-section steel channel. It did not take advantage of the new space-frame technology that was emerging, and effectively doomed the car to be heavier than much of the competition. At the rear there was a short extension to the chassis, made from square-section tubing. This was used to carry the spare wheel and fuel tank, and to support the bodywork.

The open-topped bodywork was formed from lightweight magnesium-aluminium alloy, and was a full width design with accommodation for a driver and passenger as dictated by the sports-car regulations, although the car was usually raced without a passenger. A single DB3 coupé was built in 1952 to try to reduce the drag of the open car.

### *The DB3 Suspension*

The DB3's front suspension bore a passing resemblance to that of the DB2 in that it was a trailing arm design, but it differed in several significant ways; at the rear a completely different design was used. At the front there were two trailing arms, the lower one pivoting on a roller bearing mounted in a casting bolted to the end of the front cross-member. Each arm was sprung by a torsion bar, which was enclosed in the front cross-member. As each arm's pivot centre was the same, the two torsion bars, which ran the length of the cross-member, had to be angled up and their end mounts skewed to give them clearance. To ensure the optimum length of the torsion bar, the end of each bar was mounted above the opposite side pivot, and was slightly offset longitudinally so each bar cleared the other. This meant the torsion bars were offset both vertically and horizontally to the pivot, so to ensure the suspension operated correctly, the splined pivot ends of the torsion bars were fitted in a 'universal' joint comprising a four-sided bronze block with radiused sides; this ran in a second 'box' in the pivot and allowed unrestricted and smooth movement of the pivot and torsion bar despite the angles involved.

The top link was effectively a longitudinally mounted wishbone, with the two front ends pivoting on the Armstrong lever-type damper that was bolted to the top of the front cross-member and the single end fixed to the suspension upper swivel joint. The two arms provided lateral as well as fore and aft location. Like the DB2 suspension, the pivots of both front dampers were linked with a torsion bar that acted as an anti-roll bar. The bottom link was a single trailing arm.

The DB3's rear suspension was not related to the DB2 system. Building on Eberan-Eberhorst pre-war experiences at Auto Union, and his post-war work at ERA, the DB3 had a de-Dion type system, with the two rear hubs linked with a large diameter tube, the tube located transversely by Panhard rod, and the differential fixed to the chassis' rear extension. The differential was connected to the hubs by driveshafts with universal joints at each end and a sliding spline to take up changes in length as the hub moved up and down. Each hub was located longitudinally by a pair of parallel trailing arms, one above that of the axle line, the other below, and springing was provided by transverse torsion bars that operated on the lower link's front pivot. The left-hand lower link pivot was positioned above the right-hand-side one, and so the left link's torsion bar was positioned above that of the right-hand link, eliminating the need for the sliding block arrangement seen on the front suspension. Telescopic dampers were fitted on the rear of the hub carrier, with their tops bolted to the chassis.

**The DB3 at Silverstone on 9 May 1953, with Geoff Duke at the wheel.**

Braking was by drum all round, with 13in-diameter twin leading shoe units with alloy 'Alfin' drums and light alloy back plates at the front. At the rear the inboard Alfin drums were 11in in diameter and were mounted close to the differential; they were cooled by air ducted from under the body. The brakes were operated hydraulically using two separate circuits, split front and rear. The cable-operated handbrake mechanism was incorporated in the drum.

### *The DB3 Engine*

The DB3 was powered by Willie Watson's straight six engine in Vantage specification as used in the DB2, but with a number of modifications to improve the power. The unit had an 8.16:1 compression ratio, and breathed through three twin-choke Weber 36DCF5 down-draught carburettors, with a forward-facing air intake on the bonnet to ensure that cold air was fed into the carbs. The head was tweaked with larger port throats, 1.375in (3.5cm) on the inlet and 1.25in (3.2cm) for the exhaust. The sump was cast in Electron light alloy and incorporated fins to help cool the oil; a separate oil cooler was also fitted. All-new exhaust manifolds were fabricated from steel tubing, with the separate manifolds for the front 3 and rear 3 cylinders. These manifolds merged into a single pipe that led down to the single silencer placed on the left-hand-side sill, which had two pipes exiting just in front of the rear wheel.

Finally the front of the timing cover was modified to lower the engine's profile and allow for lower bodywork, and the cooling system was fitted with a remote header tank mounted on the bulkhead, again to cater for a lower bonnet line. In this tune the engine produced a healthy 140bhp at 5,200rpm.

The engine capacity was raised to 2.9 litres by enlarging each pair of cylinder bores asymmetrically and offsetting the con rod small ends.

The cars were originally fitted with the tuned 2.6-litre unit, but for their appearance at the 1952 Monaco Grand Prix a larger 2.9-litre version of the engine was fitted. However,

**On 9 May at Silverstone, the DB3 had to retire.**

on all three cars this engine suffered big-end bearing failure in the race, and the team reverted to the Vantage spec 2.6 unit for subsequent races. The cars were originally fitted with a David Brown five-speed gearbox, but this proved to be unreliable so most cars were retrofitted with the DB2's four-speed unit.

### *The DB3 in Competition*

The DB3 made an inauspicious debut with the Aston Martin works team in competition in September 1951. Having missed that year's Le Mans, and after a brief day of testing at MIRA in Nuneaton, the prototype was shipped off to Northern Ireland to compete in the Tourist Trophy (TT) race at Dunrod on 15 September. Driven by Lance Macklin, it failed to finish. The race record gives the reason for this failure as 'bearings', and these had failed thanks to an oil leak from its Electron alloy sump. Things got better in 1952, with the full team of four

**The DB3 driven by Lance Macklin.**

DB3s entered in the Silverstone sports-car race on 10 May 1952, driven by Geoff Duke, Reg Parnell, George Abecassis and Lance Macklin. Geoff Duke's car, no. 24, suffered from steering failure and did not finish, but the remaining three finished first, second and third in class, with only a 'C'-type Jaguar driven by Stirling Moss getting the better of them. Duke followed up his unsatisfactory debut with a fourth place at the Berne sports-car grand prix behind the all-dominating Mercedes.

Further problems dogged the team at the 1952 Monaco Grand Prix. All three of the cars entered were fitted with 2.9-litre engines, and all suffered con-rod failures, with Parnell's car crashing after skidding off the track on its own oil, and then being hit by other cars. This car was quickly repaired by Henri Chapron's coach works in Paris and resulted in a shortened rear end, when the car was nicknamed 'bobtail'. With new standard 2.6-litre engines fitted the two remaining cars were joined by a new DB3 Coupé for that year's Le Mans. Reg Parnell and Eric Thompson drove the new Coupé, but went out with transmission failure after a mere two hours, and Dennis Poore and Pat Griffith in their Spyder had a water pump failure and retired after just three hours. The final car, driven by Lance Macklin and Peter Collins, lasted twenty-two hours before it was retired with axle failure, the casing having split, losing all the oil. The race was won by the Mercedes W194 of Herman Lang and Fritz Reiss, with the W194 of Theo Helfrich and Helmut Niedermayer coming second. The privately entered DB2 driven by Peter Clark and Mike Keen came a creditable seventh.

The DB3's mechanical woes continued through the season. With three DB3s entered in the Goodwood 9 Hour race in September, Collins and Griffith's car came in first after covering 283 laps, but Parnell and Thompson's DB3, while fitted with a modified 2.9 engine, suffered a disastrous fire during a pit stop, forcing its retirement. The third DB3, driven by Abecassis and Poore, suffered from clutch failure after some 162 laps, and did not finish. In the following year, 8 March 1953, just a single DB3 fitted with a 2.9-litre engine competed at the US Sebring 12-Hour race, driven by Parnell and Abecassis; they came in second (but first in class) behind the Cunningham C4/R Chrysler driven by Walters and Fitch. On 26 April 1953, Parnell and Louis Klementaski's DB3 came in fifth (overall and in class) in the Sports two-seater class in the Mille Miglia. This was to be the last works outing for the DB3 as it was replaced in the works team by the DB3S.

In total, ten DB3s were built in 1952 and 1953, with only one (no. 7) being fitted with the coupé-style body.

The DB3 was run by the works for two seasons, 1952 and 1953, and marked the return of Aston Martin to top-level racing. The car was designed as a sports racer with the ultimate

**Reg Parnell driving the DB3.**

aim of winning the most famous endurance race, the Le Mans 24 Hours, outright. The DB3's first season was not particularly successful – while it did win some races and was not badly placed in others, the season was marred by a lot of mechanical issues, which caused all three cars entered in the 1952 Le Mans not to finish. The team quickly realized that the car simply did not have the power-to-weight ratio to be truly competitive with the emerging competition, the DB3's weight of 2,163lb (981kg) being too high for its power of 140bhp, especially if compared to the contemporary 'C'-type Jaguar. While the 'C' type was only slightly heavier than a fully race trimmed DB3 at 2,072lb (940kg), its 3442cc XK engine was giving some 200bhp, so the Jaguar had a much better power-to-weight ratio. This impression was reinforced by the early stages of the 1953 season, which again saw a mixture of success and failure. As a result the team quickly adopted the DB3S to replace the DB3 by the end of April 1953.

## The DB3S

The DB3 was succeeded by the DB3S early in 1953. John Wyer in *Racing with the David Brown Aston Martins* recounts how he and the team were not happy with the DB3, and how they knew the car was too big, and had been, in his words, 'rather disappointing'. In January 1953 Willie Watson came to Wyer and suggested they modify the chassis by cranking in the sides to reduce the width of the car, and use tubing with reduced wall thickness to save weight. Development was quick, especially as the car used the DB3 front suspension, engine and gearbox; otherwise it had a tweaked rear suspension with a bevel gear differential. The new car was ready for testing at Monza in May 1953, and the team were pleased to find that the redesign had resulted in a weight reduction of some 165lb (75kg) over the DB3, which straightaway resulted in a much more competitive car. Testing showed a 3.5–4 per cent performance increase over the DB3 with the same power.

The DB3S made its public debut at Le Mans in June 1953, when the team fielded three cars, with the prototype as a

**The DB3 Coupé pictured at the Goodwood Revival in 2019.**

**At the 2019 Goodwood Revival: a pair of DB3Ss being readied to race.**

'spares' car in case of mechanical mishaps. This was really too soon after the initial testing, and while the cars were built and prepared to Wyer's and Aston Martin's high standards, there was just not enough time to have them shaken down properly, and none of the three actually finished the race. However, the DB3S went on to major success in the rest of the 1953 season, and continued as the works and private entry car until the advent of the DBR1 in 1958.

The DB3S chassis was similar in design to the DB3, but was lighter, and allowed the fitment of lower bodywork to cut drag. The tubing used was of a thinner gauge: the DB3S chassis used 16-gauge (1.6mm) wall thickness tube instead of the 14-gauge (2.0mm) tube used on the DB3, and 12-gauge (2.052mm) walled tube where 14-gauge (2.0mm) was used on the DB3. The chassis itself was slightly narrower and shorter than the DB3, so used less material and therefore cut down the car's frontal area and drag.

The DB3S's open-topped bodywork was designed and styled by Frank Feely and was formed from magnesium-aluminium alloy. Like the DB3, it was a full-width design with accommodation for a driver and passenger as dictated by the sports-car regulations, although the car was usually raced without a passenger. Thanks to the changes to the chassis, the overall bodywork was lower than that of the DB3, and is generally

**At the Goodwood 77th Members Meeting: a pair of DB3Ss show early and late grilles. HSK 110 is a 1955 DB3S/105, while 62 EMU DB3S/6 from 1954 came second at Le Mans twice (1955 and 1958).**

**The DB3S had smooth and attractive lines. The large cutaway behind the front wheel was to extract hot air from the brakes and engine bay.**

considered to be more attractive than the previous car, with a lightness of line and delicacy that was missing on the DB3.

While the majority of the twenty DB3Ss built were open-topped, two DB3S Coupés were factory built for the 1954 Le Mans race; however, both cars crashed in the race, after which they were both returned to the factory and converted back to open-topped configuration. A further three closed coupé bodies were built by the factory in 1956, towards the end of production.

The DB3S inherited the DB3's trailing arm front suspension, but had a modified version of its de-Dion type rear suspension. The new rear used twin trailing arms and the transverse torsion bars as seen on the DB3, but the DB3S system had a central slide rather than the DB3's panhard rod to provide transverse location. The DB3S also had outboard rear brakes. While the prototype DB3S, introduced to the public in 1953, carried over the DB3's drum brakes, in the middle of 1955 the cars were fitted with 11.5in-diameter Girling disc brakes all round.

The drivetrain of the DB3S was virtually the same as that of the DB3, using the same Lagonda straight six in the same state of tune as the last DB3. While it shared the DB3 gearbox, the rear axle was changed from the DB3 hypoid gear type to a David Brown-designed and made spiral bevel unit housed in a light alloy casting.

### *The DB3S in Competition*

The DB3S's debut at Le Mans in 1953 was inauspicious. Three cars were entered, and all three failed to finish. Parnell and Collins' car had an accident in lap 16, Abecassis and Salvadori's suffered clutch failure at seventy-four laps, and Thompson and Poore's died thanks to ignition failure at a late 182 laps. However, the rest of 1953 was a spectacular success for the DB3S as the cars scored a number of successes: a second at the March Sebring race, a first and second in the 3-litre class at Silverstone in May, a first at the Empire Trophy race in the Isle of Man in June, and then first places at Silverstone in July, at the Goodwood 9-Hour race in August and the Dunrod TT in September. All in all it was a successful year.

By comparison the following year was rather a disaster, with many retirements, and successes limited to a third place in the Buenos Airies 1,000km race in January, first, second and third at Silverstone in July, and a second, third and fifth at Aintree in October. 1955 was a lot better, with wins at Spa in May, Aintree in July, and at the Goodwood 9 Hours and at Oulton Park, both in August. At Le Mans the team had second and first places in the 3-litre class. In the final year of the works' use of the DB3S the team had wins and a second at Silverstone in May; first, second, third and fourth at Oulton Park; first and second at Goodwood; a second overall and first in the 3-litre class at Le Mans; and second places at Silverstone in July, Spa in May, and Rouen in July.

### *The DB3S: Conclusion*

The DB3S was undoubtedly more successful than the DB3 in competition, though it was still not good enough to win the crown sought by Aston Martin: an overall win in the Le Mans 24-Hour race. The DB3S was run by the works between 1953 and 1957, and was replaced with the all-new DBR1, which is described in the next chapter. While the DB3S was reasonably successful, its DB3-derived chassis and suspension made the car too heavy to be truly competitive. The DB3S replacement, the DBR1, would have an all-new space-frame chassis, front wishbone suspension, de-Dion rear suspension, the new 240bhp RB6 engine, and a significant weight reduction to give Aston Martin a competitive car.

## The Lagonda

As an adjunct to the DB3S, in 1954 Aston Martin were intent on developing a sports racing car that could compete at the very top level of motor sport, namely the unlimited sports-car class with engines over 3 litres. However, the effort needed to develop a car and engine, as well as run the then current DB3S, was beyond the strength of Aston Martin – John Wyer was quoted as saying that he should have stood up to the management: 'We cannot do all these things with any hope of success. We must follow a policy of concentration and not dispersal over too many fronts.' However, he didn't do this, and the result was a dilution of effort in the racing programme away from the DB3S and into the Lagonda V12 project, designated DP155.

The DP155 was intended to be a Ferrari beater, and was powered by a Willie Watson-designed V12 engine, which followed the design principles used in the LB6. Like the LB6 engine, the new V12 had the main bearings carried in LB6-style alloy 'barrels', but made the mistake of using alloy for the crankcase rather than the cast iron used on the LB6. On the LB6 the cast-iron crankcase expanded less than the barrels, which took up the clearances and let the engine run with good oil pressure – to quote Wyer again, 'it held the whole engine together'. On the V12 the cast-alloy crankcase expanded at the same rate as the alloy barrels, resulting in clearances that were too wide, and oil pressure issues from the start. The dry-sump, 60-degree V12 unit had a bore and stroke of 82.55 × 69.85mm, giving a capacity of 4484cc and moving to an over square design, unlike the LB6's over-square dimensions with its 78mm bore and 90mm stroke. The cylinder heads were light alloy, and the unit had chain-driven, twin overhead cams operating 2 valves per cylinder. In testing the V12 gave a maximum power of 312bhp, although 350bhp was expected.

One DP155 was entered in the 1954 Le Mans but did not finish, crashing at the Essess after sixty-five laps. Why it crashed wasn't clear, but Wyer recounts that they found a sheared key where the steering arm went into the hub carrier, and this could have been the cause.

The engine was fitted into a chassis based on that of the DB3S but with a longer (100in/2,540mm) wheelbase: the main longitudinal tubes were 5in (13cm) in diameter, while cross-members were made from 4in (10cm) diameter tube. The front suspension was by trailing arms with torsion bar springs, and at the rear there was a de-Dion set-up with torsion-bar springing and telescopic dampers, and a David Brown 8.75in spiral bevel final drive with open driveshafts and brakes mounted on the hubs. Brakes were Girling drums all round, with 'Alfin' bi-metal drums. Fronts were 13in in diameter and 2.5in wide, and the rears were 12in in diameter and 2.5in wide.

In the 1956 season the Lagonda's chassis was replaced with a space-frame design – Feltham's first, and the Lagonda-designated DP166. This was described as a 'centre shaft' design, with the driver and passenger sitting 'outside' the central frame. The car was fitted with Girling disc brakes and wider wheels; otherwise it retained DP155's suspension. The works took a single Lagonda P166 to the 1956 Le Mans, where they found the Lagonda lapped the course only a couple of seconds more quickly than the best DB3S. Driven by Parnell and Poore, the Lagonda did not finish as the fuel filler was not properly sealed after a fuel stop, leading to the car running out of petrol on its 93rd lap.

The Lagonda's space-frame chassis was given a new lease of life in 1957, when it reappeared as the experimental DBR2, powered by the Tadek Marek 3.7-litre straight six designed for the upcoming DB4. The DBR2 was similar in appearance to the DBR1, but under the skin there were significant differences, primarily the DBR2's dated suspension layout. The easiest way to distinguish a DBR2 from the DBR1 is that the DBR2's exhaust pipe exits under the passenger door, while on the DBR1 it exits under the driver's door.

# KEY FIGURES

The years after World War II were marked at Aston Martin by the purchase of the company by David Brown and the amalgam with Lagonda; also the company finally got into its stride and starting to produce its sports and GT cars in the sort of numbers that helped to give the company some financial stability – helped, of course, by the resources of the David Brown Corporation.

## David Brown

Sir David Brown should need no introduction to any Aston Martin fan – notably his initials formed the names of what would become the most famous line of British (or indeed any) sports/GT cars. The dynasty started with the DB2, and was carried into the 2020s with the DB11, DBS and DBX cars in the Aston Martin range.

David Brown was born in Huddersfield, Yorkshire, on 10 May 1904 to Frank and Caroline Brown. His grandfather, also David Brown, had set up David Brown Limited as a pattern manufacturer in 1860, later named David Brown and Sons (Huddersfield). The grandfather died in 1903, the year after the company had moved to Park Works, Huddersfield, and under the stewardship of his sons, Percy and Frank, expanded into the manufacture of gears, complete gearboxes, bearings, shafts and worm-drive gears, as well as complete gear-cutting equipment and tools. The company also had its own foundry and was making steel and non-ferrous castings.

It was into this versatile and wide-ranging engineering company that a seventeen-year-old David Brown was indentured as an apprentice in 1921. Brown's apprenticeship meant that he was moved around the company's various departments, then in 1922 he was posted to South Africa to assist the distributor with installing the company's equipment in the gold fields.

In 1928 he was sent to the USA, Europe and Africa to study business management, and in 1929 he was made a director. On the death of his Uncle Percy in 1931 he was appointed joint managing director, and in 1932 became sole managing director. His first contact with Aston Martin came when he supplied Bertelli with the gears for the 1930s rear axles.

In 1936 Brown diversified into the production of tractors, joining forces with Harry Ferguson and setting up a new separate company wholly controlled by him, David Brown Tractors. Production of the jointly designed Ferguson-Brown tractor started in his Huddersfield factory. In 1939, having broken up with Ferguson who took his tractor designs to the USA for Ford to produce, Brown's own tractor design, the David Brown VAK1, was put into production at a factory that was new to the company, at Meltham in West Yorkshire.

During World War II, the factories known as David Brown & Sons and David Brown Tractors were turned over to war production. The former produced gears and gearboxes for many military applications, including the Merritt-Brown tank transmissions, while David Brown Tractors made tractors, aircraft tugs and track layers. During and after the war, tractor production rose steeply, so by the end of the war Brown

**David Brown's DB4 started the line of cars that would be the most recognizable Aston Martins – the DB4, DB5 and DB6.**

**David Brown where he loved to be: at Le Mans. Pictured in June 1952, under the Aston Martin sign on the pit wall are (*left to right*) Lance Macklin (crouched down), Peter Collins, David Brown and John Wyer.**

had a successful industrial conglomerate and was himself a very wealthy man; this meant that he had the resources to buy Aston Martin and Lagonda in 1946. The new company, Aston Martin Lagonda Ltd, was, from an administrative perspective, the Automotive Group of David Brown Tractors, and was formally named David Brown Tractors (Engineering) Automobile Division. The name did change from time to time, reflecting changes to the parent group; thus in 1951 the David Brown Corporation was formed, and the car company's name changed to The David Brown Corporation (Aston Martin Division) – though by the early 1960s the company was referred to simply as Aston Martin Lagonda Ltd.

Brown's tenure at Aston Martin was, from all accounts, very 'hands on'. He dictated policy, his first decision being the production of the open-topped 2-litre Sports, rather than a four-door saloon like the Atom; then he instigated the adoption of the Lagonda engine, rather than Claude Hill's proposed 6-cylinder unit to power the first car to carry his initials – the DB2 – as well as overseeing the increasing of the Lagonda engine's capacity from 2.6 to 2.9 litres. With these early decisions he set the scene of how the company was to run, and his influence was felt on the design of all the cars that bore his initials. Luckily with the resources of his successful businesses behind him, and of course while Aston Martin was successfully producing cars, he was also able to contribute to, or underwrite the costs of product developments if needed. And he had the resources to provide items such as gearboxes, and to build the cars' platform chassis in his other factories.

Through the 1950s and 1960s Brown oversaw what can only be described as Aston Martin's glory days. And the dream

**The first car to carry the DB name was the DB2 of the 1950s. This is a 1952 DB2.**

only came to an end due to the world economic issues: in the early 1970s he was exposed financially after he had invested heavily into the next generation of tractor design and a major increase in manufacturing capacity when the world recession cut demand for tractors. He had to sell the tractor-making part of his concern, and, much to his regret, was also forced to let Aston Martin go to help the liquidity of the main group, selling it to property developers Company Developments in 1972 after twenty-five years of ownership.

Brown was married to childhood sweetheart Daisy Muriel Firth in 1926; they had two children, David and Angela, who both entered the family business. Angela went on to marry Aston Martin works racing driver George Abecassis, while Brown divorced Daisy in 1950, and married his secretary Marjorie Deans. This marriage also ended in divorce, and Brown was married for the third (and last) time in 1980 to his personal assistant Paula Benton Stone.

Brown was knighted for services to industry in 1968 for the export performance of his various companies.

When the then Labour government nationalized Brown's Vosper Thornycroft in 1977, merging it with British Shipbuilders, Brown left Britain in disgust and moved to the tax haven of Monaco's Monte Carlo. In January 1990 he sold his shareholding in the David Brown Corporation for £46 million, but retained a role as honorary president. Brown returned to the Aston Martin fold when, while living in retirement in Monaco, he was approached by then Aston Martin Chairman Walter Hayes to approve the use of his initials in the name of the new DB7. He was given the honorary title of Life President, and was apparently to have his initials used for the model name. Sir David Brown died at the age of eighty-nine on 3 September 1993, only a few weeks after he had seen the new DB7 launched.

## John Wyer (Race Team Leader)

John Wyer was born in Kidderminster, UK, on 11 December 1909. After completing an engineering apprenticeship at Sunbeam, he joined Solex Carburettors. At the end of World

**The last car to carry the DB name was the DBS V8, introduced in the late 1960s.**

**The Aston Martin race team before the 1950 Le Mans. Standing behind the DB2 VMF63 are Jack Fairman, James Stirling, George Abecassis, John Wyer, Eric Thompson, Lance Macklin and James Watt.**

War II he joined his friend Dudley Folland's garage/team Monaco Motor and Engineering Company based in Surrey, where he oversaw their racing activities and competed in a number of UK and continental races. He became Aston Martin's competition manager in 1949.

Among other achievements he oversaw the redesign of the DB3 to create the lighter and more successful DB3S, fitted disc brakes to the DB3S in 1955, and oversaw the development of the DBR series of cars that would take Aston Martin to victory at Le Mans and win the company the World Sports Car series. His first victory at Le Mans came with the DBR1 in 1959, by which time he was actually general manager at Aston Martin and Reg Parnell was competition manager. In the same year he also won the 1,000km Nürburgring race, which he won three years on the trot.

Wyer left Aston Martin in 1963 to join Ford and run Ford Advanced Vehicles (FAV) in Slough – makers of the GT40. While the GT40 was unsuccessful in its first two years of competition, with the participation of Carroll Shelby and Holman Moody it won Le Mans on its third try in 1966. Ford Advanced Vehicles was shut down by Ford in 1967, and Wyer joined forces with John Willment to form J.W. Automotive Engineering (JWA). JWA took over the former FAV factory in Slough and continued to build GT40s for Ford; it raced GT40s under the sponsorship of Gulf Oil as well as creating the Mirage M-1, which won at the 1967 spa 1,000km race. JWA moved to running the works Porsche 917s in 1970 and 1971, before switching back to building and racing the Ford Cosworth-powered Gulf-Mirage, eventually winning at Le Mans in 1975 with drivers Jackie Ickx and Derek Bell.

Wyer retired from the automotive word in 1976. He died in April 1989 in Phoenix, Arizona.

## Professor Robert Eberan von Eberhorst (DB3 Designer)

Born in Austria in October 1902, Robert Eberan von Eberhorst studied engineering at the Vienna technical university, and graduated with a Masters Degree in 1927. He then moved to Germany and joined the Institute for Automotive Engineering at Dresden Technical University as a research assistant and PhD student.

He moved to the racing department of German car makers Auto Union after being approached by Ferdinand Porsche, who was then chief engineer in the racing department. Based in the Horch works in Zwickau in Saxony, he served initially as a development engineer before becoming head of the racing engine department. After Porsche left in 1938, von Eberan was promoted to chief engineer, and oversaw the development of the V12-powered Auto Union Type D Grand Prix car.

The cars competed with some success in the 1938 and 1939 European seasons, coming first in the 1938 Italian Grand Prix and the 1939 French Grand Prix. Eberan finally completed his doctorate in 1940, and during the war worked in Dresden on the Tiger tank and the testing of the V1 and V2 rockets. At the end of the war he fled from the advancing Soviet forces into the Allied-occupied zone of Austria, and joined forces with Ferdinand Porsche's son Ferry in Gmünd, Austria, to work on the design and development of what would become the Porsche 356. He quickly moved to Cistilla in Italy to work on their racing programme alongside Carlo Arbarth, but then moved to the UK, joining ERA in Dunstable. Here he designed the layout of the ERA Formula 2, 2-litre 'G'-type Bristol-powered car, and also designed the semi space-frame chassis for the Jowett Javelin-Jupiter open-topped sports car.

In 1950 he moved to Aston Martin to design the DB3. He left Aston Martin and the UK in 1953, returning to Germany to rejoin Auto Union as their technical development manager. In 1956 he returned to academia, first as the Head of Mechanical Engineering at Frankfurt's Battelle Institute, then in 1960 he joined Vienna University to head up the university's Combustion Engine and Automotive Engineering Institute. He retired in 1965, but continued to publish various engineering papers. He died in 1982.

## TECHNICAL DESCRIPTION

The DB2 was a two-door coupé or convertible, and the DB2/4 and Mark III had two doors and a rear hatchback, and were also available as a two-door convertible with a conventional boot. The cars had a tubular steel chassis on which was mounted an aluminium body, and in DB2 form were two-seaters, and in the longer hatchback DB2/4 guise had two further small seats in the rear. The cars were front-engined with a 6-cylinder dohc engine, all based on the original Lagonda unit in 2.6- or 3-litre form. There was a four-speed manual gearbox, and a live rear axle. Front suspension was by trailing arm, and the live rear axle was controlled by two trailing arms on each side, and a transverse panhard rod. The suspension was fitted with coil springs and lever-arm dampers front and rear.

## ASTON MARTIN DB2 / DB2/4 / DB MARK III SPECIFICATION TABLE

**Layout and chassis**
Front-engined, rear-drive, four-seat sports tourer. Semi space-frame chassis constructed from square-section tube. Open top body unstressed and made from aluminium alloy

**Engine**

| | |
|---|---|
| Type | Aston Martin overhead valve |
| Block material | Cast iron |
| Head material | Cast iron |
| Cylinders | 6 in-line |
| Cooling | Centrifugal pump with water/ antifreeze mix |
| Bore and stroke | 2.6 unit: 78 × 90mm<br>3-litre unit: 83 × 90mm |
| Capacity | 2.6-litre unit: 2580cc<br>3-litre unit: 2922cc |
| Valves | 2 valves per cylinder, operated directly via bucket tappets from chain-driven double overhead camshafts |
| Compression ratio | Standard 2.6 units: 6.5:1<br>Vantage 2.6 and 3-litre unit: 8.2:1 |
| Carburettor | Standard 2.6 units<br>Vantage 2.6 and 3-litre unit |
| Max. power | Standard 2.6 units: 105bhp @ 5,000rpm<br>Vantage 2.6: 125bhp @ 5,000rpm<br>3-litre VB6J unit: 140bhp @ 5,000rpm<br>3-litre DB/A unit: 162bhp @ 5,500rpm with single-pipe exhaust<br>3-litre DB/A unit: 178bhp @ 5,500rpm with twin-pipe exhaust |
| Max. torque | Standard 2.6 unit: 133lb ft @ 3,000rpm<br>Vantage 2.6 unit: 150lb ft @ 3,000rpm<br>3-litre unit: 178lb ft @ 3,100rpm |

**Transmission**

| | | |
|---|---|---|
| Gearbox (manual) | David Brown 4-speed synchromesh on 2nd, 3rd and top gear | |
| Clutch | Borg and Beck 9in dry single plate 9-spring unit | |
| Ratios (DB2–4) | 1st: | 10.90:1 |
| | 2nd | 7.38:1 |
| | 3rd | 4.95:1 |
| | 4th | 3.73:1 (optional 4.1 and 3.5) |
| Reverse | 10.9:1 | |
| Final drive | Hypoid bevel | |

**Suspension and steering**

| | |
|---|---|
| Front | Independent by two trailing links on each side; coil springs. Transverse torsion bar links upper arm pivot to act as anti-roll bar. Upper suspension pivot doubled up as lever arm piston damper |
| Rear | Live rear axle with twin trailing arms on each side, transverse panhard rod, coil springs, lever arm piston dampers |
| Steering | Steering box, drag link and track rod system |
| Wheels | 600 section on 16in wire centre-lock wheels |

**Brakes**

| | |
|---|---|
| Type | Girling hydraulic front and rear cast-iron drums<br>Hydraulic disc front brakes fitted from DB Mark III from chassis 1401 |
| Size (front) | 12in (30.5cm) diameter by 2.25in (5.7cm) width cast-iron drums, twin leading shoe operation<br>12in diameter (30.5cm) Girling disc brakes |
| Size (rear) | 12in (30.5cm) diameter by 1.65in (4.2cm) width drums, single leading shoe operation |

**Capacities:**

| | |
|---|---|
| Fuel capacity | DB2: 19gal (86ltr)<br>DB2/4 to DB Mark III: 15.5gal (70.5ltr) |
| Oil capacity | 12 pints (6.8ltr) |

**Dimensions**

| | |
|---|---|
| Track | |
| Front: | 54in/1,372mm |
| Rear: | 54in/1,372mm |
| Wheelbase | 99in/2,515mm |
| Overall length | DB2: 162.5in/4,127mm<br>DB2/4 Mark I: 169.25in/4,299mm<br>DB2/4 Mark II and Mark III: 171in/4,343mm |
| Overall width | 65in/1,650mm |
| Overall height | 54in/1,372mm |
| Weight | DB2: 2,452.8lb/1,112.6kg<br>DB2/4: 2,632lb/1,193.9kg<br>DB2/4 Mark II: 2,744lb/1,244.7kg<br>DB2 Mark III: 2,820lb/1,279kg |

**Performance (DB2/4 3-litre)**

| | |
|---|---|
| Top speed | 120mph (203km/h) |
| 0–60 | 10.5sec |

CHAPTER 5

# CONSOLIDATION AND EXPANSION: 1957–1965

By 1957, the replacement for the DB2 series of cars was almost ready to go into production, and the production of cars was now established at Newport Pagnell. The service department and race shop remained at Feltham – but the writing was on the wall for both departments.

The introduction of the DB4 gave Aston Martin an outstandingly successful car, which quickly established itself as a fine Grand Touring car, with performance that matched its looks. The car was the start of a line of models that would see Aston Martin into the 1990s, and would establish Aston Martin in the public eye.

It also introduced to the British public an iconic Italian trademark that would always be associated with Aston Martin to the present day – Superleggera; and its appearance in the third James Bond film *Goldfinger* started the long-running association between Aston Martin and the Bond film franchise.

Finally in 1959 Aston Martin won the Le Mans 24 Hours race outright, and also took the World Sportscar Championship. Racing from then on would concentrate on variants of the DB4 production cars, which would see more success into the 1960s.

## THE COMPANY

Although the DB4 was soon to be placed into production in 1958, the company continued to produce the DB2 Mark III into 1959 while they got production of the DB4 properly underway.

**Probably the most famous model of Aston Martin is the DB5. This is Chris Bland's, which is used as a GT car, just as the makers intended.**

**The predecessor to the DB4 was the DB2 – this is Tim Slow's Mark III, and the styling ancestry of the DB4 is apparent.**

**The DB4, 5 and 6 all used the newly designed Aston Martin straight-six engine. With its all-alloy crankcase and head, and its double overhead camshafts, it was state of the art in the 1960s.**

With the introduction of the DB4, Aston Martin had a marvellous new flagship – but it was not without its problems, reflected by the number of changes made in its first few years of production, and the emergence of a new 'Series' virtually every year. Add in the 1961 four-door Lagonda Rapide, based on the DB4 but with a de-Dion rear end, and it was a miracle that anything got produced at all, let alone a world beater such as the DB4.

In the meantime, Aston Martin was selling every DB4 (and then the DB5) they could produce in the early 1960s, and despite producing limited numbers of Lagondas between 1961 and 1964, over 1,000 DB5s were produced between 1963 and 1966. With the DB5 Aston Martin had ironed out all the detail issues with the DB4, and this meant that the company could devote its engineering resources to designing the DB6 as a proper four-seat GT car in 1965.

**The DB4 was an all-new design, sharing nothing mechanical with the DB2. While it was styled by Touring, it still had a family resemblance to the DB2.**

**Not only was the DB4 an accomplished GT car, it also excelled at racing, both back in the day and in historic racing today. Here a DB4 takes part in a historic race.**

## THE ENGINES

The DB4, 5 and 6 were all powered by an all-new straight-six engine that first saw the road in the DBR2/370, which made its debut at Le Mans in 1957. The engine was completely new and bore no relationship to the previous Lagonda unit used in the the DB2 series. Designed by Polish émigré Tadek Marek, the design was conventional apart from the use of a cast-alloy block, a design decision forced on Aston Martin due to a lack of capacity in the UK specialist casting industry to produce a cast-iron block.

Wyer described how he believed that the engine would have been more refined if the block had been made of iron, and felt that the engine was inferior in terms of smoothness and quietness when compared with the Jaguar XK unit. However, he qualifies these disadvantages with the statement that the use of alloy for the block meant they had the basis for a light and strong racing engine. He also said that while he and Marek originally agreed to design the engine as a 3.0-litre unit to meet the then current Sports Car World Championship racing regulations, but allow for potential for growth in size to 3.5 litres, Marek took the cautious approach and actually designed the engine with the larger capacity. This meant the unit had a square bore and stroke of 92 × 92mm so it could potentially be reduced in size to meet the 3-litre target.

In the event, the Le Mans regulations removed the 3.0-litre capacity limit in 1957, and while Aston Martin did try a short-stroke 3-litre version of the unit with a bore and stroke of 92 × 75mm, giving 2996cc, it was not successful. However, the unit's capacity for expansion in size meant that the eventual maximum capacity the factory used was a hefty 4.2 litre, utilizing a bore and stroke of 98 × 92mm and an actual capacity of 4160cc.

**The DB4 engine was designed by Tadek Marek. This engine is being rebuilt with throttle bodies for modern electronic fuel injection at Chicane in Bramshill, Hants.**

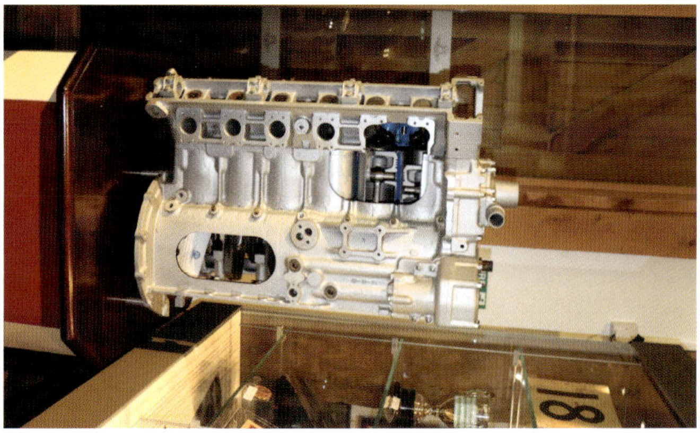

**This sectioned block at the AMHT barn shows a pair of cylinders and pistons on the right, and the main and big end bearings on the left.**

The engine was significantly more powerful than the DB2's unit, and was more than able to give the new DB4 the performance that its right up-to-date styling suggested. Another indication of the modern thinking applied to the engine was the use of a square bore and stroke ratio. This meant that the engine broke away from the British obsession with long-stroke engines, which stemmed from the 'RAC rating' tax regime imposed on cars in the 1920s and 1930s.

**Looking from the rear of the engine, the camshafts are visible, as are the spark-plug wells.**

**In this close-up the cylinder liners are visible, as are the small holes drilled in the block sides to drain out oil or water if the seals on the bottom of the cylinders fail.**

Originally produced with a bore and stroke of 92 × 92mm, giving a capacity of 3670cc, the unit had a compression ratio of 8.2:1 and produced a claimed 240bhp at 5,500rpm, along with 240lb ft of torque at 4,250rpm. Later versions gave more power, and the final Vantage units fitted to the DB6 (and the DBS) were rated at 325bhp at 5,750rpm and 290lb ft of torque at 4,500rpm. When fitted to the short-lived Lagonda Rapide in the early 1960s the unit was bored out to 96mm while retaining the standard 92mm stroke, giving a capacity of 3995cc.

The engine block was cast in RR50 specification light silicon aluminium alloy, designed for use in sand castings, with 4.4in (11.2cm) cylinder centres.

The block was designed with relatively thick walls of 0.31in (0.79cm), and there were no flat surfaces in it in order to aid strength and rigidity. The block was fitted with centrifugally cast wet chrome vanadium iron liners that were top located in the block by an integral flange that was held in place by the cylinder head. Three grooves were machined in the lower outside face of the liners. The top and bottom grooves each contained a synthetic rubber 'O' ring, the top sealing against the water jacket, the bottom against engine internal pressure. The remaining central groove communicated with the outside world via holes drilled in the block. This meant it was possible to identify if either of the the 'O' rings were failing.

The crankshaft was carried on seven plain steel-backed copper/lead main bearings 2¾in (3.23cm) in diameter that were conventionally fitted to the block using caps, each of which was held in place by a pair of bolts rather than the Lagonda unit's alloy sandwich system. The seven main bearings varied in width according to their position on the crank: the front bearing measured 1.28in (3.26cm), the centre measured 1.54in (3.91cm), the rear 1.32in (3.35cm), and the remaining four 1.03in (2.62cm).

The centre main bearing cap carried a set of thrust washers on both its sides to set the crankshaft end float. The crankshaft itself was nitrated to resist bearing wear, and had a torsional vibration damper fitted on its nose. While the big end's crank pin length was 1.375in (3.49cm), the actual bearing width was 1.03in (2.62cm) due to the relatively large radiused fillets allowed on each side of the bearing surface to prevent stress cracks. The main and big end plain bearings were supplied by Vandervell.

The light alloy cast pistons were carried on forged steel connecting rods, which were polished by the factory to remove any scratches that could promote stress cracks. Each piston had two compression rings fitted above a single oil scraper ring, and the gudgeon (or wrist) pin was located by circlips and was mounted in a plain bearing in the connecting rod.

The oil pump was placed on the left-hand side of the engine behind the timing cover on the right-hand side of the block, and was driven from the nose of the crankshaft by a dedicated duplex chain with its own hydraulic tensioner. The pump supplied pressurized oil from the sump via the oil filter assembly to the main oil gallery that ran along the right-hand side of the block, and pressure was regulated by a spring-loaded relief valve. The oil gallery fed the pressurized oil to the individual main bearings, from which, via drillings in the crankshaft, it was supplied to the big end bearings. Finally the oil fell from the big ends into the sump. Secondary drillings supplied oil into the head where it lubricated the camshaft bearings directly and, by splash, the cam lobes and tappets. The oil filler was prominently placed on the front top of the engine.

The one-piece cylinder head was also cast from RR50 silicone alloy, and the combustion chambers were hemispherical. The camshafts ran directly in the head, and each was fixed in place with four individual cam caps, each bolted to the head with two studs. Each cam lobe operated its valve by acting

**Looking at the front of the engine the duplex chains used to drive the camshafts and the oil filler are clearly visible.**

directly on a bucket-type tappet. There were 2 valves per cylinder, the inlet valve was fitted with a synthetic rubber 'O' ring seal, and the middle section of the exhaust guide was exposed to the water jacket to aid cooling. The dual-coil valve springs were held in place with a top cap and cotters, and the hardened valve seat was pressed into the head casting.

**On the top of the head, the valve springs sit in recesses, under which are the valve guides.**

Each valve was angled at 40 degrees to the vertical; the inlet valve-head diameter was 1.88in (4.77cm) and the exhaust was 1.68in (4.27cm). The valve adjustment mirrored the system used in the Lagonda engine: the valve stems had to be ground back to compensate for decreased clearance, and the tappets were available in a number of differing depths, with each depth identified by colour, the shortest being yellow, followed by black, red and green.

The cams were chain driven, with a two-stage drive mechanism located in the timing cover. The crankshaft drove a vertical duplex chain, which drove an intermediate shaft mounted in the timing case at half engine speed. A manually adjustable idler sprocket in the timing case was used to tension this chain. A second duplex chain was driven from the intermediate shaft and snaked up to drive the two chains. An adjusting idler sprocket was mounted on an eccentric shaft between the two camshaft drive sprockets and sat above the chain to manually adjust this chain's tension.

Attractive polished alloy cam covers were bolted on to the top of the engine to cover the camshafts and their driving sprockets. A large alloy casting was bolted to the front of the head and carried the large oil filler cap. A pair of breather towers were fitted on each side of the oil filler cap. Both inlet and exhaust ports were individually sited on the head, six on each side, with the inlet to the right-hand side and the exhaust to the left. The distributor was fitted to the top rear of the engine and was driven by a skew gear fitted to the end of the inlet camshaft.

As the block sides extended some 4in (10.76cm) below the crank centerline, the flange to which the alloy sump casing was bolted was unbroken. The rear bowl sump was very rigid in its own right, and when bolted to the block with thirty-two set screws made a significant contribution to the block stiffness. When the engine entered service in the DB4, there were some issues with a loss of oil pressure. This was due to the design of the main bearings – as the engine warmed up the steel crankshaft, steel bearing caps and aluminium alloy crankcase expanded at different rates, which resulted in increased clearances between the crankshaft and the bearings. This was eventually overcome by running the engine at relatively high oil pressures – up to 100psi when cold and 75psi when running at normal temperature and fitting an oil cooler.

## Engines: The DB4GT Unit

The first major development of Marek's straight-six engine was the racing unit built for the DB4GT model. With only some seventy-five units built it was a rare engine, which was developed and produced from 1959. With a twelve-plug head and triple Weber carburettors, and a compression ratio of 9:1, it gave 302bhp at 6,000rpm.

**At the AMHT barn, a complete DB4GT engine with its free-flowing tubular exhaust manifold.**

**The Vantage specification engine fitted to Chris Bland's DB5. Note the triple SU carbs.**

**The AMHT's DB4 GT motor from the front – note the three twin-choke Weber carburettors.**

## Engines: The New Straight-Six Vantage

As seen with the DB2, Aston Martin offered a tuned version of their standard engine, and called the new specification 'Vantage' or 'Special Series'; it first appeared in the DB4 in 1962. The Vantage specification was designed for road-going cars and was between the 'standard' specification and the full race unit seen in the DB4GT. The Vantage specification gave 304bhp at 5,750rpm and 255lb ft of torque at 4,500rpm, giving a significant power hike of some 41bhp and an extra 15lb ft of torque over the standard engine from the standard cars. This increase in power was achieved through a major set of modifications to the standard engine. At the top end, the compression ratio was raised from 8.25:1 to 9.0:1 by a combination of new pistons and a lightly machined cylinder head.

The diameter of the valve heads was increased in size, up to 2in (5.08cm) for the inlet and 1.875in (4.76cm) for the exhaust. The ports were enlarged to allow for better breathing, and the standard engine's pair of SU carburettors was replaced with three 2in SU HD8 carbs, fitted on three two-branch inlet manifolds. The new carburettor set-up was fed air from a new intake plenum chamber, which gave better breathing, and the distributor's advance curve was modified to suit the new engine's tune. Surprisingly, the camshaft profiles and valve timing remained the same as that on the standard car. Initially the Vantage engine gave 266bhp at 5,750rpm, and was first fitted to Vantage versions of the DB4 Series IV.

## Engines: The 4-Litre Straight Six

Originally developed in 1961 to power the short-lived Lagonda Rapide, the 4-litre version of the Tadek Marek-designed straight six also powered the Series V DB4 and the DB5, DB6 and the DBS. With a capacity of 3995cc, which was achieved by increasing the bore of the 3.7-litre units by 4mm, the new version had a bore and stroke of 96 × 92mm. With three SU carbs and a compression ratio of 8.8:1, the engine gave a huge 282bhp at 5,500rpm, accompanied by 288lb ft of torque at 3,850rpm.

# THE CARS

## The DB4

The DB4 was a replacement for the DB2, although the two models ran beside each other for some months after the start of DB4 production. Work had started on a DB2 replacement

**Rodney McMahon's DB4 shows off its nose featuring the traditional Aston Martin grille.**

in the early 1950s, and the first fruits of that labour resulted in the 'DP114' project. This was a lightly adapted DB2 Mark III, fitted with a new Frank Feeley-designed coupé style. Arguably it was a hardtop version of the DB2 Mark III convertible using DB2 Mark III running gear and chassis; however, although attractive, it really wasn't particularly striking, nor was its suspension exactly modern.

Having designed a pair of DB 2/4 Spiders in 1956, the Italian coachbuilder Touring was approached by Aston Martin to see what they could propose for a DB2 successor. However, once the decision to use Touring to style the new car was made, it meant that their 'Superleggera' system had to be used to construct the body; reusing a DB2-type chassis was found to be impractical as it could not be made stiff enough. So a new platform chassis was designed by Aston Martin man Harold Beach in just a few weeks to suit the use of the Superleggera bodywork, and this platform would serve as the basis for all new Aston Martins for the next three decades. It was made from pressed-steel panels, and was surmounted by a tubular superstructure that supported the alloy bodyshell – the essence of the Superleggera method.

In addition, the old Lagonda straight six was showing its age by then, and so the DB4 also benefited from the new Tadek Marek-designed all-alloy straight-six engine. With a new engine, chassis and running gear, the DB4 was truly an all-new design, and immediately showed great potential for both road and track. While in conventional parlance it was a two-door coupé, Aston Martin called the car (in closed form) a saloon.

### *The Chassis*

The DB4 platform chassis was constructed from pressed sheet-steel panels welded together, with a superstructure added, made from small diameter steel tube to which was connected the light alloy bodyshell. A change from the DB2 was the absence of the fully opening and easily removable front end – the DB4 had a simple flush-fitting bonnet in the centre of the front panel, making access to the engine and front suspension for deep maintenance less convenient than the design on the DB2.

A significant Aston Martin styling cue was introduced with the DB4 bodyshell: the horizontal flattened oval heat extractor vent with its single central rib in the front wing behind the wheel – and this became a styling feature that still appears on Aston Martin models up to the time of writing.

The main element of the chassis was the underlying platform, which was built up using sheet-steel pressings that were welded together. At the front the platform extended up to the wing top and bonnet opening, with a pair of box-section chassis 'legs' built up from steel pressings on the bottom of the

**The DB4's steel platform chassis.**

**Looking inside a DB5, the footwell for the rear passengers is visible behind the front seat runners.**

**The 'Superleggera' badge on the bonnet sides was a neat nod to the body construction method of the DB4 and DB5. Strictly speaking the DB6 didn't use the method, but the badge remained on early DB6s.**

platform, joined at their front by a fabricated steel cross-member, which in turn carried the front suspension. The engine bay was enclosed by sheet-steel inner wings that extended up from the chassis 'legs' and were welded to the bonnet opening's reinforcing steel tubular surround, creating a strong and rigid box. The bulkhead created a second 'box' made from steel panels that ran the width of the chassis and up to the bottom of the windscreen; the floor pan ran back from the lower front of the bulkhead and was reinforced by the sill structure under each door opening and the transmission tunnel.

Box-section steel members reinforced the 'A' pillars, while at the 'B' pillar a substantial transverse box section linked the bottom of the 'B' pillar to the floor and the rear wheel arches. The floor pan was divided into two sections, front and rear, which were divided by a transverse box section. The front of the floor pan covered the driver and front passenger area, while the rear element covered the passenger compartment. The front floor panels had elongated oval pressings to add rigidity and reinforcement, and their outer edges were welded to the inner edge of the sill structure about halfway up the sill panel. The top edge of the rear of the front floor panel formed the top edge of the central transverse box section, and the bottom was formed by the front of the rear floor panel, giving a step in the floor at the 'B' pillar. This meant the floor level towards the rear was lower than the front, which gave room for the rear seat occupants' legs and feet. The rest of the rear floor was flat, apart from the central transmission tunnel, and the floor's outer edges were welded to the bottom of the sill line.

Behind the rear floor pan the rear bulkhead incorporated the rear wheel arches, and between these was a shaped pressing that combined two individual seat bases separated by the transmission tunnel, and an angled seat back. Further back the platform formed the boot floor, with a spare-wheel recess in its centre and a box section behind each wheel arch to support the rear of the car. The chassis was strong but undeniably heavy, mainly because it was designed in a hurry once the decision to go to Touring for the body design was finalized, and Touring needed the new structure to base their body design on.

The construction was not dissimilar to that used on the DB2 body, where the bodyshell was supported on 'z'-section steel formers with welded-on tubes to strengthen the structure, but effectively discarded the steel formers. In the Superleggera system, the overall shape of the body is defined by the space frame of small tubes, and the lightweight alloy body is draped over and supported by the space frame. The edges of the body are fixed to the steel tubes by bending or

**This view of the stripped-out interior of a DB5 shows the network of tubing used to support the body panels in the 'A' pillar and roof.**

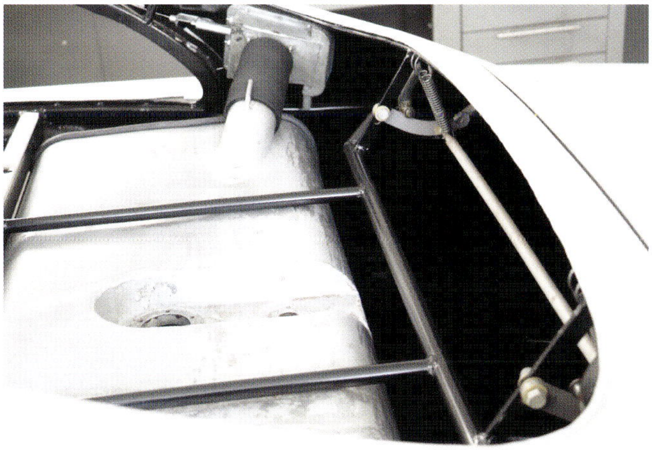

**Looking through the rear window of the DB5, the Superleggera tubing superstructure can be seen, as well as the boot-lid hinges mounted on the superstructure.**

**The bonnet opening of the stripped out DB5 shows the steel perimeter frame that forms the opening and is supported by the Superleggera tubing.**

**Looking forwards into the boot, the inner wheel arch is formed as part of the chassis, and the rear wing is supported by the Superleggera tubing. Note that the outer wheel arch has not been installed.**

swaging the alloy around the tube by riveting the alloy to a flange welded to the tube. The flange also helped to impart some extra strength to the space frame.

In order to prevent corrosion between the steel tube and alloy body, insulation in the form of either hessian or rubber is used to prevent contact between the two metals, otherwise galvanic corrosion would occur. Where the larger panels rest on the framework, the hessian or rubber covering also prevented fretting and vibrating, as well as providing insulation. On the DB4 the tubular body-support structure ran from front to rear.

### *The DB4 Exterior Bodyshell*

At the front of the car there was a tubular structure to carry the nose of the bodyshell, which was welded to the front of the chassis platform.

On the top of the front of the platform was the bonnet opening's perimeter frame, formed from square-section steel tube, which was welded to the inner wings. The rear of the bonnet perimeter frame was connected to the bottom of the windscreen tubular surround with three short joining tubes, welded in place. The windscreen opening was formed with tube and steel sections, and was welded to the bulkhead and the tops of the 'A' pillars. The main element of the small diameter, round-section tubular structure ran from the top of the windscreen back to the rear panel.

The edges of the structure, across the top of the windscreen and along the roofline over the doors, were formed from steel channel, and on each side of the roof, a few inches inboard of the steel channel, there was a longitudinal tube running from the windscreen top rail back to the rear window aperture. These longitudinals were connected to the top of the steel channel by seven transverse tubes. Three of these transverse tubes ran from side to side of the structure, with the front one just behind the windscreen rail and the second above the 'B' pillar, which meant there was room to fit a sunroof if required. The third one was combined with the rear screen aperture. The rear screen aperture was formed from tubes, and a network of shorter tubes spanned the top of the luggage compartment, the edges of the rear wings and the boot aperture.

The long doors were fitted with manually operated windows, with no quarter lights, and on the first 140 or so cars the door windows were unframed. The later cars had framed windows although still lacked quarter lights.

The fuel filler cap was hidden behind a neat flush-fitting flap incorporated into the end of the 'C' pillar, which was opened remotely from within the car. At the rear there was a distinctive semi-circular line on the top of the boot lid, marking the join where the boot lid went from being flat to where it was raised to meet the roofline. This feature, while it disappeared on the DB6 and later cars, was resurrected, albeit rather more subtly, on the boot lid of the DB9 in a nod to Aston Martin's heritage.

The exterior of the DB4 was very clean and sleek with a minimum of ornamentation. The trademark side vents in the front wing had a single chrome central rib, and the full-width bumpers, which did not have overriders, were also chrome. The long bonnet had a power bulge running down its centre, with the open front fitted with a recessed chromed grille. The 7in (17.8cm) diameter headlamps were mounted relatively high up on the front of the wings, and a pair of smaller round lamps was situated below each one – a plain side marker or parking light, and an amber indicator. At the rear the tall, slim, combined light units seen on the DB Mark III were used, finishing off the line of the slightly finned rear wings.

### *The DB4 Interior*

The DB4 was from the outset intended to be a well specified GT car, and as such the interior had to be up to the standards of the highest cars in the class. This meant that it had to be quiet, comfortable and opulent, while providing the driver with all the information needed to monitor the car's performance and condition. So the DB4 was relatively luxuriously equipped, as befitted its GT status, and upholstered in the finest materials available.

The instruments followed the pattern established in the DB3 Mark III, and were located in a binnacle (shaped to represent a squashed Aston Martin grille) mounted in the driver's eyeline behind the steering wheel. All the instruments were made by Smiths Industries (apart from the ammeter when fitted), with a 4in (10cm) diameter speedometer and rev counter directly ahead of the driver. The layout of the minor instruments in the binnacle changed over the years, with some variations. Early cars had a pair of 3in diameter circular instruments, each containing two gauges, one above the other. When fitted, the left hand was the oil pressure set above the oil-temperature gauges, and to the right the water temperature was set above the fuel gauge. Other, later cars had individual 2in (5cm) diameter Smiths gauges fitted.

**The DB4's cockpit is designed for fast driving, with all the instruments in the driver's line of sight and all controls readily accessible.**

**The Superleggera system meant that the light alloy body was supported by the steel tubular framework, as seen here in the inside of the rear wing area.**

**The DB4 interior is comfortable and well trimmed, but is not fitted with much wooden trim. The seat backs hinge forwards to allow access to the rear seats.**

Finally, combined with the other four minor instruments, a 2in diameter Lucas ammeter was sometimes fitted above and between the speedometer and tachometer. The steering wheel had a 16in (40.6cm) diameter wooden rim with three solid spokes set at 120 degrees to each other, and was designed to run with a single spoke pointing upwards when running straight so as not to obscure the instruments. There were two stalks set on the column, the left-hand side for headlamp main or dipped beam, and the right for the indicators. Both stalks had a press button on their end to operate the headlamp flasher. The car featured floor-pivoted pedals, and the fly-off handbrake lever was mounted on the floor on the outside of the driver's seat.

The two individual front seats were separated by the transmission tunnel, and were supplied by Reutter. This German firm had, in 1953, registered a patent for car seats with a special hinge that allowed the backrest angle to be finely adjusted, as well as folding forwards to give access to the rear seats; these seats were supplied to many up-market manufacturers, including Porsche and Jaguar as well as Aston Martin, in the 1950s and early 1960s. In 1963 the company was bought by

**The DB4's rear seats are not large but can accommodate adults for short journeys, albeit in perhaps some (dis) comfort.**

Porsche and renamed 'Recaro', and today it still has a reputation for producing excellent up-market seats for sports cars. At the time of the DB4's launch the press were full of praise regarding their comfort, quality and versatility. As well as being adjustable for rake, the seat backs folded forwards to give access to the rear, and the seats were mounted on runners to give fore and aft movement.

Despite being advertised as a four-seater, the DB4 was really only an occasional four-seater. The two rear seats were divided by the transmission tunnel and were fixed in position, and were formed by upholstered cushions laid on top of the rear panel of the platform chassis sited between the rear wheel arches. These were heavily contoured into the panel, and were fitted with a central fold-down armrest sited between the two individual seats, and an armrest incorporated into the outer edge of each seat. While there was adequate foot room, provided by the lower rear floor of the platform chassis, headroom and leg room were limited, an issue recognized by the growth in length and the raised roofline of the DB6.

The one-piece door windows had no quarter lights and were frameless, sealing against the rubber seals mounted on the body, and the rear windows were fixed in place. The heater itself was mounted under the scuttle and was equipped with side vents to feed warm air to the footwells as well as vents on the leather dash top to de-mist the windscreen. A fan boosted the heater's output, the heater tap temperature control was operated by slider from the centre of the dashboard, and individual fresh air control sliders were sited on the outer side of each footwell.

**The DB4's boot features an iconic Aston Martin design feature: the semi-circular arc where the roof merges into the top of the boot.**

**The DB4's boot is surprisingly spacious, with plenty of room for luggage for two.**

The DB4 lost the utility of the DB2's load bay due to the positioning of the fuel tank behind the rear seat bulkhead, which filled the space between the cabin and the boot; this meant that the tank was much less likely to be damaged in a rear-end collision.

### *DB4 Steering, Suspension and Brakes*

The DB4's front suspension was completely new and shared nothing with the DB2, while the rear suspension shared some of the DB2's implementation but was completely different in detail. At the front the limitations of DB2's trailing arm suspension, basically wheel movement, had to be balanced against unsprung weight, and were overcome by replacing the complete assembly with a twin wishbone-based solution. This system had forged unequal length wishbones, with the top using two separate forged arms and being shorter than the bottom. The bottom wishbone was made in one piece. The front shock absorbers were Armstrong tubular items with concentric springs. The two bottom wishbones were linked with an anti-roll bar that ran across the front of the axle line. Steering was by rack and pinion, a first for Aston Martin, the rack giving 2.8 turns of the steering wheel to go lock to lock.

**The DB4's front suspension was an all-new double wishbone set-up.**

**The disc caliper was mounted to the rear of the suspension and the steering arm was at the front.**

At the rear the live axle was located longitudinally by a pair of parallel trailing arms, which were positioned on the outer end of the axle and ran forwards to location points on the platform chassis. Both ends of each arm were mounted on rubber bushes. The axle was sprung by coil springs located on the rear outer end of the axle, and the longitudinal location was achieved using a Watts linkage that was pivoted on rubber bushes on the centre of the differential housing and the chassis. The rear dampers were Armstrong lever-arm types and were mounted behind the axle. Armstrong 'Selectaride' dampers were listed as an option. These were electrically controlled and had four damping positions that could be selected by a switch in the cabin for when the car was laden.

The DB4 was originally fitted with Dunlop disc brakes all round. At the front the discs were 11.5in (29.21cm) in diameter, and the two cylinder calipers were mounted behind the axle line. At the rear, 11.13in (28.25cm) diameter discs were fitted outboard on the wheel hubs, with the calipers fitted in front of the axle line. A set of mechanical calipers mounted on the lower edge of the main calipers provided the handbrake mechanism, which was cable-operated by a fly-off lever placed on the sill side of the driver's seat. A Lockheed vacuum servo was fitted.

The wheels were Dunlop 16in knock-on, seventy-two-spoke, steel-rimmed wires that could be painted or chrome. From 1959 the Borrani alloy-rimmed wire wheels, as fitted to the DB4 GT, were an option.

### *The DB4 Engine and Running Gear*

The DB4 was powered by the all-alloy 3.7-litre straight-six engine designed by Tadek Marek. This all-new competition-bred unit replaced the Lagonda straight six seen in the DB2, and was the engine that would power successive Aston Martins through the 1960s, until it was in turn replaced by the Marek-designed V8. In the first DB4s the engine breathed through a pair of SU constant velocity carburettors mounted on a pair of three-branch manifolds. Original DB4 engines were fitted with a 15 pint (8.5ltr) sump, but this was increased on later cars.

The David Brown four-speed gearbox received the addition of an optional Laycock de Normanville electrically operated overdrive unit in April 1961, which could be electrically activated on third and top gears to drop the normal revs in third or top.

The rear axle was originally intended to use a de-Dion design, however, when tested the design was found to transmit

**The Vantage specification engine in Rodney McMahon's DB4. Note the triple SU carbs.**

too much noise and vibration, so production cars adopted a live-axle design, coil sprung and located by parallel radius arms (two on each side) with transverse location achieved using a Watts linkage. There was a choice of three differential final-drive ratios: standard was 3.54:1, with the option of 3.31:1 and 2.93:1.

## The DB4 Convertible

In keeping with Aston Martin's postwar tradition and David Brown's wishes, the DB4 Convertible was introduced in October 1961 at the London Motor Show. It was based on the DB4 Series IV, and was called the 'DB4 Convertible' rather than the slightly old fashioned 'drop-head coupé' used for the DB2. The DB4's manually operated fold-down hood was made from PVC with a plastic rear window, and could be easily opened by one person. Engineered by Harold Beach rather than Touring, when folded it fitted just about flush into a well in the rear deck and around the rear seats. The hood frame and fabric meant the rear seats were slightly narrower than the Coupé's. In order to preserve the rigidity of the car, the front and rear bulkheads in the platform chassis were reinforced, and there were also significant amounts of extra steel section applied to the sills. All in all the stiffening added some 50lb (22.6kg) to the weight of the chassis.

The well for the folded roof took up the space usually occupied by the Coupé's fuel tank, so the Convertible was given a pair of smaller tanks fitted in the rear wings, one on each side. Not only did these impinge on the boot space, but with a total capacity of 16gal (73ltr) they also carried some 3gal (13.6ltr) less fuel than the Coupé. With the soft top, the Convertible was also fitted with a slightly smaller bonnet bulge, and a new grille with seven vertical bars; both these changes would be used on the Series V Saloon. Despite the additional stiffening and the roof mechanism, Aston Martin claimed that the weight of the Convertible was the same as the Coupé, and that it shared the same dimensions. However, press reports of the time show the Convertible was some 3in (7.62cm) longer, and weighed 'nearly ½ cwt' (56lb/25kg) more than the Saloon.

**This is not just any DB4 Volante: it is the car driven by Michael Caine in the film *The Italian Job* at the Goodwood Revival in 2019, where it featured in an *Italian Job* cameo.**

## DB4 Development

In production from 1958, the DB4 was subject to a rigorous programme of improvements throughout its production until its replacement with the DB5 in 1963. Every major set of changes to the DB4 resulted in a 'Series' of the car, running from the Series II of 1960 through to the Series V in September 1962, with the dates of each Series introduction depending on the engineering improvements, rather than a fixed calendar.

The main need for improvement to the original car was to sort out a problem with the new engine's oil pressure. After prolonged hard running the oil pressure could drop, thanks to the alloy block expanding more than the steel crankshaft, resulting in increased main bearing clearances and a drop in oil pressure. Also, the side windows came in for some modifications, as the early frameless side windows proved to be difficult to seal properly, especially at speed, so after some fifty cars had been produced the cars were given chrome-plated steel window surrounds fitted to the door to make the windows close fitting and draught free.

After the first 100 or so cars were produced a light alloy radiator cowl was introduced in the engine bay to improve cooling.

### *The DB4 Series II*

The Series II DB4 was introduced in January 1960, the main change being a larger sump, which helped to alleviate the oil-pressure and main-bearing problems found on the original cars. The sump carried 17 pints (9.6ltr), some 2 pints more than the original DB4, which helped by keeping the oil cooler. However, the oil capacity and cooling was found to be still marginal, so the last of the Series II and all later cars had an even larger sump of 21 pints (12ltr) capacity, which, especially if the optional oil cooler was fitted, cured the problem – although it appeared that not too many owners asked for the optional oil cooler. The Series II was also was fitted with heavier duty, front three-piston brake calipers, larger diameter front discs – 12.13in (30.7cm) – and a radiator blind for cold weather.

**The Series II DB4 shows the sharp lines penned by Touring.**

**A nice 1960 DB4 Series II pictured at an AMOC meeting.**

The main change to the original car's bodyshell was to reverse the position of the bonnet hinge, placing it on the nose of the bonnet. This meant that if the retaining catch failed while the car was moving, the bonnet would not be blown open. The fixed rear windows of the Series I cars were changed to be opening, which helped with the interior ventilation. They had a hinge mounted on the front edge and an over-centre latch at the rear, which was fitted through the glass and restricted the opening and locked the window when closed.

### *The DB4 Series III*

The DB4 Series III was introduced in April 1961, and built on the Series II with more subtle improvements. The bonnet gained an extra stay, the rev counter was now triggered electronically rather than by cable, and the combined rear-light unit was replaced with three round lights on each side on a chrome plate. Cast-iron door hinges replaced the previous steel items. The rear red and amber light lenses were fixed in position by their chromed bezel and were identifiable by the four 'ears' moulded into the plastic to facilitate removal. From top to bottom the lights were amber for indicator, red for the combined tail and stop lights, and at the bottom a round reflector. The interior received an improved ventilation system with extra demisting vents fitted, and a cover was fitted over the clutch and brake pedal linkages. Some export cars were fitted with a 4.09:1 ratio differential. Three cars were originally fitted with the high performance DB4GT specification engine.

### *The DB4 Series IV*

The DB4 Series IV replaced the short-lived Series III in September 1961. Again there were a number of small changes: a lightly restyled nose with a new grille with seven vertical

**Rodney McMahon's 1961 DB4 Series IV in Pearl Grey.**

slats, the gearbox ratios were changed to a wider set on most cars, the single-plate clutch was replaced with a Borg and Beck twin-plate 9in unit, and the standard differential drive ratio was changed to 3.31:1, with 3.45:1 and 3.77 as options. Cars fitted with the optional overdrive were fitted with the 3.77:1 ratio.

The DB4 Vantage specification was first offered on the Series IV, with the Vantage specification engine. Most cars completed to this specification had the recessed headlights with their glass cover as first seen on the DB4GT and then standardized on the DB5 and DB6.

### *The DB4 Series V*

The DB4 Series V was introduced in September 1962. The major exterior change was to lengthen the car by 3⁵⁄₈in (9cm) to 180in (4,570mm), and to subtly alter the roofline to give rear-seat passengers a little more room. The main difference in appearance to the previous cars was the elongation of the line between the flat and raised areas on the boot lid to be an ellipse to cater for the fairing-in of the revised roofline into the boot lid. The cars were fitted with 15in diameter wire wheels rather than the previous 16in units, which, despite the raised roofline, meant the Series V was the same overall height as the earlier DB4s.

The interior gained the DB4GT-style instrument binnacle with separate minor instruments fitted, and virtually all the Series V cars had the DB4GT sloping headlights. The rear light treatment also changed. While the layout remained similar, the design of the three separate round lights mounted on each side of the rear wing first seen on the Series III were changed, with the lenses secured by two screws. The bottom reflector was replaced with a round reversing lamp, and the red reflectors were repositioned on the bumper. With the exception of the engine (which as standard was the 3.7 unit), these last DB4s were very close to being the same in appearance and specification as the DB5. The very last batch of DB4 Vantages had twin filler caps, one on each side with hinged covers on the 'B' pillar.

The DB4 built on the reputation established by the DB2 to firmly establish Aston Martin at the pinnacle of the road-going sports touring car market in the late 1950s. The model was subject to an extremely comprehensive development programme after it was introduced, with the five distinct versions appearing over a scant five years of production. This should not imply that the car was underdeveloped when it was introduced: rather, it was being produced at a time when technological advances, increasing competition from other manufacturers, and increased customer needs for comfort and practicality were being addressed.

Add in the improvements that came about as a result of racing the cars, along with the experience gained producing the high performance DB4GT and the Zagato, and the rapid state of changes is understandable. And of course the DB4 marked the arrival of Aston Martin in the forefront of road-going GT cars, with the need to keep abreast of the opposition. This market was only going to get even more competitive with the introduction of the Jaguar E-type in 1961: with its advanced, race-proven specification and extremely competitive price, the E-type represented an existential threat to all high-performance GT cars at the time. The DB4 was up to the challenge, and evolved gracefully, maintaining the model's performance and style while keeping Aston Martin's market position.

**While this is a DB5 Volante, it shows the rear bumper and lights as fitted to the last DB4 Series V.**

## The DB4GT

One of the first iterations of the DB4 line was the short-wheelbase DB4GT. Introduced to the press in October 1959, the car was intended as a sports racing car. While the DB4GT retained the DB4's looks, it had some subtle modifications, including faired-in headlights to distinguish it from the DB4. As a car aimed primarily at racing in the GT class, the DB4GT's engine produced some 64bhp more than the standard DB4, a 25 per cent increase that gave the DB4GT a scintillating performance. The car offered a major performance boost over the already fast DB4, and the 302bhp engine, close-ratio gearbox and a weight reduction of 2,706lb (1,227kg) – about 178lb (80kg) less than the standard DB4 – resulted in claims that the car could accelerate from 0–100mph and stop in under twenty seconds.

While the DB4GT was not used by the works, apart from some early testing, it had a great deal of success in the hands of club racers throughout the 1960s.

### *The DB4GT Chassis*

The DB4GT's chassis was based on that of the DB4 but had 5in (12cm) taken out of the wheelbase. The reduction was made by reducing the length of the rear passenger footwell area, which cut the rear passengers' legroom but preserved the legroom for those in the front. This reduction in length undoubtedly increased the stiffness of the overall chassis to the benefit of the

**A 1962 DB4 with a 1965 DB5 behind it, and a DB6 just visible behind the DB5. Note the change in headlights between the DB4 and DB5, and the revised roofline and side-window profile of the DB6.**

**DB4GT DP199/1 at the 1959 Le Mans, where it retired after engine-bearing failure after only twenty-one laps.**

**DB4GT chassis DB4GT/016/R racing at Cussons Classic GT event at Thruxton, 1972.**

handling, and also resulted in a significant weight loss. Otherwise the chassis platform and the associated Superleggera tubework was much the same as the standard DB4.

### *The DB4GT Exterior*

The main visible difference between a DB4GT and the standard DB4 was found in the front wings, where the headlamps were recessed and faired in with plexiglass plastic covers, which were fitted with slim chrome surrounds. While the style was adopted for the late DB4s and carried through to the DB5 and DB6, it appeared first on the DB4GT. The sidelights, which were normally sited alongside the indicator underneath the headlamp on the standard car, were repositioned to sit in front of the headlight underneath the perspex cover.

Twin filler caps were provided for the fuel tank, with the chromed 'Monza'-style quick-release caps mounted on the flat area on the top of the rear wing between the front of the boot lid and the end of the rear window. The caps were recessed into the top of the wing, and all DB4GTs were fitted with the one-piece 'cathedral'-style rear lights.

### *The DB4GT Interior*

The driver and front passenger positions remained the same as on the DB4, but the instrument binnacle was altered to incorporate individual minor dials for oil pressure, oil temperature, water pressure and fuel, rather than the large combined units fitted to the standard car. The reduction in wheelbase was achieved at the expense of the rear seats, which were replaced with a plain shelf in most of the DB4GTs produced. In the boot, most of the available space was taken up with a 30gal (132ltr) fuel tank made from light alloy, and the spare wheel.

### *The DB4GT Suspension and Steering*

The DB4GT carried over the front and rear suspension layout of the standard DB4, but had Girling disc brakes fitted all round, rather than the standard DB4's Dunlop items. The front discs were larger, at 12.06in (30.6cm) in diameter, while the rears were 11in (27.9cm) in diameter. The wheels were lightweight Borralli, wire-spoked, knock-on units. These were, like the standard DB4, 16in in diameter, had a 5.5in-width rim, and seventy-two spokes to mount the light alloy rim to the Aston Martin steel hub. As a competition-oriented car, the DB4GT was fitted with a tuned version of Tadek Marek's 3.7-litre straight six, also fitted to the DB4. With a 9:1 compression ratio, some porting work, a dual ignition system with two plugs per cylinder, three side-draft, twin-choke Weber carburettors, the unit gave 302bhp.

The transmission was a David Brown four-speed, all-synchromesh, close-ratio unit, and the car was fitted with a 9in diameter, twin-plate Borg and Beck clutch. The Salisbury differential was a limited slip 'Powerloc' unit, and there were five ratios available – 4:1, 3.77:1, 3.54:1, 3.31:1 and 2.93:1.

The DB4GT was a very potent and successful sports racing car, and did much to enhance and maintain Aston Martin's sporting pedigree throughout the 1960s.

## The DB4GT Zagato

The DB4GT Zagato was a lightweight DB4GT with an all-new lightweight body made by Italian coachbuilders Zagato of Turin. With styling by Zagato's Ercole Spada, the DB4GT Zagato's body was built at Zagato's factory and then fitted over a complete DB4GT rolling chassis in the Zagato works; the car was then transported back to Newport Pagnell for trimming and final finishing before going to the customer. With its lightweight body, crafted from the thinnest aluminium possible, minimal interior trim, no bumpers, perspex windows and no extra external frippery, the Zagato weighed about 100lb (45kg) less than the standard DB4GT.

The Aston Martin DB4GT Zagato was an exclusive version of an already exclusive and limited edition car, the DB4GT. With a list price of £3,750 – which after adding the UK's

**The DB4GT Zagato is the rarest and probably the most valuable DB4 variant. With its Zagato-styled lightweight body and its trademark 'double bubble' roof on a DB4GT chassis, the car was very competitive in its day.**

purchase tax of £1,719.19, meant a full price of £5,469.19 in early 1962 – it is no surprise that the cars were rare, especially when you consider that in late 1961 the standard road-going DB4 cost (with purchase tax) £4,084.

## The Lagonda Rapide 1961–1965

While not actually badged as an Aston Martin, the Lagonda Rapide of 1961 was very much a development of the successful DB4, and was aimed squarely at a market that David Brown was keen to enter – that of a fast, good handling and handsome four-door, five-seat saloon car. The Rapide met these criteria head on, and followed the formula pioneered by the DB4 with aluminium Superleggera bodywork on a steel platform chassis, and a totally restyled front end. While some have dismissed the Rapide as simply a long-wheelbase DB4, it was in fact very much a new design. It took the best of the DB4, such as the front suspension and body-making techniques, and mated them with a lengthened chassis, de-Dion rear suspension, a 4-litre retuned version of the DB4's straight-six engine, four-door bodywork and all-new front-end styling, and this made the Lagonda every inch the businessman's express that David Brown envisaged. It was a car that could be chauffeur driven during the working week, and then driven and enjoyed by its owner at the weekend.

### *The Chassis*

While the Rapide's steel platform chassis was based on the DB4 unit, the chassis was longer, to accommodate both a 16in (406mm) increase in wheelbase, the Rapide having a 114in (2,897mm) wheelbase as opposed to the DB4's 98in (2,489mm), and an increase in overall length of 18.75in (476mm), with the Rapide measuring 195.5in (4,966mm) in length, and the DB4 176.75in (4,889mm). Otherwise the DB4 construction principles were followed, with a superstructure made from small diameter steel tube (which included the 'B' pillars) welded on to the steel substructure, and the alloy body panels fixed to the structure using a mixture of riveting and turning, or folding the alloy over flanges welded on to the tubing.

### *The Exterior*

While the rear of the Rapide was similar in outline to the DB4, with the vestigial rear wings carrying the rear lights and the boot lid opening just above the bumper, the front end had a very different look. A pair of headlamps was mounted horizontally on the outer edge of the front wing, the outer being 7in (1.8cm) in diameter and the inner 5.75in (14.6cm) in diameter, with indicator and parking lights positioned below them. The centre of the nose was taken up with an oval grille framed with a chrome edging and a central vertical chrome strip, and running along the bottom line of the front was a pair of secondary squashed oval grilles with a large chrome central strake, the outer edge of which carried the amber indicator light. The trademark DB4 wing vent was present just behind the front wheel arch. Chrome wrap-round bumpers with overriders were fitted at front and rear.

Twin interconnected fuel tanks were fitted, one in the rear of each rear wing, giving the car a fuel capacity of 16.5gal (75ltr); the fuel filler cap was electrically operated. The spare wheel was fitted in a well underneath the boot floor.

### *The Engine*

The Rapide's engine was a bored-out version of the DB4 6-cylinder all-alloy dohc unit with a new bore of 96mm, which, combined with the standard stoke of 92mm, gave a capacity of 3,995cc. With a compression ratio of 8.5:1 and reprofiled camshafts to give less overlap, the Rapide's engine produced a healthy 236bhp at 5,000rpm and a hefty 265lb ft of torque

**The Lagonda Rapide was David Brown's luxury 'businessman's express' – a fast and comfortable four-door saloon.**

at 4,000rpm. Fitted with a pair of Solex 44PHH twin-choke carburettors, the engine was tuned to give more torque and a less peaky power delivery than the DB4 unit, making it more refined and relaxed than the unit fitted to the sports cars.

### *Transmission*

The standard equipment gearbox was the three-speed Borg Warner unit, which was controlled by a lever to the right of the steering column. Unique to the Lagonda's unit was a 'second gear hold' feature. This was activated when in top (third) gear by pressing the gear lever forwards, and would cause the box to change gear into second and hold second gear – useful for overtaking swiftly and safely. There was an option of having the David Brown four-speed all-synchromesh gearbox. A two-part propellor shaft carried the drive from the rear of the gearbox to the rubber-mounted differential, with a centre bearing.

### *Suspension*

At the front of the car the Rapide used the same twin wishbone suspension seen on the DB4, but with revised spring and damper rates to suit the saloon car rather than a sports car. The rear suspension was completely new for the Rapide and comprised a de-Dion set-up, with springing provided by torsion bars. The differential was rubber mounted, and drive taken to the hubs by sliding driveshafts with universal joints at each end. The hubs and connecting de-Dion tube were pivoted using a pair of trailing arms on each side, the top being tubular and the bottom fabricated from steel sheet and sprung by the torsion bars. A Watts linkage was used to locate the de-Dion tube transversely. Armstrong lever-arm shock absorbers were fitted.

### *Brakes and Wheels*

Braking was by Dunlop discs all round, with 11.5in (29.2cm) diameter up front, and 10⅞in units at the rear. The braking system was split into two circuits, front and rear, and a vacuum servo was fitted.

Unlike the DB4, the Rapide's 15in diameter, 6in wide road wheels were made from maintenance-free pressed steel, but retained the knock-on hubs. For safety reasons the winged spinners of the DB4 were substituted with octagonal spinners.

### *The Interior*

As would be expected of a businessman's express, the interior was comprehensively fitted out to be as comfortable and cosseting as possible. Ample leg and headroom was provided, the upholstery was in 'the finest English hide', there was Wilton carpet on the floor, walnut veneer on the dash, and separate heating for front and rear compartments. Electric windows were fitted all round, and the doors, all four of which were fitted with arm rests, were designed to open to nearly 90 degrees to make getting in and out easy. Wooden picnic tables were fitted to the rear of the front seats, and in the rear there was a central retractable arm rest with a compartment in it for 'personal requisites'. The boot was large enough to carry several suitcases, thanks in part to the wing-mounted fuel tanks.

### *Into Production*

While the Rapide was a superb design, it had taken a fair time to develop, and while expensive, offered a fine grand touring saloon that was aimed at the enthusiastic driver. However, the design had two faults. First the concept was flawed: while David

**The tradition of producing fast four-door saloons is alive and well at Aston Martin. This is a 2017 Aston Martin Rapide, showing how the model is still a sleek and attractive saloon.**

**The interior of the Lagonda Rapide was as luxurious and comfortable as any contemporary car, with wood and leather trim and picnic tables for the rear passengers.**

**The Lagonda's front end was given its own look to give the Lagonda marque its own identity.**

Brown was a keen and enthusiastic driver he was very much in the minority, and most captains of industry would rather be driven around in the back of a Rolls-Royce or a Bentley with their chauffeur doing all the driving while they got on with the job of running their company in the back. Performance, as long as it was adequate, was of little or no concern, so the market for the Rapide was very limited, and in the four years of production only fifty-five cars were actually built.

The second issue was the rear suspension. The splined driveshafts of the de-Dion set-up should have been set at 90 degrees to the fore–aft axis of the car, but were in fact set at about 87 degrees. This was just enough to make the shafts vibrate at certain speeds, and the rubber mounting of the differential itself made the problem worse. While the rubber mounts could be stiffened, to change the orientation of the driveshafts to 90 degrees would mean either changing the wheel arches or the differential box mounting cross-member. Either was an expensive job, and as the number of cars being built did not justify the expense, in 1965 the car was dropped from the range after only fifty-five were sold.

## The DB5

Introduced in 1963, the DB5 could be considered to be a Series VI DB4. However, while the last of the DB4 Series Vs were almost identical in chassis, bodywork and suspension up to the first of the DB5s, there was one significant difference: the 4-litre straight-six engine. This produced an extra 45bhp, which, despite the extra weight of the DB5, gave the car a significant performance boost over the DB4. However, probably the most important aspect of the DB5 was not the car itself, but its appearance in the James Bond film *Goldfinger*. This appearance meant that the DB5 is forever associated with Bond, and is the Aston Martin that the public recognizes and loves.

The halo effect of the Bond franchise has also spread to the DB4 and DB6, and while it has undoubtedly pushed prices up, it has also helped to preserve many of these fine old cars, which would otherwise have fallen into the scrapman's clutches. The DB5 was replaced in 1965 by the DB6, which, with a longer wheelbase and extended roof line, gave adequate space to carry four adults in relative comfort.

**The DB5 was the logical development of the DB4, with the new flush-fitting headlights the main difference in appearance.**

**Like the DB4, the DB5 was also available as a Volante with a neatly tailored hood.**

The DB5 chassis and bodywork were carried over from the DB4. The only major change was the new front wing and headlight treatment, with the DB5's unit being faired in, as seen originally on the DB4GT.

As with the DB4, the DB5 was offered in coupé and drophead coupé forms.

From the start of production, as standard the DB5 was fitted with the 4-litre version (bore and stroke of 96 × 92mm) of the Marek all-alloy straight-six engine, in what would have been Vantage tune in the DB4. Fitted with three 2in SU carburettors and with an 8.8:1 compression ratio, the engine produced 282bhp at 5,500rpm and 288lb ft of torque at 3,850rpm, to give a significant power boost over the standard DB4. The Vantage tune engine in the DB5 featured triple twin-choke Webers, as seen on the DB4GT, and produced a claimed 314bhp.

Several different options were offered for the transmission. A prospective owner could choose from a David Brown four-speed box, to which a Laycock de Normanville overdrive could be added, a ZF five-speed box, or a Borg-Warner three-speed automatic. The David Brown box had synchromesh on all four forward gears, and was the same as that fitted to the DB4. The ZF five-speed box was the same as that specified for the Maserati 5000 GT, and had a direct fourth gear, with fifth acting as an overdrive with a 0.83:1 ratio. The ZF box was not the same as that supplied to the contemporary Alvis TD21 or Reliant Sabre/Autocars Sabra, but was significantly stronger in order to handle the DB5's power and torque.

The majority of the running gear of the DB5 was identical to the previous DB4 Series V. The main exception was the change of brake-part supplier, with Girling supplementing Dunlop. The car was also fitted with dual brake circuits, split front and rear, and had servos fitted as standard.

The DB5 was the logical replacement for the DB4, and was an evolution rather than a revolution, offering the customer only minor styling and mechanical changes. However, the car's place in the history of Aston Martin was sealed thanks to its appearance as Bond's gadget-laden express in *Goldfinger*. Thanks to the film franchise, Aston Martin DB5s are instantly

**The rear of the DB5 was very similar to the last of the DB4s. This is Chris Bland's 1964 example.**

recognizable even five decades after its first appearance, and the car has had a significant and mostly good influence over Aston Martin ever since. However, it was also a quick, good handling, fast GT car in the real world, and fully deserves to be remembered for these traits just as much as Bond's car.

## The DB4 and 5 Family Summary

In both styling and method of construction, the DB4 and DB5 family were the cars that defined Aston Martin for the swinging sixties, and which were some of the most attractive that Aston Martin ever made. There is of course no avoiding the halo effect of having the DB5 starring in the Bond films – possibly the most successful product placement ever – and certainly the best of all Aston Martin's publicity efforts.

On the road it competed with exotica from the great Italian marques of Ferrari and Maserati, while at home the E-Type Jaguar ran it close when competing on the road. The DB4 was a significant improvement on the DB2, with the possible exception of losing the hatchback practicality of the earlier car; however, customer acceptance of the DB4 seemed happy with the car's two-door configuration. The security of a separate lockable boot would in many people's eyes trump the convenience and extra capacity of a hatchback, and a hatch would not feature on any Aston Martin (excluding the Cygnet) until the introduction of the Vantage in 2004.

# COMPETITION

Development of Aston Martin's racing cars started with the DB3, which led to the DB3S of 1956, described in the previous chapter; then came the DBR series introduced in 1956, which led to success at Le Mans in 1959. A single-seat grand prix racer, the DBR4 appeared in 1959.

The short-wheelbase DB4GT racer was released in 1960, followed by the Zagato-bodied cars. The 1962 DP212 and the 1963 DP214 were Le Mans prototype sports cars based on the DB4GT. The DP215 was also produced in 1963 as a GT-class racer, and competed in the 1963 Le Mans alongside the two DP214s.

## The DBR1

After the limited success of the DB3 and DB3S, it was the DBR1 that at long last gave Aston Martin an overall win at Le Mans.

Designed by Aston Martin engineer Ted Cutting, the DBR1 was a purpose-built sports racer, with no vestigial production car parts. It moved away from the tubular ladder-type chassis seen on the DB3 and DB3S, and followed the then

**The DBR1 was the sports racer that would bring Aston Martin victory at Le Mans.**

The front end of the DBR1 lost the traditional Aston Martin grille in the name of aerodynamics.

**A contemporary shot of a DBR1 being raced at Silverstone on 14 September 1957. Driven by N. Cunningham-Reid, the car came third.**

contemporary practice of having a space frame made from small diameter tubing, welded together to form a rigid and light structure. The DBR1's space frame was some 50lb (22.7kg) lighter than the DB3S's chassis, at 116lb (52kg). Front suspension was by trailing links and torsion-bar springing, while at the rear the independent suspension comprised trailing arms with a Watts linkage, transverse torsion-bar springing and a de-Dion tube. The front-mounted RB6 engine and the rear-mounted CG537 transaxle made for ideal weight distribution. The attractive all-enveloping bodywork was clearly related to the DB3S, but lacked the DB3S's rearwards extended front wheel arches, relying on a large vent in the side of the front wing to extract hot air from the engine bay.

The DBR1 was fitted with the RB6 engine seen in the last of the DB3s, and it initially used the twin-plug cylinder head designed by Eberan, although this was later replaced with an all-new head. The engine was first used in 223bhp, 2493cc specification, but was quickly uprated to 3-litre specification with a capacity of 2922cc and a power output of around 240 to 250bhp. With seven main bearings, an all-alloy crankcase, and having lost the alloy 'cheeses' used for the main bearings on the original Lagonda engine–these were replaced with conventional bearing caps in the crankcase – the RB6 unit was strong and relatively powerful. The engine drove the propshaft through a flywheel-mounted triple-plate Borg and Beck clutch to a new, rear-mounted, five-speed David Brown CG537 transaxle. This was effectively a transaxle, and incorporated a ZF differential mounted above the gearbox. However, the gearbox would be a source of trouble for the cars, with lubrication issues initially causing many failures. In all, five DBR1s were built by the factory between 1956 and 1959, with the fourth (DBR1/4) being a conversion of DBR3/1.

### *In Competition*

The DBR1's first outing for the works was on 6 April 1957 in the British Empire Trophy race at Outon Park, where the two cars came fifth and second, and this was followed on 22 April by second and third places at Goodwood. The car's first victory came at Spa on 12 May, with a first and second, and another first at the 1,000km race at the Nürburgring on 26 May, with the second DBR1 coming fifth. Le Mans resulted in both entered DBR1s retiring, but the car scored a second place at Aintree on 7 July. A first and a fourth place came along at the Belgium GP at Spa on 25 August, and a fourth and sixth place at the final race of the year at Silverstone Sports car race on 14 September.

In 1958 the DBR1 did not have a good year, with many retirements including no finishers at Sebring, the Targa Florida and Le Mans. A single DBR1, chassis DBR1/3, came first at the Nürburgring 1,000km on 1 June, but the other two DBR1s that were entered retired. The last race of the season at Goodwood was a success, with the three DBR1s entered coming first, second and third.

The DBR1 finally came good in 1959. The team only competed in five races – Sebring, Silverstone, Nürburgring 1,000km, Le Mans and the TT at Goodwood – and the season did not start well, with a retirement due to clutch failure for

**The DBR1's lines can be appreciated from the rear three-quarter view.**

the single DBR1 entered at Sebring. However, after that failure DBR1s came first at Silverstone, first and second at Le Mans, and first and fourth at Goodwood. With a win at Goodwood, Aston Martin won the World Sportscar championship.

## The DBR2

The DBR2 was based on the Lagonda DP166 space-frame chassis but was powered by the 3.7-litre DB4 engine, which had a capacity of 3670cc and a power output of around 280bhp. This was fitted with a conventional four-speed David Brown gearbox.

The car retained the running gear from DP166, with the trailing-arm front suspension and torsion-bar springs, while at the rear there was a de-Dion set-up with torsion-bar springing and telescopic dampers. The car was fitted with Girling disc brakes all round. It was run in the 1957 Le Mans, but failed to finish after the gearbox failed – while this also occurred to the DBR1 that year, the DBR2's conventional gearbox failed when the breather became blocked and the box lost all its oil and seized. It was also found after the race that some hurried modifications to the fuel system before the race had caused problems for the triple twin-choke Webers, resulting in fuel starvation, which cut engine power and caused a misfire above 5,000rpm. Despite this issue cutting maximum power by some 50bhp, the car still lapped very quickly and Wyer believed that it could have won the race that year.

**The DBR2 was very similar in appearance to the DBR1. Tony Brooks driving the DBR2 at Silverstone in May 1958, where he came in fifth.**

The two DBR2s that competed also ran at the Silverstone Sports Car race in September, coming first and third. In 1958 the cars took a first place at Goodwood on 7 April, a first and second place at the Empire Trophy race at Oulton Park on 12 April, a second place at Aintree on 19 April, a fourth and fifth at Silverstone on 3 May, and finally a second and third at Spa on 18 May.

## The DBR3

A single DBR3 was produced in 1958, designed to run in the 3-litre Sports Car class. It was effectively a DBR1 space-frame chassis that was fitted with a short-stroke 2990cc version of the DB4's Tadek Marek straight six. It ran in a single race at Silverstone in May 1958, but the engine did not produce enough power to be competitive in the 3-litre class, and at the event it ran its bearings. The car was rapidly reconfigured to DBR1 specification.

## The DBR4 and DBR5

Aston Martin had not competed in the single-seater racing classes since the 1920s and the Razor Blade, but in January 1956 Reg Parnell took a single-seater based on a modified DB3 chassis to New Zealand to use it in the winter season. This car had originally been built in 1952/53 and fitted with a 2-litre version of the Lagonda engine. However, for 1954 the 2-litre Formula 1 class was due to be replaced with a 2.5-litre limit, and Aston Martin's engineering effort was needed elsewhere in 1953, so the project was abandoned.

When they had the time and resources Aston Martin took another look at the engine, and developed a 2.5-litre version of the RB6 3-litre unit designated the RB6/250. The reduction in capacity was achieved by reducing the engine's stroke to 76.8mm and retaining the bore of 83mm, giving an over-square unit which, when run on alcohol fuel, could be persuaded to produce as much power as the 3-litre unit. So when in 1955 Reg Parnell suggested to Wyer that he could use the car with the 2.5-litre engine in the 1956 winter season in New Zealand, it was resurrected and shipped out; but a rod through the cases stopped the car in practice in the Ardmore race, and it came in fourth in the Lady Wigram racing in Christchurch. The car was basically too tall, as the chassis construction meant that the driver had to sit above the propshaft, and the works quickly lost interest.

In 1957 the works commenced a racing programme aimed at the single-seat Formula I class alongside the DBR1, producing the DBR4, but the programme suffered from delays as race-shop resources were diverted to the sports racers. The DBR4 had a narrowed DBR1 space-frame chassis and the 2.5-litre RB6/250 engine, along with a CG537 transaxle. The front suspension was a twin wishbone set-up, initially sprung using torsion bars but later changed to the conventional coils, while the rear was the DBR1 style de-Dion set-up.

The new DBR4/250 was tested at MIRA in December 1957, and was found to be competitive; but the need to concentrate on the sports cars meant that the car was not introduced for the 1958 season – a fatal mistake as the rear/mid-engined revolution was just starting. The car was introduced in 1959 but was outclassed by the new mid-engined cars; it also suffered from engine bearing problems, which, after a long and expensive investigation, were traced to the positioning of the oil-way drillings in the crankshaft – these were drilled at top dead centre as on the 3-litre engine, but when the short-stroke engine was revved to 7,500rpm, some 1,000rpm above the 3-litre unit's maximum, they caused oil starvation and failed bearings. Despite these difficulties, at the car's debut at Silverstone in May 1958 it came in a creditable second to Jack Brabham's mid-engined Cooper, and broke the Formula I lap record.

Development of the car continued, and in late 1958/early 1959 a new 80-degree cylinder head was fitted to the R – but it was rather a disaster, necessitating a change to Lucas fuel injection as the inlet ports emerged from the head at a compound angle, precluding the use of the usual twin-choke Webers. However, the fuel injection resulted in a loss of top-end power.

The DBR5 was the result of a chassis redesign: it sported a smaller and lighter chassis than the DBR4, and had a two-piece propshaft to lower the driveline and hence the driver's seating position, helping to reduce drag. While it retained the DBR4's front double-wishbone suspension, it was fitted with independent rear suspension, and the David Brown transaxle was replaced with a Maserati 5M-60 unit. Unfortunately the new suspension meant that the DBR5 lost the good handling characteristics of the DBR4. Three DBR4s and two DBR5s were produced.

The DBR4 and DBR5 only raced over two seasons, 1959 and 1960, and overall results got worse as the seasons progressed and the mid-engined cars asserted their superiority. In their first race at Silverstone one of the two DBR4s came a creditable second, but the other car retired when a conrod broke. At the Dutch GP on 31 May both DBR4s retired due to conrod failure, then at the British GP in July one came in sixth,

**The single-seat DBR4 was just too late to go racing in Formula I – by 1959 the rear/mid-engined cars were starting to dominate.**

**The DBR4 was a good-looking racer, but based on a narrowed DBR1 chassis, the car was too little, too late.**

**Developed from the DBR4, the DBR5 was lighter and smaller, but was just not competitive against the lighter and nimbler mid-engined cars.**

while the second retired, this time due to valve trouble. In the Portuguese GP in August the cars came sixth and eighth. Only three races were entered in 1960, with a retirement for the DBR4 and a tenth place for the debut of the DBR5 at Silverstone in May; at the Dutch GP on 6 June a single DBR5 failed to qualify, and finally at the British GP in July one DBR5 came eleventh, and the second retired. At this point Aston Martin took the decision to withdraw from Formula 1 racing as the cars were clearly not competitive.

## The Le Mans Projects DP212, DP214 and DP215

After Aston Martin withdrew from racing with the victory at the 1959 Le Mans, but then the 1959 and 1960 Formula 1 débâcle, their competition flag in sports-car racing was kept flying by the DB4GT and Zagatos run by private individuals and teams across the world's sports-car racing. However, many of Aston Martin's customers and concessionaires wanted the company to return to racing, and especially racing at Le Mans. John Wyer recounts in his book *Racing with the David Brown Aston Martins* how the French concessionaire, Marcel Blondeau, in particular was insistent that the company returned to the international racing scene. The result was a small run of 'Development Project' – or DP – numbered cars aimed firmly at the 4-litre prototype class at the Le Mans 24 Hour race: one DP212, a pair of DP214s, and a single DP215, all produced between 1961 and 196. DP212 competed at the 1962 Le Mans, and the two DP214 and DP215 competed in the 1963 Le Mans and various other races in the season. The principal opponent to the DP cars was Ferrari's GT cars, starting with the 250 GTO.

### *DP212*

Development Project (DP) 212 was the first result of this dealer pressure, and was built between late 1961 and early 1962, making its debut at the 1962 Le Mans. Essentially the car's appearance at Le Mans was as a (to quote Wyer) 'reconnaissance (exercise), as we had been out of racing for two years'. It was entered in the 4-Litre Prototype class that was new for that year; the engine was a bored-out 3.7 unit that displaced 3996cc, and was fitted with Weber 50DCO carbs to give 330bhp, with DB4GT-derived double wishbones up front and a DBR1-style de-Dion and torsion bars set-up at the rear. However, the car was based on the DB4GT, and the steel platform chassis was, to quote Wyer, 'a cut and shut' DB4GT, which, despite having been lightened by using alloy floors and thinner section steel in some box sections, proved to be too heavy.

The two-door coupé body was an extremely attractive design, formed from 20-gauge magnesium/aluminium alloy and with an attractive fastback style and very smooth lines, and was very modern looking with little carryover from the DB4. Originally it was fitted with a long sloping tail, but wind-tunnel tests showed that this caused considerable rear-end lift, so the rear of the car was shortened to give a Kamm-type tail. The body was built around the half-completed chassis at the factory, rather than being built after the chassis was completed.

Running the car at the 1962 Le Mans proved that while it was quite fast, it did not handle particularly well, and that the handling issues were down to the aerodynamics. Also, as it was largely DB4GT based under the attractive body, there was little scope for further development, especially in weight reduction. So the decision was taken to produce a pair of all-new cars, similar in appearance to DP212 but with more scope for lightening and suspension development.

### *DP214*

The next two cars, labelled DP214, while still classed as being based on the 'production' DB4GT, had a significantly modified

**The DP cars marked Aston's return to endurance racing in 1961. DP212 was a development of the DB4GT, and is seen here driven by Tony Dron at the Goodwood Revival, September 2000.**

**DP214 was much more than a rebodied DB4GT: it had an all-new chassis under the aerodynamic bodywork.**

**DP214 under heavy braking, driven by Colin Crabbe on 28 August 1966.**

**DP214 at the 77th Members meeting at Goodwood.**

**The engine bay of DP214 showing the 4-litre DB4-derived engine.**

understructure, to the extent that it was arguably all new. The DB4-derived chassis of DP212 was replaced with an all-new structure built up from box-section girder frames. Wyer was quoted as saying the running under the Four Litre Prototype rules the 'new chassis was strictly illegal but we didn't think anyone would look too hard, and so it proved'. Otherwise the DP214 cars were fitted with the DB4GT derived 3.7-litre engine bored out to be 3996cc, the David Brown S432 four-speed gearbox and a Salisbury live rear axle. Both the cars at Le Mans suffered from piston failure with the tops breaking off pistons on both cars. Once the cars were fitted with forged pistons they acquitted themselves well in the rest of the 1963 season.

### *DP215*

The final car of the series, DP215, also had an all-new girder-frame chassis that incorporated extensive cross-bracing, and a dry sump, DB4-derived 4-litre engine. The bonnet line of DP215 was lower than that of DP214 thanks to the dry sump engine, but otherwise the body shape was identical to DP214. However, mechanically DP215 was fitted with the CG537 transaxle used on the DBR1, which proved troublesome.

### *Competition Results*

The DP cars were run by the works between 1962 and 1963. Only DP212 competed at Le Mans in 1962, and failed to finish thanks to a broken piston after seventy-nine laps. The two DP214s and DP215 ran in the 1963 Le Mans, where both DP214s retired with broken pistons, and DP215 also retired with gearbox problems. DP215 was then run at the French Grand Prix at Rheims on 30 June, where valve problems caused several gear changes to be missed and forced its retirement after only four laps. The two DP214s were run at the Tourist Trophy race at Goodwood on 24 August, where one was placed seventh and the other retired with valve problems; however, this was quite a good result, as an oversight on the homologation of the cars meant they had to run with narrow tyres and rims rather than the wider ones they used at Le Mans.

The car's luck then changed, as both DP214s entered finished first and seventh at the 3-Hour Coppa Intra Europa at Monza on 8 September, and finally achieved a DP214 first and second at Montlhéry on 22 September.

### Competition Conclusions

In the late 1950s Aston Martin achieved what much of the racing effort expended up to 1959 had been aimed at – an outright win at the Le Mans 24 Hours race. The small company's DBR1 beat off the competition from Ferrari, Mercedes and Jaguar to achieve the win in 1959, marking the pinnacle of Aston Martin's racing exploits to date and giving the company a major marketing boost. The win demonstrated the company's engineering excellence, and served to give sales a major boost at the time.

## KEY FIGURES

Although the DB2 was selling successfully throughout the 1950s, Aston Martin were fully aware that they would have to introduce a new road car if they were to remain successful into the 1960s and beyond. This resulted in the design and development of the DB4, the first model of a line that would serve the company well through the 1960s. With a new platform chassis, new suspension and a new engine, the DB4 was the result of inspired design work by teams led by two outstanding engineers: Tadek Marek and Harold Beach.

### Tadek Marek

Polish émigré Tadek Marek was responsible for the two engines that saw Aston Martin through the 1960s and onwards to the 1990s: the straight six and the V8. He was born in Kraków, Poland, in 1908; his mother, Ada Markowa, was a medical doctor and his father, Zygmunt Marek, was a lawyer and member of the Polish parliament. Marek's father died in 1931, and his mother remarried Makesymilian Rutkowski, a professor of medicine and a surgeon. After school, Marek studied engineering at the Berlin Institute of Technology (incidentally the first German university that adopted the title 'Technische Universität', or Technical University) based in the Charlottenburg suburb of Berlin. After graduating in 1933, he worked for the Polish state-owned military engineering works, Państwowe Zakłady Inżynierii (PZInż), where he was involved in designing a heavyweight motorcycle for the Polish armed forces, the Sokół 1000, powered by a side-valve 45-degree 'V'-twin engine of 995cc. This motorcycle's design was based on an earlier Polish bike, the CWS M55, which was in turn based on a Harley Davidson frame and an Indian 'V'-twin engine. He later helped to design the engine for the civilian Sokól 600 motorcycle, a 598cc single-cylinder unit that was in essence half of the larger Sokól 1000's V-twin.

Marek had moved from PZInż to the Polish motor conglomerate Lilpop before the German invasion of Poland, which precipitated World War II; as the Germans and Russians overran Poland he joined the Polish army, escaped, and was interned in Romania. From Romania he set up a diplomatic convoy to transport members of the Polish government in exile to Paris, and got himself a job with engine manufacturers Hispano Suiza in the south of France near the Pyrenees; as the threat of occupation increased he fled France via Spain and Morocco, finally making it to England in 1941. There he was involved in the development of the Meteor tank engine, and met his wife to be. After the war he and his wife worked for the United Nations Relief and Rehabilitation Administration (UNRRA) in Germany. In the late 1940s he returned to the UK to join Austin, where he apparently worked on engine design. In 1954 he joined Aston Martin as a designer.

After his revision of the Lagonda Six, Marek embarked on the design of an all-new straight-six engine of 3.7 litres

**Tadek Marek's masterpiece – the straight-six Aston Martin engine, here in Chris Bland's DB5.**

capacity. This engine, again a dohc straight six, was to power the DB4, 5, 6 and 'S' through the 1960s and into the early 1970s, and had a great reputation for performance, smoothness and reliability.

Marek's second engine for Aston Martin was the all-alloy V8, the design of which started in 1963, with the first examples running by the end of 1964. Derivatives of the V8, ending with the supercharged Vantage unit with its 6.3-litre capacity and 600bhp, would power Aston Martins from the 1970s all the way to the year 2000, astonishing proof of the engine's qualities and a testament to Tadek Marek's engineering prowess.

As well as engine design Marek was involved in most aspects of product design and development work during his time at Aston Martin. He was always keen to carry out 'extra curricular' activities – he dived into the design and engineering of the full size James Bond DB5 with, to quote Dudley Gershon, 'mischievous joy', and he was also heavily involved in the design and construction of the miniature 'James Bond' convertible DB5 made for Prince Andrew, which was presented to the Queen and Prince Phillip when the royal couple visited the Newport Pagnell works in April 1966.

Marek bought a cottage in Terracina, near Naples, with his wife in the early 1960s, and spent several holidays renovating it. He retired from Aston Martin in 1968 and moved to Italy. He returned to England in 1979 due to failing health, and died in 1982 after a long and happy retirement.

## Harold Beach

Harold Henry Beach was one of the unsung heroes of Aston Martin through the 1950s and 1960s, and he laid the foundations for the company's successful products that carried it through to the 1990s and the DB7. Born in Acton, London, on 15 February 1913, Beach started his working life as an apprentice in the engineering department of Barkers, based in Kensington, Central London. Barkers were the famous coach builders who were renowned for some of the best Rolls-Royce car bodies ever built. While training as a draughtsman and engineer, he quickly caught the the eye of the company owner, Viscount Curzon, and he was soon working on Curzon's racing stable, which included such exotica as Alfa Romeo, Mercedes, Bugatti and the 1.5-litre 8-cylinder Grand Prix Delange – the best in Beach's eye.

His time at Barkers ended in 1933, when, with the depression starting to bite, Beach realized that Barkers would soon go out of business. He therefore got a job as draughtsman at William Beardmore, a builder of commercial vehicles based in Wimbledon, West London, where he spent three

**Tadek Marek (right) is shown a V8 at Newport Pagnell by Mike Loasby in 1976.**

## TECHNICAL DESCRIPTION

The DB5 was a two-door coupé or two-door convertible, and was designed to be a fast GT car. The cars had a steel platform chassis with small-diameter tubular frame used to support the all-aluminium body using Touring of Milan's patented 'Superleggera' method. The cars were four-seaters, although the space for the rear-seat passengers was limited. The cars were powered by the 4-litre version of the Tadek Marek-designed, all-alloy, dohc 6-cylinder engine, and drive through a five-speed gearbox made by ZF. Front suspension was by double wishbones with coil springs and telescopic dampers, and the rear live axle was located fore and aft using trailing arms and transversely using a Watts linkage. The rear was sprung using coil springs and damped with lever-arm dampers. Disc brakes were fitted front and rear.

## DB5 SPECIFICATION TABLE

| | |
|---|---|
| **Layout and chassis** | Front-engined, rear-drive, 2-plus-2 Sports/GT car. Closed two-door body, Superleggera lightweight body on a steel platform chassis |
| **Engine** | |
| Type | Aston Martin twin overhead camshaft, 2 valves per cylinder |
| Block material | RR-50 specification light silicon aluminium alloy |
| Head material | RR-50 specification light silicon aluminium alloy |
| Cylinders | 6 in line |
| Cooling | Centrifugal pump with water/ antifreeze mix |
| Bore and stroke | 96 × 92mm |
| Capacity | 3995cc |
| Valves | 2 valves per cylinder, operated directly via bucket tappets from chain-driven double overhead camshafts |
| Compression ratio | 8.8:1 (Vantage tune: 9.0:1) |
| Carburettor | 3 × 2in SU |
| Max. power | 282bhp @ 5,500rpm |
| Max. torque | 288lb ft @ 3,850rpm |
| **Transmission** | |
| Gearbox (manual) | ZF five-speed, all synchromesh |
| Clutch | Laycock 9in single-plate diaphragm spring unit |
| Overall ratios | 1st 2.7:1 |
| | 2nd 1.76:1 |
| | 3rd 1.23:1 |
| | 4th 1:1 |
| | 5th 0.83:1 |
| Reverse | 3.31:1 |
| Final drive | Hypoid bevel, 3.77:1 |

| | |
|---|---|
| **Suspension and steering** | |
| Front | Independent by dual wishbone with coil over dampers. Anti-roll bar |
| Rear | Live axle with two parallel trailing arms on each side, transverse location by Watts linkage. Coil springs and lever-arm dampers |
| Steering | Rack-and-pinion |
| Wheels | 15in wire centre-lock wheels |
| **Brakes** | |
| Type | Girling hydraulic front and rear discs |
| Size (front) | 11.5in (29.2cm) diameter disc |
| Size (rear) | 11.13in (28.2cm) diameter disc |
| **Capacities** | |
| Fuel capacity | 19gal (86.4ltr) |
| Oil capacity | 23 pints (13ltr) |
| **Dimensions** | |
| Track | |
| Front: | 54in (1,372mm) |
| Rear: | 53.5in (1,359mm) |
| Wheelbase | 98in (2,490mm) |
| Overall length | 181.5in (4,610mm) |
| Overall width | 66in (1,676mm) |
| Overall height | 52.5in (1,334mm) |
| Weight | 3,450lb/1,565kg |
| **Performance** | |
| Top speed | 141mph (227km/h) |
| 0–60 | 8.1sec |

years designing commercial vehicles. He then joined up with another ex-Barkers employee, James Ridlington, who made various components for Rolls-Royce and other motor manufacturers. It was here that Beard became more involved in racing, designing an all-alloy body for cotton-mill owner E. R. Hall's Rolls-Royce works supplied 3½-litre 6-cylinder Bentley, which competed in various races in the UK.

When the war started he moved to work for Hungarian engineer Nicolas Straussler, who dabbled in military vehicles and various other military machines. He eventually left Straussler's in 1950 for Aston Martin, tempted by an advertisement in *the Daily Telegraph* for a 'Design Draughtsman for the David Brown Tractors (Engineering) Automotive Division at Feltham'. Having had four jobs in the motor industry up to this point, he was to stay at Aston Martin until he retired.

Beach's first job at Aston Martin was to design the DB2 replacement; however, the appointment of Von Eberhorst as Chief Engineer meant that Beach's ideas for the replacement of the DB2's dated trailing arm suspension with an up-to-date wishbone system was discarded, and the eventual DB2/4 was little more than a stretched DB2. Beach then worked on DP114, the DB2 Mark III replacement. In 1956, when Von Eberhorst left, John Wyer was appointed Works Manager and Beach was promoted to Chief Engineer. Wyer decided that the styling of the prototype DP114 was not different enough from the DB2/4, and proposed that Aston Martin went to Italian coach builders Touring for a new body design, Touring having already produced bodies for the DB2.

Beach went out to Milan to liaise with Touring, who immediately pointed out that DP114's perimeter frame was not strong enough to support the use of their trademark Superleggera bodywork. Beach designed a platform chassis that was to become Aston Martin's road-car platform for the following four decades, and in 1957 the DB4 prototype was unveiled, with Beach's platform chassis and suspension (although the de-Dion rear end was replaced with a live axle) and Marek's all-new straight-six engine.

Beach's work at Aston Martin continued with the designs of the DB5 and DB6, which utilized his platform chassis in ever-increasing lengths to provide more internal room, as well as cutting the chassis length to shorten the wheelbase of the DB4 GT. In the early 1960s he extended the width of the basic platform chassis to create the DBS, which at long last incorporated Beach's preferred de-Dion rear end. Beach remained with the company after David Brown sold it to Company Developments. In 1973 Beach was made Director of Engineering, and after the failure of the Company Developments-owned company, continued to work in engineering (albeit not as a director) for Aston Martin after its rebirth in 1975. He eventually retired in 1978 at the age of sixty-five.

His legacy is huge: responsible for the platform and running gear of the DB4 through to the DBS, his expertise laid solid foundations for what would be seen as the company's golden era in the 1960s, and the products that would aid the company's survival through the troubled 1970s and 1980s. Harold Beach was described by Geoff Courtney in his book *The Power Behind Aston Martin* as being 'a quiet and talented innovator who made his mark simply by doing an outstanding job', which sums him up nicely. Beach died at the age of ninety-six on 24 January 2010.

CHAPTER 6

# THE DBS YEARS: 1966–1975

The introduction of the DBS in 1967 marked the start of a series of changes for Aston Martin that would have a profound effect on the company fortunes.

First of these was the change of emphasis of the cars. The DBS was a very different car to the DB6 – it was bigger and heavier, and its width of some 72in (1,829mm), while normal today, was considered to be too wide by many observers. The DBS was a further step on a path set by the DB6. The DB4 (and to a greater extent the DB4GT) was a relatively small, compact sports car that was fun to drive but still had GT aspirations, while the DB5 and DB6 were longer, less wieldy cars that tended more towards the GT market, rather than being a pure sports car. The DBS carried this transformation further forwards, with its increased size, and initially while powered by the 6-cylinder engine, it lacked the performance of the previous cars and was placed firmly in the GT class, with its sporting pretensions sacrificed on the GT altar.

Secondly was the sheer expense incurred by the company in the 1960s. Not only was a new V8 engine being developed, but also a new car needed to be developed to house the engine, albeit based on the platform of the existing DB6. All this cost money, and when combined with the instability of the economic situation in the late 1960s, added unwanted uncertainty to the company's position.

**The DB6 was in production when the larger and longer DBS was introduced. This is Tim Slow's lovely Series 1.**

**The DBS was longer and wider than the DB6, and was a true Grand Tourer. However, the 6-cylinder engine gave the car less performance than the DB6.**

Finally the vagaries of the international economic situation were having unwanted effects on the viability of Aston Martin itself. David Brown's parent company was also under pressure in the late 1960s, with major investments in increasing tractor production capacity, which soaked up precious resources, making it hard to divert funds to Aston Martin. The economic and commercial uncertainty finally led to David Brown unwillingly selling Aston Martin in 1972 to Company Developments, a property company. Despite selling off the company sports ground for development, the increasingly bad economic situation resulted in severe problems for Aston Martin, which led to the company having to call in the liquidators in 1975.

## THE COMPANY

By 1966 Aston Martin had settled in at Newport Pagnell, and production of the DB5 was proceeding. Aston Martin always did a lot of work in-house, and the production of the cars was a well run and efficient operation. Dudley Gershon, the Engineering Director, gave a description of the production process in his book *Aston Martin 1963–1972*, and it can be summarized briefly here.

### The Production Process

The chassis platforms would arrive at Newport Pagnell from their production at David Brown's Huddersfield factory. Each platform would be checked on a jig and then mounted on a production trolly in the structure shop, where the bodywork superstructure was built up and welded on to the basic platform, again using jigs. The complete chassis was then 'pickled' – a process that removes all impurities such as rust, scale, stains and inorganic contaminates from the surface of a metal structure – and then painted in a small tunnel, and then moved into the body shop. There the body was fitted to the chassis, using preformed sub-assemblies that had been made up and assembled in the adjoining panelling shop.

The fully panelled chassis was then inspected and crack tested, then moved to the paint shop where it was pickled and painted with several layers of undercoat, and a couple of colour coats. The painted chassis and body assembly was then moved to the production line, where the car was built up in some twenty-four stages. Here all the main components were fitted, some of which (for example the engines) would have been built up beforehand in their own specialist areas. The finished car was then road tested, and after final rectification of any faults, would be brought back into the paint shop for the final top coats and the rectification of any scratches, dents or other assembly damage. The car was then fitted with accessories, such as bumpers, badges and mirrors, and given a final check before despatch to the customer's dealer.

**From the front the DB6 looks much the same as the DB5. The split front bumper is the only significant change.**

The engine was built 'in house'. The engine build started with the machining of the raw head and block castings, and all the small working components were machined and, where possible, assembled into sub-assemblies. The crankshaft, connecting rods, flywheel and clutch were balanced, and then assembled into the crankcases with the liners, pistons and rings. The head, which was assembled separately with its valve guides, valve gear and camshafts, was then fitted, and the engine assembled. The complete engine was taken to the test bed where it was run for around six hours, tested on the brake to check the power output, and if satisfactory sent on to the assembly line for installation.

The interior trim was similarly produced in the trim shop and then sent to the line for fitting. The resulting production process was a good balance of craftsmanship and simple assembly skills, and allied to the exemplary engineering that underlay the car's mechanical elements, meant that the cars produced were exceptionally good quality. Gershon recounts how there was rarely a day when an existing or potential customer wasn't shown over the line. As the cars had to be sold at a premium, the company was careful to promote the skills involved in hand building the cars, as well as the engineering excellence of the underlying mechanicals; with competition from the likes of Jaguar with their E-Type, Aston Martin could not afford to scrimp on either the engineering or the finish of the completed car.

## A Perfect Storm

In late 1966 Aston Martin was hit by a perfect storm, which threatened the company's existence. The combination of a sluggish economy, the then Labour government raising purchase tax on cars from 21 to 23 per cent, and rumours of a new model to replace the DB6, meant that sales of the DB6 slumped. These factors meant that by early 1967 Aston Martin had some 200 unsold DB6s stockpiled around Newport Pagnell. David Brown took the radical decision to cut the price of the DB6 from just over £5,000 to £4,000, which stimulated sales and raised demand for the cars; in this way the backlog was cleared, and production could continue at the economical rate of some 200–300 cars per year.

In 1968 the company brought the new larger and wider DBS to market alongside the DB6, but as the company's new quad-cam V8 engine was not ready, it was launched with the straight six under the bonnet. The straight six was less powerful than the proposed V8, and the DBS suffered from complaints that its performance was only at best equal to that of the DB6. It would be another year before the V8 was ready and the DBS V8 could be rightly considered to be a suitable flagship for the company's range.

At the end of 1971 David Brown sold Aston Martin Lagonda to the UK-based property firm Company Developments. This was due to a number of factors, the main ones being the costs of an expansion of the group's tractor production, followed by a worldwide slump in demand, which put pressure on the group, and meant the luxury of running an Aston Martin was no longer possible. Brown payed off Aston Martin's debts, said to be around £5 million, and sold the company for a nominal £101 to Company Developments in a bid to ensure that it would have the best chance of survival.

As was typical of the times, the directors of Aston Martin at the time of the purchase were replaced by members of

**A pair of V8s from the post-David Brown era with their single-headlight noses sitting next to a blue DBS V8 with the earlier David Brown-era twin-headlamp front end.**

**The DBS V8 was very similar to the 6-cylinder DBS, but the V8s were fitted with alloy wheels, which could take the power of the V8 engine.**

the new owners' organization – so William Wilson became Chairman, replacing David Brown, the Managing Director post was taken by G.E. Fletcher, Dudley Gershon as Technical Director was replaced by H. Pollack, and Charles Warden was appointed Financial Director. Continuity was maintained by the promotion of Harold Beach to Director of Engineering, and Company Developments then raised a significant amount of capital by selling the Aston Martin sports ground for housing development. However, the company was spending money fast in order to make the V8 emissions compliant, and the tenure of Company Developments was short – on 31 December 1974 the production side of Aston Martin Lagonda was shut down, while the service side was kept running with a skeleton staff under the management of a receiver.

After some months of uncertainty, in August 1975 an international consortium of four businessmen – Britain's Alan Curtis, American Peter Sprague, Canadian George Mindon and Britain's Denis Flather – bought the company, setting it up as Aston Martin Lagonda (1975). Importantly the new owners were all serial Aston Martin owners and understood the unique appeal of the cars, and production of complete cars was restarted in the autumn of 1975. Under the new ownership the new company was set to weather the rest of the 1970s.

## THE ENGINES

### The Tadek Marek V8

As the production of the DB5 and then the DB6 continued through the 1960s, the Tadek Marek-designed straight six continued to give both the power and reliability needed to keep the cars at the forefront of performance and reliability. However, cars were getting larger and, more importantly, heavier as customers called for more sophistication, comfort and performance.

**Having designed the straight-six engine that took Aston Martin through the 1960s, Tadek Marek then designed the quad-cam V8 that would take the company through to the 1990s.**

Power-sapping additions such as air conditioning and power steering were becoming more important, especially in vital export markets, and as well as the usual challenges from Ferrari and Maserati, a number of new competitors were starting to emerge who were invading Aston Martin's niche market for the sophisticated GT car. At home Jenson's new Interceptor was introduced in 1966, and the AC 428 Frua quickly followed, both cars being attractive and viable competitors to the DB6, while abroad in Italy Monteverdi showed their own Frua-styled 'High Speed' model at the 1967 Frankfurt Motor Show.

The two common features of these three cars were their up-to-date Italian styling, and their use of out-of-the-box American V8 engines. The US engines may not have been as technically advanced as the British or Italian dohc straight sixes – or even Ferrari's V12 – but what they lacked in sophistication they more than made up for with capacity. Never before had the saying 'these's no substitute for cubes' been

**The V8 sitting in a Virage Volante from the 1990s.**

truer, and couple this with the credibility gained by the Ford GT40 wins at Le Mans in 1966 to 1969, and the presence of a massive, crude but powerful pushrod V8 under the bonnet became a thing to boast about.

With this competition in mind Aston Martin needed a new car that would have to be bigger and more sophisticated than the DB6, which meant that a bigger, more powerful engine would be needed to power the next generation of its cars – and that engine would have to be a V8.

The Aston Martin V8 was designed by Tadek Marek, initially ably assisted by design engineer Alan Crouch, who took over when Marek retired in 1966; design work started in 1963. The design brief was to keep as many of the good aspects of the straight-six design as possible, which meant as far as possible retaining the existing type of combustion chamber, valve gear and bottom-end bearing sizing, all of which had worked well in the previous engine and simplified the design of the new unit.

The engine was, like the preceding straight six, an all-alloy unit with the crankcases and cylinder heads cast from LM8 aluminium alloy, and the angle between the two banks of cylinders set at 90 degrees. The crankshaft was carried on five main bearings, and each crank pin carried two connecting rods, each serving a different cylinder bank. The engine weighed about 30lb (13.6kg) more than the straight six, but initially produced approximately 360bhp, some 10 per cent more than the straight six's 325bhp in Vantage specification. Initially the engine displaced 5.4 litres and powered the DBS V8, and it remained in production up until the year 2000, powering the last version of the Virage in 6-litre, 32-valve twin-supercharger form.

### *Technical Description of the Aston Martin V8 Engine*

The first production version of the new Aston Martin V8 engine had its two banks of cylinders set at 90 degrees to each other, the block and cylinder heads were cast lightweight alloy, there was a five bearing crank, a bore and stroke of 100 × 85mm, and it displaced 5340cc. Each cylinder was served by 2 valves, which were operated by chain-driven camshafts, two per cylinder head. The crankcase was extensively ribbed, especially around the bell housing area, and each main bearing had webs incorporated around the bearings and extending downwards to the sump joint to help support them. The cylinder centres were slightly larger than those used on the straight-six engine to make the coolant passages between the cylinders as large as possible. The sump was a large and rigid alloy casting that was bolted to the bottom of the crankcase with twenty-six bolts and screws, which aided the rigidity of the crankcase.

The engine was fitted with wet liners, which meant the outer surface of the liners was exposed directly to the water jacket, and were made from centrifugally cast iron by Hepworth and Grandage. The liners were of the 'top hat' type, and were held in position in the block by the clamping pressure of the cylinder-head gasket against the top of the liner. Like the straight six, the bottom of the liner was sealed with two 'O' rings, with a gap between them open to the atmosphere to identify if the 'O' rings were leaking.

The crankshaft was a forged chrome molybdenum steel item produced by Laystall, and the crankshaft throws were spaced at 90 degrees to each other to achieve perfect primary and secondary balance. The addition of counterweights to each end of the shaft took care of the primary coupling forces to completely balance the engine. All the journals were nitrided, and the main bearings were 2.75in (6.98cm) in diameter and 1in (2.54cm) wide. The big-end journals were 2.25in

**While wide, this front view of the Marek V8 shows its otherwise compact design. The timing case is on the front of the engine.**

(5.71cm) in diameter and 2.1in (5.33cm) in width. Each journal carried two conrods, and each big-end bearing was $^{15}/_{16}$in (2.38cm) in width.

All the engine's timing gear and ancillary drives were taken off the nose of the crank and driven by duplex chains. Two sprockets were fitted to the crank, the inner one looking after the timing, and the outer one providing drive to the oil pump.

The rotary oil pump was mounted in the front of the sump, ahead of the main bowl, and it was connected to the oil strainer positioned at the bottom of the sump bowl. Oil was pumped up into the block through internal drillings to the full-flow oil filter and then into the crankshaft oil gallery, where it was distributed to the main bearings and, via drillings in the crankshaft, on to the big ends. The pistons and small ends were splash lubricated, and additional drillings directed oil from the main gallery in the block up to the heads to lubricate the camshafts and valve gear.

Connecting rods were 'H'-section EN19 steel forgings. These were cleaned up after forging, but were not polished. The small end was a bronze bush, and the gudgeon pin floated in the bush, and was retained in the die-cast alloy piston with circlips. Each piston had three piston rings, the top two for compression and the bottom an oil scraper. Oil drain holes were positioned on the piston's side just below the scraper ring. The top edge of the piston was domed to promote squish in the combustion chamber, and there was a pair of cutouts on the edge for valve clearance.

The timing sprocket on the crank drove the duplex primary timing chain, which operated a half engine speed intermediate sprocket mounted in the top of the timing case, level with the bottom of the 'V' of the engine. Behind the intermediate sprocket was a pair of duplex sprockets that drove the secondary chains – one per head – that drove the camshafts. The intermediate sprocket was attached to a driveshaft that was taken backwards in the 'V' of the engine to drive the fuel-injection pump.

Each of the camshafts ran directly in the head, with the front bearing being double width to cater for the extra load imposed by the drive. The camshaft operated directly on bucket tappets to open the valves. As on the 6-cylinder unit, the valve clearances were set at the factory, and could only be adjusted by either grinding the top of the valve stem or fitting a different-sized tappet bucket – four sizes were listed.

The valves, 2 per cylinder, were angled at 64 degrees to each other, 32 degrees to the vertical axis of the cylinder. While the straight-six unit had its valves set at 80 degrees separation, retaining this angle would have resulted in too large an increase in the width of the engine, so this compromise angle was specified. The valve gear was similar to the straight six, with each valve being operated directly from the camshaft using bucket tappets.

**Another view of the V8, this time the AMHT's example housed in the barn. It shows the large cam covers with 'ASTON MARTIN LAGONDA' cast in.**

The distributor was driven by a skew gear mounted on the front of the right-hand-side exhaust camshaft.

On the outside of the engine there was a torsion damper fixed to the nose of the crankshaft, and a multiple pulley with four grooves. This drove double 'V' belts to the water pump mounted in the timing case, and a remotely mounted power-steering pump. A third groove on the water-pump pulley drove a single 'V' belt that drove the alternator, which was mounted on the right-hand side of the unit.

After Marek retired in 1966, subsequent development of the V8 was carried out under the eye of Senior Design Engineer Alan Crouch, who had been engaged in the design of the engine from 1963.

## Development Problems

The prototype engines were fitted to a couple of modified DB5s, with suitable 'adjustments' to the chassis and front suspension, and a larger bonnet scoop to get them to fit. Later, one car also aquired a de-Dion rear end as part of the DBS development programme. The testing soon threw up some problems with the original design. Firstly the conrod bolts and connecting rods were found to be prone to failure, but by beefing up the connecting rod cross-section and rebalancing the crankshaft to take into account the extra weight, the problem was solved.

The second problem, which was a lot more serious, was the block distorting, which resulted in the sealing surface of the block fretting against the lower cylinder liner edges, and also set off incipient cracking at the main bearing housings. In addition, in the highly tuned racing engines run at Le Mans by Lola, it was found that there could be distortion of the head

**The black front air dam was the only way of identifying the DBS as a V8 from the front. This 1971 example shows the original style, twin headlamp front end shared with the 6-cylinder DBS.**

face when the engine ran very hot. These issues were rectified by strengthening the block, adding reinforcing ribs along the stress points, and also beefing up the area around the main bearing housings.

In addition, all 'pull' stresses were removed from the head face by using long bolts to fix the heads in place: these were threaded into the bottom deck area of the block. This also stopped the 'panting' effect between the head and the block, which had added to the fretting issue. These modifications also meant that the engine could be increased in size to 5.4 litres. A lot of the work was carried out by Alan Crouch, a development engineer who would later work for Ricardos. The result of the development work on the V8 meant the engine was capable of coping with significant increases in capacity and power output, and it remained in production until the late 1990s. The last Aston Martin to be fitted with the Tadek Marek-designed V8 was the Virage-derived V8 Coupé, which only ceased production in 1999; this meant that the engine was produced in various forms for over three decades.

## THE CARS

During the 1960s a number of changes were made to the Aston Martin model range. DB5 was replaced in 1966 with the longer DB6, but this was very much a light revision of the DB5, and was very much a stop-gap. While Italian styling house Touring designed a DB5/6-based two-seater, named the DBS, for Aston Martin in the mid-1960s, the big change of the period was the emergence of the William Towns-designed DBS, which went on sale in 1968 with the 6-cylinder engine, as the intended V8 engine was not ready. The V8-powered DBS was eventually released in 1969, but before that a yellow 6-cylinder DBS badged as a V8 and fitted with V8 alloy wheels featured in the television series *The Persuaders*, while a 'real' DBS V8 featured in the then current Bond film *On Her Majesty's Secret Service* in the DBS V8's launch year, 1969.

The V8 Series 2 was announced in 1972 and named simply the 'Aston Martin V8', as the company was now owned by Company Developments so the 'DB' badge was dropped. A limited run of V8-based four-door Lagondas based on a stretched V8 chassis and the William Towns four-door design was built in 1974.

### The '170mph' (275km/h) DBS Two-Seater Car

While the DB6 was being developed as a four-seat derivative of the DB5, Aston Martin was also looking in the opposite direction, with the development of a short-wheelbase version with two seats and a 4-litre, Vantage specification, straight-six engine as standard to create a true sports car. This derivative would give Aston Martin a balanced two-car range: a four-seater GT with the DB6, and a true two-seat sports car. With a stated top speed of 170mph (25km/h), the two cars made were clad in a very pretty body, styled and built by Touring of Milan.

The model was designated MP226, and the cars were badged 'DBS'; it was based on a shortened DB6-derived platform that retained the DB6's longer wheelbase, but had shorter front and rear overhangs that would be able to accommodate the proposed V8 engine in the front and have a de-Dion rear end. With the proposed V8, the rear of the engine and the gearbox would be mounted lower and further back in the chassis to promote sleeker lines. However, the V8 engine was not ready by the time the two prototypes were built, and due to the reduced front overhangs, the straight-six engine had to be

**The original DBS was a mid-1960s concept car based on the DB6 and designed as a two-seat sports car.**

Front and side views of the original mid-1960s DBS.

fitted further back than it was in the DB6. This did introduce a couple of slightly impractical features, in that the engine had to be taken out of the car before the head could be removed, and there was no room for a heater – but practicality was not allowed to get in the way of style where Italian concept cars were involved!

The body was a two-door coupé, with a typically 1960s vibe and a slightly ungainly rear, where the large rear window sloped down to the oddly reversed tail panel. One of the two cars was fitted with a front air dam to cut down the front-end lift, with four slots 'cut' into the rear three-quarter panel while the rear inboard discs overheated merrily. One prototype was a left-hand drive painted in a dark red (Black Cherry), and the other was a right-hand-drive version also painted in red, but this time Dubonnet Rosso.

That the design was not progressed with had several suggested reasons: Touring was going out of business anyway; Lamborghini 'leaned' on the coach works as the design was too similar to the 'Flying Star II' design that was based on a Lamborghini GT 400 chassis; and finally they had taken too long to produce a design, so the new William Towns-designed DBS concept was now Aston Martin's main development thrust.

## The DB6

The DB6 was the successor to the DB5 and was in essence a stretched version of the earlier car, which gave adequate legroom to rear-seat passengers. Introduced in 1966 and remaining in production until 1971, the DB6 marked the movement from the sports GT car epitomized by the DB5, to a pure GT car, which while being slightly longer and heavier than the DB5, gave the customer significantly more interior space, providing a practical four seats for adult passengers as well as plenty of luggage room. The two-plus-two-seat GT car would be Aston Martin's main market for the following thirty-five or so years until the advent of the two-seat Vantage in 2005.

### *The Chassis*

The DB6 chassis remained much the same as the DB5, and was a steel platform with a tubular steel superstructure to support alloy bodywork. The extra length of the car was provided by inserting 4in (10.2cm) into the lower floorpan behind the front seats, giving the passengers more leg- and footroom. Otherwise the platform remained much as the DB5, although the top rear radius arm locating mounts were altered to accommodate the shorter top links needed to provide the additional legroom.

Developed from the DB5, the DB6 had an extended roofline, larger rear window and completely new cut-off rear end. The changes made the car into a true four-seat Grand Tourer.

The DB6 retained the construction methods used on the DB4 and 5, retaining the platform chassis, but the circular cross-section tubes used for the Superleggera body were replaced with square-section tubes, which resulted in better torsional rigidity over the longer structure. Later Mark I DB6s lost the 'Superleggera' badges on the bonnet edges, but it is not clear if this was due to the change to square tubing or because Touring had by then gone bust. While the front end of the DB6 was all but identical to the DB5, there were two obvious changes from the DB5: a revised roofline and an all-new tail. The height of the roofline was extended backwards, giving the rear-seat occupants extra headroom, which with the extended wheelbase gave extra head- and legroom to the rear-seat passengers.

### *The Exterior*

Externally, apart from the slightly raised rear roofline, the main distinguishing feature of the car was its all-new tail. This was cut off flat, forming a Kamm-style tail, which, combined with a built-in lip spoiler on the top of the cut-off, improved the car's aerodynamics and increased downforce at the rear, and cut down drag. The spoiler also made a significant improvement to the car's high speed stability. As an example

**The DB6's flattened 'Kamm' tail was so designed to help the aerodynamics. A split bumper was also fitted.**

**At the front the DB6 was very similar to the DB5. This is Mark Seligman's 1967 Series I.**

of racing improving the breed, the DB6's tail was obviously derived from the DP212 and DP214 Le Mans cars.

While the front lights were basically the faired-in DB5 type, the rear lights were one-piece combined light and indicator units, which came courtesy of the Triumph TR4 and were mounted on small plinths incorporated in the flat rear panel. A single centrally mounted reversing light was positioned low down between the split rear bumper. The front bumper was also produced in two halves, with the number plate mounted in the gap. Below the number plate was a new air intake for the oil cooler, which was larger than that used on the DB5.

### *Steering, Suspension and Brakes*

The DB6 was fitted with the steering, suspension and brake layout as used on the DB5, so had the twin-wishbone front and live axle with trailing links and coil springs as seen on the previous car. Power steering was offered as an extra. However, there was one change made to the rear suspension: the parallel trailing arms used to locate each side of the live axle were revised, primarily to allow for more room in the passenger compartment. The top link on each side was reduced in length from 17in (43cm) to 12in (30cm), and its front mounting moved backwards, so it did not infringe on the width of rear seat. The change gave an extra 4in (10cm) to the rear-seat width, which, when combined with the extra length of the cockpit, meant it was practical to seat two normal-sized adults in the back seats. The shortened top link length meant that the links no longer operated as a parallelogram, but this did not appear to have any effect on the handling or roadholding.

### *Engine and Transmission*

The DB6 retained the 4-litre engine and transmission options seen on the DB5. This meant the standard set-up was triple SUs, giving a claimed 282bhp. Vantage specification was also offered, with triple twin-choke Weber carburettors replacing the SUs. Later in 1969 the DB6 Mark II was sold with the Brico electronic fuel-injection system as an option. While the system did not offer any performance gains, it did improve emissions. The ZF five-speed, all-synchromesh gearbox was carried over from the DB5, and a Borg Warner three-speed automatic box was a no-cost option.

### *The DB6 Mark II*

Introduced in 1969, the DB6 Mark II was an evolution of the original model, with most changes made to provide commonality with the DBS. So the car had new DBS-style seats and wider, 6in wire wheels, while the wheel arches gained subtle flares to accommodate the wider wheels – a simple recognition point between the Mark I and Mark II models. Optional

**Just as in the DB4 and DB5, the straight six is a tight fit under the DB6's bonnet.**

**The DB6 Volante was originally based on the shorter DB5 chassis, but it was quickly produced on the longer DB6 chassis with the Kamm tail, such as this example.**

Brico fuel injection, as used on the DBS, was also offered on the Mark II.

Apart from being based on the longer DB6 chassis, the convertible DB6 – named the Volante – differed from the DB5 convertible in one important factor: it had a power-operated hood. To accommodate the hood and its folding mechanism the single 19gal (86.4 ltr) fuel tank of the standard car was replaced by a pair of smaller tanks, containing a total of 16gal (72.7ltr), mounted each side of the boot behind the rear wheel arch; this slightly reduced the boot capacity. Otherwise it was much the same as the DB6 saloon, retaining the DB6's cut-off rear end with its built-in spoiler on the boot lid, and obviously benefiting from the increased rear legroom thanks to the increased wheelbase.

Three types of Volante were produced alongside the DB6 saloon. The first model, introduced in October 1965, was based on the shorter DB5 platform, and while it shared the DB6's nose, it continued to use the DB5-style rear. Only thirty-seven of these short-chassis Volantes were built. During 1966 the first Volante was replaced with a Volante based on the longer DB6 platform, which also shared the DB6 Kamm-style rear end. One hundred and forty examples were produced before the third variant of the Volante was introduced alongside the DB6 Mark II in 1969. This final version had the Mark II's wider wheels and flared wheel arches. Available for only one year, thirty-eight were produced.

### The DB5 and DB6 Estates

In 1965 the works had created a one-off estate car for David Brown that was based on a DB5. Primarily designed to take Brown's dogs and polo gear, the car was not 'properly' designed *per se*, but was created by the talented staff at Newport Pagnell working by eye from sketches. By extending the roofline and revamping the interior an eye-catching car was created: a three-door estate with a rear hatch. However, as the existence of the car became known, demand meant that the factory made a few more DB5 estates during late 1965 and early 1966, with the work being carried out essentially by hand and eye with little formal tooling.

With the introduction of the DB6 demand continued, but the task was even more onerous as the lengthened DB6 would mean a comprehensive redesign and retooling (such as there was), and would divert skilled staff away from producing standard production models. The problem was solved by enlisting Aston Martin's London-based distributors, H.R. Owen, who had their own coachbuilding facility and were willing to take on the job. The coachbuilders took on the task of building the estate cars based on a complete DB6 chassis at a rate of around two per week for three to four months, delivering fully trimmed and painted cars back to Newport Pagnell for final test and inspection before the factory organized their delivery to the customer. However, it was eventually decided that the disruption this caused to the production process was really not worth the trouble, so the estate was quietly dropped as a product in mid-1966, around thirty DB5 and DB6 estates having been made in total.

### A 'New Look' Car

One little-known episode in the development of the DB6 occurred in late 1966: rather than replacing the car with an all-new design, an evolutionary approach to the development of a new car was adopted, with production scheduled to start in late 1968. As the rear end of the DB6 was significantly different to the DB5, a modified front end was mooted that had a lower bonnet line, achieved by adding some 6in (15cm) to the length of the nose, and having the headlights fitted lower and covered with flatter glass cowls to create a lower, forward bonnet line and give the front end a new, sleeker look. The new front end would be different and more 'modern' than the DB5-derived front end on the DB6, marking out the car as a new model that could replace the DB6. In addition, as the prospect of a new V8 engine was firming up, the whole car would need to be widened by some 3in (7.6cm) to fit the new engine.

A prototype of the new look car but in standard width was built by June 1966, but the car was never proceeded with. Firstly, marketing questioned if the car was different enough to the DB6 to be sold as a new car, and David Brown objected to the extra length ahead of the front wheels, which he felt would make the car awkward to park. Finally, regulations in some markets would not allow the sleek faired-in headlamp cowls, so the whole project was quietly dropped.

**DB6 badging used a distinctive font – this is a Mark II. The small built-in tail spoiler is apparent.**

### *DB6 Evolution*

The DB6 was the result of the continuous and logical development of the DB4 concept. Like so many families of cars, its character changed, from the DB4's as a two-plus-two sports coupé, through the more refined DB5 sports tourer, and into the DB6, a Grand Tourer capable of taking four adults far and fast. As such, the DB6 marked Aston Martin's progression from being a pure sports-car manufacturer to being a manufacturer of high performance GT cars – and this set the scene for the DBS and DBS V8 that followed it.

## The Wide Car: The 1968 DBS

Rather than going to an Italian styling house for the DB6 replacement, notwithstanding the two Touring 'DBS' two-seaters that had been produced in 1966, the stylist William Towns was responsible for the shape of the DBS. Originally taken on as a designer of the car's interior, Towns was a talented body stylist in his own right. To further his cause, Towns would leave sketches of cars lying around so the management would see them; this led to him being given the brief to design the DB6 replacement. Knowing that David Brown wanted two new models – a four-door Lagonda and a two-door Aston Martin GT – Towns knew that it was harder to stretch a two-door design to produce a decent-looking four door than it was to go the other way. Doing the design this way meant that the longer car would retain a suitable length-to-width ratio, and the shorter car would have a stubbier, more aggressive and powerful look.

However, this was in late 1966 when Touring had gone bust, the UK was undergoing a credit squeeze, and Aston Martin sales were dropping – so Towns was instructed to concentrate on the shorter two-door Aston Martin design, and shelve the Lagonda. The result was the DBS, which hit the market in 1968, but Towns' Lagonda design was reprieved and actually appeared as the V8-powered Aston Martin Lagonda Series I in 1974.

Overall the DBS was some 10in (25.4cm) longer and 6in (15.24cm) wider than the DB6, and the increase in size, especially the width, gave rise to some uncomplimentary comments at the time. Geoff Courtney recounted in his book The *Power Behind Aston Martin* how David Brown described how a mistake had been made in the chassis jigs, which meant the chassis was 3in (7.62cm) wider than the drawings; and when the mistake was discovered it was too late to change. This can only have increased the weight issues of the new platform, as well as contributing to the car's width.

### *The Chassis*

The chassis of the DBS, while retaining the overall design of the DB6 unit, was widened by 6in (15cm) from that of the DB6 for two reasons. First, the engine bay had to be able to

**An early 6-cylinder DBS still on its wire wheels.**

**The DBS may have been big and heavy, but it was also very safe. This picture of the original DBS crash test was used by Aston Martin as a sales aid.**

accommodate the new V8 engine – the top end of the new engine was of course wider than the straight-six unit, and the width was compounded by the need to accommodate the exhaust manifolds, which were sited on each side of the unit, increasing the overall width needed in the engine bay. Second, the increase in power of the planned V8 over the straight-six engine meant that wider wheels front and rear would be needed, and so the front and rear wheel arches, and by default the overall body width, would need to be extended to cover them.

Widening the chassis also threw up a problem of stiffness: the new platform needed extensive additional bracing to be added to return the chassis stiffness back to that of the DB6 – and this added to the weight of the basic chassis. Obviously the rear was different to the previous design to accommodate the DBS's new de-Dion rear suspension, but apart from that, and the increased width and length, the chassis was much the same in layout as that used in the DB4 to DB6, and was constructed in welded sheet steel in the same way.

### *The Bodywork*

The William Town's styled alloy bodywork was a big departure from the DB6, and made an emphatic statement that Aston Martin was moving on from its previous designs. The two-door saloon was a true four-seater and, thanks to the extra width and wheelbase, offered a great deal more room than the DB6. The front grille retained the traditional Aston Martin appearance, but was innovative in that the twin headlamps and combined side light and indicator cluster were placed inside the outer edges of the grille aperture, making the whole front end quite bluff and aggressive. The look was finished off by the delicate chromed grille strakes, and the bold chrome surrounds for the individual headlights. A full-width chrome bumper sat under the grille, while the side lights and indicators cluster sat on the outer edge of the headlights.

**The front of the DBS cleverly incorporated the headlights into the outer edges of the traditional but flattened Aston Martin grille design.**

**The first DBSs had air extractor vents on the sides of the 'C' pillar, as seen here.**

The fastback rear meant the car had a steeply raked rear windscreen, complemented by the sloping boot lid, which led to a flat tail. Modern integrated rear-light clusters, shared with the somewhat more mundane Hillman Hunter, were fitted to the rear panel above the full-width chromed rear bumper. Under the bumper the number plate was flanked by a pair of reversing lights, and a pair of exhaust pipes poked out at each corner of the lower back panel.

The styling retained a classic Aston Martin cue in that each front wing carried a squashed oval air extractor vent with a chromed bar running along its centre line, just as on the DB4, 5 and 6. The car moved away from the Superleggera method of body construction, and instead used a number of steel pressings to mount and support the body panels on the platform chassis.

### *The Interior*

The overall approach to the interior was carried over from the DB6, with leather upholstery and good quality carpeting, and a separate instrument binnacle in front of the driver. However, the binnacle was wider and shorter than that seen on the DB6, with the main instruments, the speedometer and tachometer flanking a single central oil-pressure gauge, and two groups of two more minor instruments placed outboard of the main instruments. In the DBS the main panel was backed with wood trim, meaning Aston Martin was bowing to customer pressure for the traditional 'wood and leather' interior associated with British sports cars for so long.

Rather an anachronism were the pedals. These were carried over from the DB6 and were floor mounted, unlike most of their contemporaries, so pivoted at their base. This led to some comments in the press about them having a different and somewhat old-fashioned feel. While they worked well and the floor mounting meant they were securely mounted, their positioning made access to the master cylinders awkward. The fluid reservoirs were remotely mounted in the engine bay.

### *The Running Gear*

The big change to the running gear from the DB6 was the adoption of a de-Dion rear end. This was a development of the system used on the ill-starred Lagonda Rapide of the mid-1960s, and used roller bearings in the splines of the half shafts to overcome the 'sticking' issues experienced with the Rapide's sliding spline design.

Brakes were Girling discs all round, with dual circuits, one serving the front, the other the rear, with twin servos giving assistance to both circuits. Fronts were 11.46in (29.1cm) in diameter, while the rears were 10.38in (26.3cm). The rear calipers were mounted inboard close to the differential, with the discs bolted between the output shaft flange and the driveshaft. Six inch-wide, 15in-diameter chromed spoked wire wheels were fitted to the DBS with knock-on hubs and eared spinners.

The DBS was originally intended to be fitted with the new V8, but circumstances dictated that the Tadek Marek straight six would have to be fitted. This was offered in two states of tune, the triple SU-equipped unit giving 282bhp at 5,500rpm, or the Vantage version fitted with tripe twin-choke Webers, which gave a healthy 325bhp.

The car was available with a ZF five-speed all-synchromesh manual gearbox, or a Borg Warner Model 8 three-speed automatic.

### *The DBS Vantage*

The final incarnation of the 6-cylinder DBS was simply named Vantage. Previously the name 'Vantage' had been used as a

**Thanks to the increased width of the car, intended to make room for the V8, there is plenty of room around the straight-six engine.**

high performance version of the then current Aston Martin model, but in 1972 Aston Martin introduced the 'Aston Martin Vantage' as a model in its own right. This was basically a straight-six powered version of the AM V8, with the new nose and revised boot layout, with the air-extractor grilles repositioned from the 'C' pillars to behind the rear window, and fitted with wire wheels rather than the V8's alloys. By now the company was owned by Company Developments Ltd, and the use of the 'DB' moniker had ended; therefore a new name had to be applied to the revamped DBS. So in a complete reversal of the use of the Vantage name to that point in time, the new Vantage was introduced as the 'baby', or entry model of the Aston Martin range, with a performance lower than that of the flagship V8 but with a price that was also lower.

### *The DBS and Going Forwards*

The 'Wide Car' development resulted in a car that would serve Aston Martin well for the next two decades. The DBS and the V8 that followed it would be the models that would carry Aston Martin forwards after David Brown relinquished his hold on the company, and would set the pattern of Aston Martins through the 1970s and into the 1980s as being purveyors of expensive, hand-crafted automobiles with a performance that was up there with the best of the other supercar manufacturers. It has to be said that the DBS was not Aston Martin's finest model as it was powered by the old straight-six engine, so overall performance was lower than that of the DB6 it replaced. However, like the V8, it was a big, bold, expensive, exquisitely styled, hand-built supercar in its own right: it was a desirable car in its day, and is still a much sought-after classic today.

## The DBS V8

The DBS V8 was introduced in 1969, and with its 170mph (273km/h) top speed, 0–60 time of 5.7sec and 0–100 time of 12.5sec, it was the car that Aston Martin wanted to produce right from the start. Aston Martin claimed (probably rightly) that the DBS V8 was the fastest four-seat car in the world. The car was well received by both the press and the customers, and was a very impressive example of its kind. The sheer performance of the car was staggering for the time, and the complete package, with its combination of stunning looks, supreme performance and hand-built quality, was unmatched. The car was just right from the start, and this was reflected in the way it survived as Aston Martin's performance product all the way into the 1990s.

### *The Chassis and Exterior Bodywork*

The DBS V8 carried over the platform chassis from the DBS unchanged. To create the DBS V8, there were three subtle changes made to the DBS's exterior bodywork. At the front of the car there was a spoiler or air dam, mounted underneath the full-width front bumper. Painted matt black to make it less prominent, and made from glass fibre, the spoiler was designed to reduce front-end lift at high speed, and to direct cooling air on to the front brakes. It also had the additional benefit of reducing drag slightly.

The other two changes were found on the rear quarters of the DBS V8, and were designed to improve the car's ventilation system. The air extractor vents used on the rear three-quarter panel of the DBS were removed, leaving the panels smooth, and air was extracted from the interior via a long 'ladder' grille incorporated in the bodywork between the bottom of the rear window and the rear of the boot lid. Badges proclaiming the 'V8' were fitted to the front wing side vents. The DBS V8 interior was virtually identical to the DBS.

### *The V8 Engine*

The V8 engine filled the DBS's engine bay. Initially the car was fitted with Bosch mechanical fuel injection, which resulted in the distinctive 'bunch of bananas' inlet manifolds leading from the two separate plenum chambers mounted on the outside

**With the introduction of the DBS V8 in 1969, the wire wheels were replaced with alloys – but otherwise very little changed externally other than badging.**

**The wing strakes gained 'Aston Martin V8 DBS' script when the DBS V8 was introduced.**

**The DBS V8 was originally fitted with Bosch fuel injection, which gave the car its 'bunch of bananas' inlet manifold.**

of the engine under the air boxes, which fed the fuel to the individual inlet ports in the 'v' of the engine.

### *The Gearbox*

The DBS V8 could be fitted with a manual or automatic gearbox. The manual option was a ZF all-synchromesh five-speed gearbox with an 'H'-gate action for second to fifth, with first to the left and up, and reverse left and down. The manual car was fitted with a 10in (25cm) diameter hydraulically operated clutch. The automatic option was the American Chrysler Torque Flite three-speed unit with torque converter.

### *The Running Gear*

While the DBS V8 inherited the DBS running gear, there were some tweaks made to accommodate the increased performance. The brake discs were increased in size all round, the fronts to 11.5in (29.21cm) in diameter, and were fully ventilated. At the rear the solid brake discs were 10.8in (27.4cm) in diameter. The DBS's wire wheels were not strong enough to handle the greatly increased torque of the V8 engine so were replaced with bolt-on cast-alloy wheels mounted on five studs, which at 7in (17.8cm) wide were 1in (2.54cm) wider than the wires. The wheels were also designed to produce turbulent air around the calipers to aid cooling, as well as acting as an extra heat sink for the brakes.

Otherwise the suspension remained largely unchanged, with double wishbones up front and the de-Dion set-up with Watts linkage at the rear. The front spring rates were increased from the DBS's 90lb per inch to 95lb per inch, and at the rear the four-position, electrically adjustable Armstrong 'Selectaride' shock absorbers were given a wider damping range to allow for the increased performance. Power-assisted steering was initially offered as the only option on the car, but was standardized for the 1971 model year.

**From the rear three-quarter view only the alloy wheels, the lack of vents on the rear three quarter and the long vent across the rear panel show that this is a DBS V8.**

### *Going Forwards*

With the introduction of the DBS V8, Aston Martin at last united the last of the DB-era cars with the engine that would see Aston Martin through to the turn of the millennium. The DBS was, of course, designed for the V8, and it was the engine that defined the character of the car. The V8 would, in its various manifestations, carry the Aston Martin flag through the 1970s and 1980s, remaining defiant in the presence of various supercars. The V8 would often snatch the crown from the various Italian mid-engined cars that were vying for dominance of the performance market. It may well have been old fashioned and outdated, but it could still put its ever-increasing power down when it mattered, and its traditional front engine and rear-wheel drive gave it an 'olde worlde' charm that the mid-engined cars could not emulate.

Considering that its lineage went back to the 1950s and the DB4, the V8 simply cemented the validity of the design of the DB-era cars. Its combination of performance, style, tradition and class carried the car through the decades and ensured the survival of the company until its eventual rescue by Ford in the 1990s.

## Company Developments: The Aston Martin V8 (Series 2 and Series 3)

With the sale of Aston Martin to Company Developments, the first fruit of the new company was a light revamp of the DBS V8, resulting in the new company's Aston Martin V8, unveiled in April 1972. One result of the change of ownership was the dropping of the 'David Brown' and 'DB' naming and badging – the Aston Martin wing badge lost the 'David

**The ultimate development of the classic V8 nose – in this case on Chris Youell's 1984 V8 Vantage, showing the single headlamp and narrower traditional 'grille' shape. The Vantage had the grille filled in so as to improve aerodynamics.**

Brown' lettering, and the cars lost all the 'DB' badges, creating the Series 2 model. The revamp of the DBS V8 had been in train for some time before the sale of the company, and the resulting Aston Martin V8 had some mechanical changes and a number of restyled features. Mechanically the car retained the Bosch fuel-injection system but the inlet side was modified. The most obvious of the styling changes was the new nose, with a pair of recessed 7in (17.8cm) diameter headlamps on either side of a narrower grille, which was also recessed into the nose.

The grille retained the traditional Aston Martin shape, and the restyle tidied up the nose of the car and set the style that would remain as the V8 through to its replacement with the Virage. Inside, the main instrument binnacle remained, but the outer two minor instruments on each extremity were staggered, rather than being in line, to reduce the width of the unit, and the backing was plain black rather than wood. The centre console was also redesigned, with the top part still carrying the clock and window switches, but it was integrated into the passenger side, while the separate lower part incorporated a pair of air vents, below which were the ventilation controls and on the base the radio. The row of rocker switches on the bottom of the centre panel was replaced with a row of push switches mounted on the horizontal panel in front of the gear lever.

The Aston Martin V8 Series 3 was introduced in 1973, after only around 288 Series 2 cars had been built. The main change, which was needed in order to meet emissions regulations, was the replacement of the Bosch fuel-injection system with four downdraught, twin-choke Weber carburettors. The change necessitated a new bonnet with a larger power bulge on the bonnet, needed to clear the carbs and their air box. The carbs upped the power initially, with a healthy 310bhp, but power was sapped by increasingly rigorous emissions standards, reaching only 288bhp by 1976. In 1977 the engine was retuned (to 'Stage 1' specification), with new camshafts and a new exhaust system giving the car 305bhp.

## Company Developments: The Aston Martin Lagonda Series 1

The styling of the DBS/V8 had always been intended to cater for a four-door version, and a prototype of what would become the Aston Martin Lagonda Series 1 first appeared in 1969. Intended for Sir David Brown's personal use, the car was based on a DBS but was powered by the V8. The car had all its extra length, some 12in (30cm), added to the wheelbase, retaining the standard dimensions of the V8 in the boot and bonnet area. This prototype retained the DBS-style front end with its twin headlamps and large grille. The car was not put into production immediately; when the company was sold the production models finally appeared in 1974. To differentiate them from the two-door V8 they sported a revised front end. This retained the new V8's recessed headlights, but the grille was revised to lose the traditional Aston Martin shape, and had the top squared off to form a plain flattened oval.

In the centre of the oval there was chrome trim to outline a central grille, with a single central vertical chromed strake and a pair of horizontal styling chromed strakes running from the side of the central grille to the outer edges.

The overall styling was very subtle, and it is easy to miss that the car had four doors. Unfortunately the car was even

**The Aston Martin Lagonda sported a nose similar to that of the mid-1960 Lagonda Rapide.**

**The short-lived four-door Aston Martin Lagonda (Series 1) was based on the DBS; only seven cars were sold between 1974 and 1976.**

less successful than the preceding 1960s Lagonda. Launched at the Earls Court Motor Show in October 1974, sales were very slow, and only seven cars found customers before production was stopped in June 1976.

## IN COMPETITION

Even though by this time Aston's glory days competing on the world stage had ended, the company was involved in a Le Mans attempt in 1967. Its contribution was a pair of V8 engines that were supplied to Lola to power the Lola T70 Mark 3. Unfortunately, although the V8 had the potential to provide good power, it was nowhere near as reliable as that used by the opposition, which was usually powered by souped-up American V8s. A Lola T70 Mark II was used as a test car for the engine in 1966, but the engine blew up just after a couple of laps with John Surtees driving; so Aston Martin went back to the drawing board, coming up with a revised V8 that was fitted to a pair of Lola T70 Mark IIIs.

The cars were entered by Lola Cars and Team Surtees, but in the race both cars suffered engine failure early on. Surtees and Hobbs were driving car number 11, which failed at lap 3, supposedly with piston failure but actually with main bearing housing failure, while Irwin and DeKlerk were driving car number 12, which had engine failure at lap 25 when the shaft driving the fuel pump (the engines had mechanical fuel injection) sheared. However, this engine showed no sign of the bearing housings failing when the block was crack tested. Other reports in the press later attributed both engine failures to sparking-plug problems and a detached crankshaft vibration damper, but they also reported that there was 'lozenging' around the main bearing areas of the crankcase.

The Aston engine in the Lola was quietly replaced with a Chevrolet unit after Le Mans, and the T70 went on to an illustrious record in the Group 7 and Can-Am race series.

## KEY FIGURES

### William Towns, DBS Designer

William Towns was born in 1936, and brought up in the Lake District in the North of England. After leaving school at the age of eighteen having completed his 'A' levels, he took up an engineering pupilage (effectively an apprenticeship for candidates who had 'A' levels) at the Rootes group, where he quickly specialized in styling, working on the team who created the Hillman Super Minx, among other achievements; he also produced drawings of what would become the Hillman Hunter before he left in 1963. Moving to Rover as a stylist, his crowning achievement was the second Rover BRM Le Mans gas turbine car, along with a great deal of detail work on the production cars under the eye of David Bach, Rover's chief designer at the time.

He moved to Aston Martin in 1966 as a 'seat designer', but with the intention of improving the marque's overall style. The result was that Towns ended up designing the complete DBS as well as the four-door Lagonda variant before he left Aston Martin to go freelance in the middle of 1968. He made this move because, as he said in an interview he gave to *Car* magazine: 'I could see myself, the designer, becoming the "regulations man", as the company had to take into account the plethora of safety regulations being introduced by the Americans.'

Towns set up his own design studio, 'Interstyl', and carried on doing work for Aston Martin as a freelancer; this included the new front end for the V8 Coupé with the single 7in (17.8cm) headlamps, as well as a revamped back end – this was not adopted. In 1976 he was given the brief from Aston Martin to design what would become the new wedge-shaped Lagonda. As with the DBS, he was briefed to produce two-door and four-door proposals. Importantly the brief was to feature the existing platform chassis but with a modified front subframe, which allowed for a much lower body line.

After reviewing the proposals Aston Martin chose to produce the four-door version, and the new Lagonda was born.

**William Towns, the designer of the DBS, also produced the Hustler, a modular mini-based kit car from the 1980s.**

**On the right is Alan Curtis, centre is Keith Martin, and left is William Towns. The picture was taken at the launch of the Bulldog at 'The Bell' in Aston Clinton on 27 March 1980.**

Towns also designed the 1980 Aston Martin Bulldog concept car, and a proposed new smaller car, christened simply the V8. Other projects he worked on outside Aston Martin included the Reliant SS2 and the Scimitar Sabre, as well as the mini-based Hustler kit car. Towns died of cancer in 1993.

## Dudley Gershon, Engineering Director

Between 1963 and 1972, Dudley Gershon, C. Eng, MI Mech.E, MI Prod.E, AMBIM, FIWSP worked for Aston Martin, initially as the Service Manager and later as Director of Engineering. William Morris, of Morris Motors fame, was his uncle, but to avoid charges of nepotism when he started work in the motor industry he was apprenticed at Riley, and he continued his engineering and management career at Riley until the outbreak of World War II, when he joined the army. After the war he continued serving in the army in technical engineering and management roles.

His first job on leaving the services in 1963 was as Service Manager at Aston Martin. Initially he oversaw the movement of the Service Department at Feltham to the Newport Pagnell facility, and was then involved in the design and engineering of the company's products. Having become a director in 1966 he had to leave Aston Martin in 1972 when the company was sold. He became a freelance consulting engineer, and worked for many high performance car manufacturers. He wrote a book on his experiences at Aston Martin, *Aston Martin 1963–1972*, which gives many insights into the company during the 1960s.

## TECHNICAL DESCRIPTION

The DBS was a two-door coupé and superseded the DB6 as a fast, comfortable GT car. The DBS was based on a lengthened and widened DB6 steel platform chassis, and its William Towns-designed all-alloy body was mounted on the chassis with a tubular superstructure. The car was a roomy four-seater and had a decent-sized boot for luggage. It was designed to have the new V8 engine, but was initially fitted with the straight six, albeit in Vantage tune as standard, giving the car a performance that was slightly less than that of the DB6. Up front it was very similar in layout to the DB6, with twin wishbones, coil springs and telescopic dampers, but the rear end was all new with a de-Dion set-up, with twin parallel trailing arms for longitudinal location and a Watts linkage for transverse location. The car was fitted with disc brakes all round.

## DBS SPECIFICATION TABLE

| | |
|---|---|
| **Layout and chassis** | Front-engined, rear-drive two-plus-two sports/GT car. Closed two-door lightweight alloy body on steel platform chassis |
| **Engine** | |
| Type | Aston Martin twin overhead camshaft, 2 valves per cylinder |
| Block material | RR-50 specification light silicon aluminium alloy |
| Head material | RR-50 specification light silicon aluminium alloy |
| Cylinders | 6 in line |
| Cooling | Centrifugal pump with water/antifreeze mix |
| Bore and stroke | 96 × 92mm |
| Capacity | 3995cc |
| Valves | 2 valves per cylinder, operated directly via bucket tappets from chain-driven double overhead camshafts |
| Compression ratio | 9.4:1 |
| Carburettor | 3 × 45DCOE Weber twin-choke |
| Max. power | 325bhp @ 5,750rpm |
| Max. torque | 290ft lb @ 4,500rpm |
| **Transmission** | |
| Gearbox (manual) | ZF 5-speed synchromesh on all gears |
| Clutch | Borg and Beck 9.5in single-plate 9-spring unit |
| Overall ratios | 1st 2.97:1 |
| | 2nd 1.76:1 |
| | 3rd 1.23:1 |
| | 4th 1:1 |
| | 5th 0.834:1 |
| Reverse | 3.31:1 |
| Final drive | Hypoid bevel, 3.73:1 |

| | |
|---|---|
| **Suspension and steering** | |
| Front | Independent by dual unequal-length wishbones with coil springs over telescopic dampers. Anti-roll bar |
| Rear | De-Dion axle located by parallel trailing arms and Watts linkage. Coil springs, 'Selectaride' adjustable lever-arm dampers |
| Steering | ZF-assisted rack-and-pinion |
| Wheels | 15in Dunlop wire centre-lock wheels |
| **Brakes** | |
| Type | Girling hydraulic front and rear discs |
| Size (front) | 11.46in (29.1cm) diameter disc |
| Size (rear) | 10.375in (26.3cm) diameter disc |
| **Capacities:** | |
| Fuel capacity | 21gal (95.5ltr) |
| Oil capacity | 24 pints (11.9ltr) |
| **Dimensions** | |
| Track | |
| Front: | 59in (1,499mm) |
| Rear: | 59.5in (1,511mm) |
| Wheelbase | 102.5in (2,603mm) |
| Overall length | 181.25in (4,604mm) |
| Overall width | 72in (1,830mm) |
| Overall height | 44in (1,117mm) |
| Weight | 3,785.6lb (1,717kg) |
| **Performance** | |
| Top speed | 141.5mph (228km/h) |
| 0–60 | 7.1sec |

CHAPTER 7

# TURBULENT TIMES: 1975–1987

The period between 1975 and 1987 was turbulent, with many changes to the company's management and finances. There were high spots – for example, while the V8 Saloon continued to be developed, a second string was added to the company's range, the striking wedge-styled Lagonda. And when Victor Gauntlett, through Pace Petroleum, joined the company it became a little more stable – and eventually Gauntlett paved the way for the takeover by Ford, which would ultimately save the company.

## THE COMPANY

Having been bought out of receivership in the middle of 1975 by the international consortium headed up by Alan Curtis, Aston Martin Lagonda (1975) had got the V8 saloon back into production and had a healthy order book. Producing between four and six cars a week, the company needed a second model, and so in February 1976 the design and build of the prototype William Town's styled four-door Lagonda was started. The intention was to show it at the 1976 Earls Court Motor Show, a deadline that the company met, albeit with a non-functioning prototype.

In 1977 MD Fred Hartley resigned, and consortium member Alan Curtis, who by now owned 42 per cent of the shares of the company, was appointed as the managing director in March.

In 1980 the company was sold again to Tim Hearley's CH Industrials (CHI) and Victor Gauntlett's Pace Petroleum. The following years were the norm for Aston Martin, with continual money worries, and various injections of cash needed to keep the company afloat. However, production continued throughout the period and a good number of cars were produced – although the model range was limited to the V8 and the Lagonda. There was talk of incorporating MG into the marque when Austin-Rover closed the Abingdon factory but that came to nothing, although Aston Martin did modify an MGB designed by William Towns to promote their bid to buy MG. By July 1980 sales had fallen and a recession had set in, forcing Aston Martin to cut back the workforce, making some forty-five people, 10 per cent of the workforce, redundant.

In 1981 Aston Martin set up an engineering service subsidiary, Aston Martin Tickford, which carried out tuning and luxury enhancements to several makes of mainstream cars, including the Ford Capri and Rover Metro, as well as selling engineering expertise to other mainly automotive companies.

Victor Gauntlett had been selling off various subsidiaries of his Pace Petroleum empire to keep up with Aston Martin's need for investment, and eventually agreed in 1983 to selling his complete stake of Aston Martin to ALL Inc., a company set up by the shipping tycoon Peter Livanos with Greek shipowners Nick and John Papanicolaou. This meant that ownership of Aston Martin was split 55–45 per cent between ALL Inc. and CHI. A further deal in 1983 resulted in ALL Inc.

**One of the big surprises of the 1970s was the introduction of the Aston Martin Lagonda. It was probably the most distinctive car of the 1970s and 1980s and was a surprising success for Aston Martin.**

**The diversification of the Tickford subsidiary by Aston Martin led to Tickford upgrading existing cars to give them both styling and performance boosts. Typical of this work was the Tickford Capri.**

exchanging CHI's shares in Aston Martin by transferring their 50 per cent ownership of Tickford, leaving ALL Inc. owning all Aston Martin and CHI owning Tickford. In 1984 Nick and John Papanicolaou's shipping business was in financial straits, and Livanos's father bought their stake in ALL Inc. At the same time Gauntlett bought back into Aston Martin with a 25 per cent stake. This still left the company in need of substantial investment if it was to survive, but left the way clear for Ford to eventually take a stake in the company over the next few years.

## THE CARS

The years 1976 to 1986 were bumpy ones for Aston Martin, but the cars they produced were some of the high points of the company's ranges. While the new Towns-styled Lagonda saloon prototype was shown at the October Earls Court Motor Show in 1976, it would be a couple of years before the company got it into production, thanks mainly to delays in developing the computerized instrumentation. Development of the V8 continued, and the high performance V8 Vantage was introduced in 1977, which placed Aston Martin back on the peak of the performance race. Aston Martin rediscovered the money-making appeal of the coachbuilt special when they introduced the V8 Zagato coupé in 1986, a restyled short-wheelbase conversion based on the V8 and available in coupé or convertible body styles.

### The Aston Martin V8 Series 4 (Oscar India) and Series 5

The Series 4 Aston Martin V8 appeared in October 1978 in what was called 'Oscar India' specification. The name was derived from the NATO phonetic alphabet – the car's code name was 'October Introduction', which was shortened to 'OI' and then transposed into Oscar India. The main visual change was the small integrated spoiler on the boot lid and the air scoop on the top of the bonnet changed into a power

**The stalwart of the Aston Martin range throughout the 1970s and 1980s was the V8. The ultimate version was the Vantage, touted as the world's fastest four-seat car.**

bulge, with the open front of the Series 3 car's air scoop being closed off. Inside the cabin became plusher, with more wood trim on the dashboard. From 1980 cars destined for the American market were fitted with large, impact-resistant bumpers.

Mechanically the Oscar India cars were much the same as the previous Series 3 cars, with Weber carbs and usually fitted with a three-speed Chrysler Torqueflite automatic gearbox. The Oscar India cars were replaced in January 1988 by the Series 5, which were fitted with a new fuel-injection system from Weber/Marelli. This meant there was plenty of clearance under the bonnet so the power bulge was dispensed with. Production of the V8 ended in 1989.

## The V8 Vantage

With the V8 Coupé firmly established as a fast, good-handling GT car, the Aston Martin V8 Vantage hit the market in late 1977, and rapidly earned itself the title of the 'fastest production car tested by *Motor*' when the magazine tested the manual version in its 25 April 1981 edition. Re-introducing the Vantage name as the highest performance model of the range, it more than fulfilled the role. The Vantage was powered by a tuned version of the existing V8, with a compression ratio raised to 9:1 (up from the standard units 8.3:1), hotter cams, larger inlet valves, new inlet manifolds and larger Weber carburettors (48mm choke diameter compared to the standard 42mm) breathing through a revised airbox. This betrayed a traditional approach adopted by chief engineer Mike Loasby to tuning the unit, to give the car a 0–60 time of 5.4sec (the standard V8 being 7.5sec) and a top speed of, to quote Aston Martin, around 170mph (274km/h) – the standard V8 achieving 147mph (237km/h).

At the time Aston Martin did not quote power outputs, but the press at the time estimated it to be some 40 per cent up on the standard car to give the performance achieved, and the power output claimed in the German market was 390bhp, with the standard car pushing out 306bhp. Later cars were further tuned to give a claimed 405bhp. Torque figures were also up by an estimated 10 per cent. From the outside the new model was recognizable thanks to a blanked-off front grille and bonnet bulge, a larger front-end air-dam, and a bolt-on rear spoiler; these changes were all wind-tunnel designed to keep the car stable at the higher speeds it was capable of. Slots in the front air-dam fed air to the brakes and the main radiator.

The brakes were revised, with larger ventilated and slotted discs all round, and the car rode on larger 255/60 VR 15in-diameter radial tyres on 7in-width alloy wheels. The suspension was boosted with Koni telescopic shock absorbers all round, a larger diameter front anti-roll bar, and revisions to the geometry of the de-Dion back end to promote a suitable roll steer effect. A Volante version appeared in 1987, which must have given toupee makers pause for thought.

The Vantage placed Aston Martin firmly at the top of the 1980s performance tree. While many felt it to be somewhat of an anachronism, its combination of four-seat comfort coupled with its outstanding performance and surprisingly docile nature, meant it was hard to categorize – *Autocar* called it a 'hairy-chested sportscar of surprising sophistication', a description that suits the car very well. The model sold well in Aston Martin terms, with some 534 built by the time production ended in 1989.

**The Vantage featured subtle styling modifications, including the deeper air dam and blanked off grille. This is Chris Youell's 1984 car.**

**The Vantage's V8 engine fills the engine bay, and is fitted with four twin-choke downdraught Weber carbs.**

**The V8 Volante was introduced in 1978. It was a clean, neat design although the hood did not fold down completely flush with the rear deck.**

**Inside the Lagonda seems to be all traditional wood and leather until you see the space-age instruments.**

## Aston Martin V8 Volante

Looking back to the appeal of the open-top Aston Martin, last seen in the DB6 Volante, Aston Martin first produced a soft-top version of the V8 in June 1978, just before the introduction of the Series 4 'Oscar India' V8 Coupé; however, the Volante featured the Series 4 bonnet from the start, but not the built-in rear spoiler. The car's production was initially sent to the USA, with sales on the home market only starting the following year. The Volante Series 2 was introduced in January 1986 alongside the Series 5 V8, and like the coupé, was fitted with Weber/Marelli fuel injection and lost the bonnet bulge.

## The Aston Martin Lagonda Series 2

The Aston Martin Lagonda of 1976 was a radical interpretation of the classic Aston Martin four-door saloon. During David Brown's tenure the Lagonda badge appeared on the Rapide four-door saloon, but achieved limited sales success. After the company was sold the DBS-based Lagonda of the early 1970s was even less of a sales success than the 1960s car. The styling of both cars was obviously derived from the existing two-door cars, but their high performance never really hit the spot with the customers. Aimed at captains of industry, the sporting character of the marque probably put off potential buyers, with most potential customers opting for the luxury products of Rolls-Royce and Bentley, leading to too few customers who appreciated and bought into the Lagonda's sporting Aston Martin underpinnings.

**The Aston Martin Lagonda Series 2 was designed by William Towns, and is probably the epitome of the 'wedge' school of car design typified by the Lotus Elite, the Esprit and the TVR Tasmin. This is a Series 4 with slightly softened lines.**

After the brief appearance of the DBS-based, Towns-styled Lagonda Rapide (retrospectively called the Lagonda Series 1) of 1974, the appearance of a new four-door Lagonda (named the Series 2) at the 1976 Earls Court Motor Show came like a bolt from the blue. The new car brought two startling things to the market: a staggeringly different body style with no resemblance to any previous Aston Martin, and a space-age interior with instrumentation never seen before on a car's dashboard.

The new Lagonda, while still aimed at the 'captain of industry' market, was also set to tap into a relatively new market – that of the oil-rich gentleman of the Arabian peninsula. As the Gulf States were rapidly building themselves into modern societies thanks to the ever-increasing revenues generated from their oil sales, their large and ever-growing ruling families were becoming Westernized, and hungry for the best that the West could offer. With its unique modern styling, underpinned by its well proven mechanicals, and all hand crafted in the best Aston Martin traditions, the Lagonda was a huge success.

The new wedge-shaped saloon was truly jaw dropping, with its long and low looks, and razor edges that were unlike anything previously seen on the road. The luxurious interior presented a dashboard adorned with gas-plasma displays and touch-sensitive switchgear, dragging the marque into the twenty-first century. The new car was named the Lagonda

**The wedge styling of the Lagonda meant it had a tiny grille surrounded by driving lights and indicators, and pop-up headlights.**

Series 2 to distinguish it from the DBS-styled car, and gave the unequivocal message that after its recent troubles, Aston Martin was back in the game.

Despite being virtually all new, development of the Lagonda, from its inception to the prototype appearing at the 1976 Earls Court Motor Show, took a staggeringly short time of nine months, with development starting in February 1976 and the prototype being presented to the public in October 1976. Now even though William Towns' body styling was all but ready before the development started, and the show car wasn't actually a proper runner, this was still an incredible achievement by Mike Loasby and his small team of engineers. Unfortunately the fine tuning of the design, and especially getting the complex electronic instrumentation up and running, led to major delays, and the first car only reached its customer in 1978.

### *The Chassis*

The sheet steel chassis of the Lagonda Series 2 was designed by Mike Loasby, and while it was based on the concept of the platform chassis, like that seen on the DBS – itself of course of the Harold Beach design first seen on the DB4, and used in long-wheelbase form for the 1974–76 DBS-based Lagonda saloon – it was an entirely new design.

Not only did it have to cater for the increased length of the car, but also for the extra stiffness needed for the longer four-door configuration, and it also had to allow for the significantly lower nose-line of the new car. The basic structure of the new chassis was a pair of longitudinal box-section members with an additional pair of upper box sections at the front, passing each side of the engine. A bolt-on panel was used to join these and reinforce the structure below the propshaft tunnel, and a steel hoop ran round the 'B' pillar to give roll-over protection and improve body stiffness. On the front of the platform there was a bolt-on transverse member to stiffen up the front suspension mounts, and the new chassis was designed to support the all-alloy body to avoid any stresses affecting the bodywork.

The Lagonda chassis showed the versatility of the concept, with extra length inserted into the wheelbase to make room for four adult passengers and the four doors needed to serve them in this class of car, as well as providing plenty of room for a large and secure boot.

### *The Bodywork*

The striking Lagonda bodywork, styled by William Towns, was a three box design and was hand crafted in aluminium and was, in line with the design trends of the time, much sharper than the V8's, with straight lines and well defined edges and corners giving the car the wedge look so popular in the 1970s. The bodywork was hand formed from aluminium and was attached to the steel chassis and superstructure mainly using rivets.

The long and low look of the design was enhanced by the flat front panel, which housed a small traditional grille flanked by rectangular auxiliary driving lights, fog lights and indicators. The grille was slightly higher than the lights and a major styling point was the way the raised centre section of the bonnet line ran diagonally back from each side of the grille to the 'A' pillars, while gently merging into the side panels until disappearing at the rear of the bonnet. On the Series 2 and 3 cars

**The rear three-quarter view of the Lagonda is rather ungainly to some eyes. The overall shape is attractive and very advanced for its time.**

**The pop-up headlamps used by the Series 2 and 3 Lagondas were installed in the bonnet. This was unusual but it meant easy access to the mechanism.**

**The Lagonda's touch-operated switches and digital displays eventually worked, but were criticized for lack of feel, and the displays as being difficult to see in sunlight. This is the Series 3 set-up.**

the headlamps were pop-up, with two semi-rectangular units on each sides. They were located in wide pods mounted on the front edge of the bonnet panel.

The four-door centre section accommodated the passengers with some comfort, and behind the passenger compartment was a long and flat boot. The boot lid formed a vertical rear panel in which the rear lights and the number plate were situated, and gave a nice low lip to the spacious boot.

With its wheelbase of 115in (2,921mm) and overall length of 208in (5,283mm), the car was significantly longer than the Aston Martin V8 (length 183in 1,207mm) but its height at 52in (1,321mm) was 1in (254mm) lower than the V8. However, despite the loss of height, the extra length meant there was plenty of room for the passengers.

### The Interior

The leather-trimmed interior was undeniably luxurious and comfortable; however, the main feature was the futuristic dashboard, with its touch-sensitive switches and gas-discharge displays. Peter Sprague was one of the consortia that owned the company; he was also the head of US firm National Semiconductor, and this gave the company access to specialist expertise, and to the touch-sensitive switches as supplied by National Semiconductors. Development of the complete system was done at Cranfield University, but they struggled to produce a working system. Aston Martin eventually turned to the Texas-based Javalina Corporation, a company specializing in aircraft instrumentation, to get the original system up and running.

While the system was comprehensive and worked, it had a lot of criticism from the contemporary press: they found the displays hard (if not impossible) to read in direct sunlight, also that the touch switches were impossible to locate by feel, and they disliked the digital presentation of information. This was the main aspect of the car to be modified throughout its production, and as it matured, more conventional instruments and switchgear would replace the gas-discharge displays and the touch-sensitive buttons.

### Suspension

While the front suspension followed the V8 twin-wishbone layout, the set-up's geometry was altered to suit the Lagonda's ride and handling parameters, and the lower wishbone was modified to be much wider, with its front arm mounted much further forwards on the chassis than on the V8, acting almost as a trailing arm. Coil springs with concentric dampers made by Koni were fitted front and rear, with the rear dampers self levelling. At the rear the suspension was by de-Dion tube, but the V8's radius arms of unequal length were replaced with ones of equal length. On the V8 the unequal-length radius arms meant the de-Dion tube would act like an anti-roll bar and the suspension would stiffen up as the travel was used up, but on the Lagonda the equal-length arms meant there was no stiffening of the suspension.

### The Engine

The Lagonda engine had to be modified from that used in the V8 saloon to enable it to sit under the low nose of the Towns' body design. While the core of the engine remained largely unchanged, the sump, air-intake manifolds and the air box all had to be modified to drop the overall height of the unit. Internally the V8 unit was fitted with new camshafts, and larger inlet and exhaust valves were fitted to flatten the torque curve, making the engine more tractable and more in

**Under the Lagonda's bonnet sat the classic Aston Martin V8. It needed some modifications to the intakes, air box and sump to fit under the Lagonda's low bonnet line.**

keeping with the Lagonda's limousine persona. Sources for the power and torque of the engine vary, but it appears that the revised engine put out 280bhp at 5,000rpm, as opposed to the standard V8 saloon's 310bhp at 5,500rpm – but it had greater torque of 360lb ft, as opposed to the saloon's 301lb ft.

The Lagonda's standard transmission was a three-speed Chrysler Torqueflite automatic gearbox, which drove the car through the 3.07:1 differential.

## Lagonda Production and Development

The Lagonda took a long time to get into production, mainly because of problems with the computer used to control the instruments; but Aston Martin managed to overcome almost all the issues, and the first production Lagonda was delivered to Lord and Lady Tavistock, the Duke and Duchess of Bedford, at Woburn Abbey in Bedfordshire on Monday 24 April 1978. After this well publicised event, development continued to iron out many minor issues as cars were delivered.

The short-lived Series 3 Lagonda was introduced in January 1986 and was fitted with Weber/Marrelli fuel injection, and

**From the front the Lagonda is an attractive and imposing car. This is a Series 3.**

**The last of the Lagondas, the Series 4 had a styling update to soften the lines; also the pop-up headlamps were disposed of, and conventional lights repositioned in the nose.**

vacuum fluorescent (in fact cathode ray tube) displays for the instruments, along with a two-spoke steering wheel.

The Series 4 was introduced at the Geneva Motor Show in March 1987, and was the result of a softening-up of the styling by William Towns, as the sharp-edged wedge look was rapidly falling out of fashion. Along with the softened lines the cars lost the pop-up headlamps, which were relocated on a slightly larger front panel each side of the grille, and the fog lights under them repositioned in a larger front bumper. Inside, the instruments and touch-sensitive switches were finally replaced with conventional rockers. Under the bonnet, Weber sequential fuel injection was fitted. Also 16in wheels replaced the 15in ones of Series 2 and 3.

**The Bulldog's interior was very much a leather-coated cocoon for two people. Lagonda-style digital instruments were fitted.**

## The Bulldog

The Bulldog, project designation 'K9', was started in 1976, but the project was put on ice with the departure of chief engineer Mike Loasby to De Lorean. Restarted in 1979, the project was intended as a 'technical exercise', designed to show off the company's capabilities – and the result was certainly striking. The car was an extreme wedge design by William Towns, with gull-wing doors. The headlamps, five in all, were mounted in the middle of the bonnet line, and exposed by a drop-down panel in front of them.

The interior was a strict two-seater, luxuriously fitted out with Connolly leather and Wilton wool carpets, air conditioning, and Lagonda-style electronic instruments, though these reverted to conventional rocker switches for minor functions. The light alloy bodywork was mounted on a tubular space-frame chassis, which was originally intended to have de-Dion-type suspension front and rear, but in fact emerged with conventional V8-style wishbones up front and de-Dion at the back. The space frame was based on a backbone of three 4in (10cm) diameter tubes, with extra strength provided by a fully structural roof panel and two 'A' pillars fitted on each side.

**The Bulldog was a technology demonstrator, and Aston Martin's first mid-engined design. Powered by a V8 equipped with a twin turbocharger, the Bulldog's design speed was 200mph (320km/h).**

The wheelbase was a long 109in (1,754mm), and the car was powered by a mid-mounted, twin Garrett AiResearch turbocharged V8 fitted with Bosch mechanical fuel injection, and drove through a five-speed ZF transaxle, making it the first mid-engined car to be fitted with a de-Dion axle. The engine was fitted with forged Cosworth low-compression pistons, giving a compression ratio of 7.35:1 to allow for the high boost pressure needed to produce around 650bhp: this powered the car to just under 200mph (320km/h) at the MIRA test track. The single example produced has undergone a complete restoration, with the aim of seeing if it can break 200mph – the original design speed.

## The V8 Zagato

The Aston Martin V8 Zagato was introduced in 1986, and marked the return to Aston Martin collaborating with Italian Carrazzeria Zagato, a relationship first garnered with the lightweight competition-oriented DB4GT Zagato of 1960. Inspired by Ferrari's limited edition 288 GTO, a high-performance version of the then current 308GTB, which took the 1984 Geneva Motor Show by storm, Victor Gauntlett and Peter Livanos – Aston Martin's joint chairman – decided to pull the same trick to raise some much needed revenue. The new Zagato project was announced at the following year's show, and the publicity was such that, even with only a styling sketch to tempt customers, fifty committed to buy a car that was projected to cost £87,000. The car's design parameters were simple: outstanding performance with a 0–60 time under 5sec and a top speed of 186mph (300km/h).

**The V8 Zagato was a rebodied V8 with a shortened chassis. Built only to order from 1986, it was available as a coupé or a roadster.**

**The V8 Zagato convertible was rare, with only thirty-seven built as compared to fifty coupés. The styling is not to everyone's taste.**

Based on the V8 Vantage, the Zagato was 18in (457mm) shorter than the V8, but retained the V8's 102in (2,590mm) wheelbase, with the reduction in length taken from the front and rear overhangs. Weighing 3,600lb (1,633kg), the Zagato was some 360lb (163kg) lighter than the Vantage, and with a claimed power output of 432bhp thanks to some engine tweaks and 50mm-throat-sized Weber carburettors sat under a large bonnet bulge. The bodywork, mainly aluminium and with foam-filled glass-fibre front and rear panels, was built by Zagato in Milan, with Aston Martin sending rolling chassis to Zagato at a rate of two or so a month.

It has to be said that the styling was inconsistent – good in parts and not so good in others. It sported the trademark Zagato 'double bubble' roof, very short front and rear overhangs, a stylized chrome Aston Martin grille flanked by a pair of rectangular headlamps, and was fitted with flush glass all round – a contributor to the very good drag co-efficient of 0.33 (originally 0.29 before the fitment of the front air-dam needed to maintain stability at high speed). Performance-wise the car just about met its brief – while the 0–60 time came in at 4.8sec, the 'official' top speed came in at 185.6mph (298.75km/h) – just a fraction under the aimed-for 300km/h. With fifty two-seat coupés and thirty-seven soft-top versions made, the car was successful, and more than met its brief to raise Aston Martin's profile in the market as well as making the company money.

## COMPETITION

Thanks to the precarious state of Aston Martin's finances there was no works-sponsored racing taking place in the time covered by this chapter (1975–1986); however, there was a well publicised private venture that was encouraged by, and had some non-financial support from, the factory. This was a short-lived partnership called Aston Martin Nimrod Racing Automobiles, formed between Aston Martin – and in particular Chairman Victor Gauntlett – and car dealer and racing driver Robin Hamilton, an ex-Rolls-Royce apprentice. Robin Hamilton had some experience of racing Aston Martins, racing a DB4GT to promote his Burton-upon-Trent based garage, then moving on to a more modern DBS V8 in 1975, competing in AMOC events. In 1977 the much modified DBS V8, with tuned engine and extensively modified and widened bodywork – and nicknamed 'The Muncher' thanks to its insatiable appetite for brake pads and discs – was entered in the Le Mans 24 Hours, where it came seventeenth overall and third in its class.

By 1980 Hamilton was in discussions with Eric Broadley of Lola, the company that had built the Aston Martin V8-powered T70 of the 1960s. The Nimrod was designed to compete in the Group C endurance racing class, and the new car was financed by Hamilton, Victor Gauntlett's Pace Petroleum, and Peter Livanos (then the Aston Martin US distributor), who each put £250,000 in the pot, forming Nimrod Racing Automobiles. However, Livanos had intended to use the Nimrod in the US IMSA series but the differences between this race series and Group C were too much so Livano withdrew.

Nimrod was based on the Lola T600/T610 chassis, modified and called the T385. The car was a monocoque made from

**The Aston Martin Nimrod was a V8-powered endurance racer from the 1980s. It achieved limited success between 1980 and 1984.**

bonded and riveted honeycomb composite and aluminium sheet, with a steel-tube space frame at the rear to carry the Aston Martin V8 engine, Hewland transaxle and rear suspension. A lightweight composite body with gull-wing doors completed the car.

The first car made its debut at the Dubai Grand Prix meeting in October 1981, and the cars made their racing debut at the Silverstone Six Hours race in May 1982, when two cars had been completed. The works car was entered by Hamilton with Tiff Needel, Geoff Lees and Bob Evens, and the second was a private entry, owned by Viscount Downe and driven by Michael Salmon and Ray Mallock. Hamilton's car retired with a broken rotor arm after 148 laps, and the second car came in sixth.

At Le Mans the same two cars entered, but Hamilton's car crashed when a rear tyre failed. Downe's car finished a creditable seventh place. In the following race, at Spa, the Hamilton car dropped a valve and did not finish, while the Downe car finished eleventh; and in the last race of the year, the Brands Hatch 1,000km, the Hamilton car did not appear, and the Downe car came eleventh. Hamilton then contested the UDS IMSA 1983 season with two cars, as by then IMSA allowed Group C cars, with limited success. At the Sebring 12 Hours their best result was fifth overall, and first in the group C class.

Meanwhile Downe's team continued to compete in Europe, with a fifth at the Silverstone 1,000km, and a retirement at Le Mans. Spa was another retirement, but the car came fourth

**Victor Gauntlett at the launch of the DB4GT Sanction II with a collection of original DB4GTs.**

## TECHNICAL DESCRIPTION: ASTON MARTIN V8 VANTAGE

The Aston Martin V8 Vantage was the ultimate development of the line that started with the 1968 DBS. While it shared the DBS's all-steel platform chassis and its attractive two-door coupé bodywork, the Vantage's V8 engine was tuned to the limit to provide the car with the title of the fastest four-seat production car – and it was many a patriotic British teenager's poster car of choice in the 1980s. Front independent suspension followed the DB4/5/6/DBS practice, with double unequal-length wishbones with coil springs and telescopic dampers, while at the rear a DBS-style coil-sprung de-Dion set-up was used, with parallel trailing arms and a Watts linkage, though telescopic dampers were used. The car had disc brakes all round, and a ZF five-speed gearbox. It was fitted with 15in diameter, 7in wide alloy wheels, shod with 255/60 tyres to handle the extra power.

## SPECIFICATION TABLE: 1977 ASTON MARTIN V8, V8 VANTAGE, V8 VOLANTE

| | |
|---|---|
| **Layout and chassis** | Front-engined, rear-drive two-plus-two sports car. Closed two-door body, all-alloy body, mounted on steel platform chassis |
| **Engine** | |
| Type | All-alloy quad-cam 90-degree V8 |
| Block material | RR-50 specification light silicon aluminium alloy |
| Head material | RR-50 specification light silicon aluminium alloy |
| Cooling | Centrifugal pump with water/antifreeze mix |
| Bore and stroke | 100 × 85mm |
| Capacity | 5340cc |
| Valves | 2 valves per cylinder, operated directly via bucket tappets from four chain-driven overhead camshafts |
| Compression ratio | 9.3:1 |
| Carburettor | 4 × Weber 42 DCNF |
| Max. power | 390bhp |
| Max. torque | Not disclosed |
| **Transmission** | |
| Gearbox (manual) | 5-speed ZF synchromesh on all gears |
| Clutch | Hydraulically operated single dry plate, diaphragm spring |
| Overall ratios | 1st 2.9:1 |
| | 2nd 1.78:1 |
| | 3rd 1.22:1 |
| | 4th 1:1 |
| | 5th 0.845:1 |
| Reverse | 2.63:1 |
| Final drive | Hypoid bevel, 3.45:1 |

| | |
|---|---|
| **Suspension and steering** | |
| Front | Independent by double unequal-length wishbone coil springs over telescopic dampers. Anti-roll bar |
| Rear | De-Dion axle located by parallel trailing arms and Watts linkage. Coil springs, telescopic dampers |
| Steering | ZF power-assisted rack-and-pinion |
| Wheels | Cast aluminium alloy, 15in diameter, 7in wide, 5-stud fixing |
| **Brakes** | |
| Type | Hydraulic-operated front and rear discs with servo |
| Size (front) | 11.5in (29.2cm) diameter vented and slotted disc |
| Size (rear) | 10.4in (26.4cm) diameter disc |
| **Capacities** | |
| Fuel capacity | 15gal (68ltr) |
| Oil capacity | 20 pints (11.4ltr) |
| **Dimensions** | |
| Track | |
| Front: | 59in (1,498mm) |
| Rear: | 59in (1,498mm) |
| Wheelbase | 102.7in (2,608mm) |
| Overall length | 180.5in (4,585mm) |
| Overall width | 72in (1,828mm) |
| Overall height | 53in (1,346mm) |
| Weight | 4,130lb (1,873kg) |
| **Performance** | |
| Top speed | 167mph (227km/h) |
| 0–60 | 5.8sec |

at Brands Hatch in September 1983. The final Nimrod racing year was 1984; three cars ran in the Daytona 24 Hours, but only one finished, in sixteenth place. Car 005 was fitted with a new body and a pair of Garret turbochargers, but it suffered piston failure at the Silverstone 1,000km race; while the two cars entered for Le Mans both crashed.

## KEY FIGURE

### Victor Gauntlett

Born on 20 May 1942 in Surrey, England, Malcolm Victor Gauntlett was an entrepreneur and an inspirational leader; he was also a popular and well liked character. With a lifelong interest in classic cars, he owned and raced a 4.5-litre 'Blower' Bentley, which under the pilotage of pre-war racer Tim Birkin had lapped Brooklands at over 100mph (160km/h).

After joining the RAF on a short service commission and learning to fly, Gauntlett entered the oil business: he joined BP in 1963, then moved to France to work for the parent company of Total, the Compagnie Française des Petroles. Having returned to work in London, in 1972 he left Total and set up his own company, Hay Petroleum Services, which traded as Pace Petroleum. Pace went on to become one of Britain's largest petrol distribution companies, as Gauntlett's policy of shrewd buying of petroleum products and distributing them efficiently to some 450 petrol stations ensured that Pace was very profitable.

Gauntlett's first interest in Aston Martin came in 1980 when he bought 10 per cent of the company for £500,000 from the consortium headed up by Alan Curtis, Peter Sprague and George Mindon. Aston Martin became his main interest, and he was appointed chairman in 1981, by which time he and CHI owned the company 50/50. As the company needed more capital to develop the model range, in 1983 Gauntlett sold a share of Pace to the Kuwaiti Investment Authority, which subsequently bought the rest of the Pace, in 1986. With sales at an all-time low, in 1983 Gauntlett had to sell his share in Aston Martin to the Livanos/Papanicolaou-owned ALL Inc – but in 1984 he returned, buying a 25 per cent share in 1984.

By 1987 under Gauntlett's leadership Aston Martin had been revived and was in a reasonable state, and Gauntlett negotiated Ford's purchase of 75 per cent of the company, though he kept himself on as chairman. In 1991 Gauntlett handed over to Ford man William Hayes; by this time the development of the new 'entry model', the DB7 – arguably the car that saved Aston Martin – was in hand. Having sold his shares in Aston Martin, Gauntlett became a trustee of the National Motor Museum, as well as becoming a consultant to a number of London banks. Gauntlett died in 2002, having lived to see Aston Martin firmly on the road to success under Ford's ownership.

CHAPTER 8

# THE FORD YEARS: 1987–2000

It is often stated, unfairly in the author's opinion, that the DB7 was nothing more than a lightly remodelled Jaguar XJS, or a 'Jag in drag' as Jeremy Clarkson called it in an episode of the BBC's *Top Gear* television programme. However, the DB7 was probably the most important car in Aston Martin's history. Not only was it made in greater numbers than any Aston Martin model before it, it also re-established the marque in the expensive (but not too expensive) GT market, opening up ownership of the cars to a much wider market than the older Newport Pagnell-produced cars could ever hope for. This was made possible by three main factors: first the acquisition of Aston Martin by Ford; second the appointment of the very influential and experienced Walter Hayes, the Ford manager with a long and distinguished record of looking after Ford's performance interests in the UK, to run the new acquisition; and finally Ford's purchase of Jaguar in 1990, which opened up the possibility of using an existing platform, based on the Jaguar XJS monocoque, as a basis for a new Aston Martin model.

## THE COMPANY

By 1986, even though Aston Martin was not losing money, the product range comprising the V8 and the Lagonda was only addressing the top end of a limited market and selling in small numbers. However, the newly introduced limited edition V8 Zagato was selling well and at a premium price, helping with the company's cash flow and demonstrating its ability to produce new, innovative and attractive cars that could still sell. It was apparent to Aston Martin owners Victor Gauntlett and the Livanos family that if Aston Martin were to survive in the long term it would need a third, cheaper product line to increase the volume of sales to a level that would generate sufficient funds to pay for the company's expansion. It was the classic business problem: the company had the ideas and the vision to create a new range, but lacked the funds to bring the vision to reality.

**The DB7 is generally acknowledged as the car that saved Aston Martin. It was introduced in 1993 and was followed by the convertible Volante version in 1994. Here an original coupé sits in front of a convertible at an AMOC show in 2021.**

The solution was to find a partner who had the money to finance the dream, and that partner would turn out to be automotive giant Ford. Ford stepped in in September 1987 and bought a 75 per cent share of Aston Martin Lagonda from Victor Gauntlett and the Livanos family; this would give the company the financial stability it needed, not only to revamp the existing products but also to start to develop a new model line.

Walter Hayes, who had retired from Ford as vice chairman of Ford of Europe in December 1989, came out of retirement when he was appointed to the Aston Martin board; he became chairman in 1991 when Gauntlett stood down and Ford bought the remaining shares in the company. One of Hayes's important achievements was in appointing David Brown as Honorary Life President of Aston Martin – which also meant that the use of the important 'DB' initials on the new DB7 was seen as legitimate to the typical Aston Martin customer.

The work on a new entry model line took second place to development of the Virage, a car that gave the company's product line a much needed boost in terms of kerb appeal, and brought to the Aston Martin line-up an up-to-date, all-new body shape. Replacing the V8, and with an eye-watering price of £120,000 in the UK on its launch (equivalent to around £275,000 in 2021), the Virage was an expensive indulgence for Aston Martin's customers, and served to underline the importance of having another, cheaper model in the range, especially as the Lagonda was dropped in 1990.

The need for a new model was underlined by the fact that sales during 1993 measured a measly forty-two cars. However, despite the poor sales figures, the next car introduced in 1993 was the supercharged Vantage: not only was it an extensively restyled and re-engineered Virage, it was also fitted with what was, at the time, the most powerful production engine produced anywhere in the world. The engine's 550bhp was complemented by a colossal 550lb ft of torque, achieved by fitting two superchargers to the car. And in 1998 the V600 was introduced, with an extra 50bhp in case 550 wasn't enough! For the faint of heart the normally aspirated Virage was restyled on Vantage lines, and renamed the V8 Coupé in 1996.

The Virage was of course available as a Volante.

The Vantage's final iteration was the twin supercharger-equipped V600. This is AMHT chairman Rob Smith's fine example.

The last of Aston Martin's traditional line of 'old school' sports cars was started by the Virage, which evolved into the totally restyled Vantage. All were powered by Aston Martin's 1960s V8 engine with 4 valves per cylinder head and various states of tune.

The defining moment for Aston Martin's future came in 1990 when Ford acquired Jaguar. Jaguar had been spun off from British Leyland and was floated on the UK stock exchange in 1984; after a successful few years during which Chairman Sir John Egan had improved profitability by concentrating on quality control, productivity and controlling costs, Ford made a successful offer to Jaguar's shareholders and bought the company. This acquisition had a major effect on Aston Martin, and would result in an all-new entry level Aston Martin, the DB7.

To produce the DB7 Aston Martin acquired the old TWR factory in Bloxham, Warwickshire, previously used to produce TWR's range of tuned Jaguars and limited number production cars such as the XK220. The factory was reconfigured for DB7 production, and reopened in 1994. The Newport Pagnell factory continued to produce the 'hand-built' range of Virage-derived cars.

In 1998, the 2,000th DB7 was produced at the Bloxham factory, while production of the hand-built cars at Newport Pagnell continued. In 1999 the V12-powered DB7 Vantage was added to the DB7 range, and this new model immediately took the majority of DB7 sales, leading to the straight six-powered car being dropped from the range in 2000.

**The Lagonda Vignale concept car was fitted with a dummy engine made from a pair of Ford Mondeo engines welded together. This led to the rumour that the 'real' V12 was made in this way, which is not true.**

## THE ENGINE: THE ASTON MARTIN V12

Aston Martin Lagonda does have some history with the V12 engine: there was a pre-war V12 built by Lagonda, the unsuccessful 1954 Le Mans Lagonda V12 based on the straight six, while the 1990 Lagonda Vignale show car was also V12 powered; however, they only appeared as prototypes. Aston Martin's first production V12 engine was unveiled to the buying public in the DB7 Vantage in 1999. The engine was a 60-degree, 48-valve four-cam V12 displacing 5935cc, which in the DB7 produced 420bhp at 6,000rpm, along with 400lb ft of torque at 5,000rpm.

In the press at the time the engine was inaccurately described as a pair of Ford Duratec V6s 'welded together', a description still bandied about today, some two decades after the engine was introduced. In fact the engine was designed from scratch specifically for Aston Martin, and the rumour concerning the pair of Mondeo V6s was the result of an earlier dummy V12 fitted in the Lagonda Vignale concept car.

The Aston Martin V12 project was financed by Jim Clark's Ford Advanced Powertrain division and was developed by a small team headed by Ford Project Design Engineer Anthony Musci. Musci had pointed out the potential failings of producing a new V12 using the Ford/ Yamaha V8 as a basis, and suggested a different approach – and Clarke asked Musci to implement this. Musci started off the project in early 1994 with an outline design using an all-new block, crankshaft and head designs, and the well

**The Aston Martin V12 engine was developed by Ford's Advanced Powertrain Division especially for Aston Martin. The 6-litre unit is reasonably compact and very powerful.**

**The V12's inner workings are visible in this cutaway drawing. Note the chain-driven four camshafts, the 4 valves per cylinder, and that each crankshaft big-end journal supports two connection rods.**

proven piston assemblies and valve train from the existing Duratec V6 – but using the larger bore 3-litre Zetec engine components.

The result was an outstanding engine that has gone on to power many Aston Martins, from the DB9 through to the current DB11 and Vanquish in its smaller, twin-turbocharged AE31 guise. It is to be hoped that this account and Musci's article will finally put to bed the story that the engine was simply a pair of Ford Mondeo V6s 'welded together' – as mentioned above – and enable owners to explain that the engine was designed specifically for Aston Martin and has a pedigree every bit as illustrious as the previous Aston Martin fours and straight sixes, and the V8.

## INTRODUCTION TO THE CARS

The cars produced by Aston Martin between 1996 and 2003 formed the basis for the company's recovery under Ford's stewardship, and gave a hint of the new direction the company would be taking. The DB7 was the kingpin of the recovery, being in production from 1994 to 1999, and was unarguably the car that saved Aston Martin. The soft-top DB7 Volante was in production from 1996, while the final iterations of the Virage line, in the shape of the V8 Coupé and Volante, were produced in Newport Pagnell until the line was replaced with the first of the truly all-new Aston Martins, the Vanquish, in 2001.

From 1986 Aston Martin was producing fewer and fewer cars: the V8, Zagato and Lagonda were discontinued, while the Virage was introduced in 1989 to replace the V8 range. The soft-top version of the Virage, traditionally named the Virage Volante, was introduced in 1990, the high performance Vantage was introduced in 1992, and the 6.3-litre V8 engine was introduced in 1993. As an aside, four DB4GT Zagato-based 'Sanction II' recreations were built at Newport Pagnell and Zagato's plant in Turin during 1991.

Everything changed with the introduction of the DB7 in 1994, and it is not unreasonable to say that this was the car that saved Aston. Slotting in below the hand-built cars, it used a Jaguar XJS-derived platform, and its supercharged straight-six engine was derived from the Jaguar AJ6 unit. The car was styled by Ian Callum, but its underpinning gave rise to the sobriquet 'a Jag in drag'. Be that as it may, the car gave Aston Martin a new model that was priced well below that of the Newport Pagnell cars, and opened up the possibility of Aston Martin ownership to a much wider market.

## THE VIRAGE FAMILY OF CARS

The Aston Martin Virage was the logical finale of the Aston Martin platform chassis line that started with the DB4 in the 1950s. The Virage was aptly summarized by *Car* magazine as 'Pretty, Powerful, but Pricey' in their first road test in 1990; it was in essence a reclothed V8, still hand-made and retaining the classic Aston V8 engine, but fitted with new cylinder heads to give 4 valves per cylinder and a useful power hike. The design was originally given the go-ahead by the company board in 1985, and was to run alongside the Zagato car. It was originally unveiled in 1987, with customer deliveries starting in 1989, while a soft top version was introduced in the October 1990 Motor Show.

### Virage Design and Development

The design and development of the Virage commenced in 1985. The name of the new car was supposed to be decided

**The Virage was an all-new design, but was still powered by the venerable Aston Martin V8, albeit in 4-valve per cylinder guise. The sleek bodywork retained the Aston Martin grille shape while appearing new and modern.**

in a works-sponsored competition, but apparently Victor Gauntlett settled on the name himself, although it was also suggested by an AMOC member. 'Virage' is French for 'corner' – an important element of any race track and so appropriate for the new Aston Martin; it also took a sly glance back to the marque's racing history. In a first for Aston Martin, the styling of the Virage was put out to a competition between five design consortia. The design brief was very open: Aston Martin gave the five contestants details of the proposed mechanical layout of the new car, and asked that it should be:

> *...a direct replacement for the existing model (the V8) in 2+2 configuration. It should not only be lighter and more aerodynamically efficient, but the shape should reinforce those statements. And it should be identifiable as an Aston Martin capable of retaining the loyalty of the traditional buyer, but appealing to a new generation.*

The end result of the competition was the award of the design contract to a team trained at the Royal College of Art (RCA), comprising John Heffernan and Ken Greenley. Both were vehicle design tutors at the RCA; they had already designed the Panther Solo, and their design for Aston Martin, while lacking any nods to previous Aston Martin styling apart from a small Aston Martin grille, was a smooth, modern and attractive design that was (from the front) recognizably an Aston Martin.

Using modern CAD methods, the team's new two-door, two-plus-two coupé design had relatively long overhangs ending in deformable bumpers, a teardrop-shaped cabin with flush glass, slim pillars, slim triangular rear three-quarter windows, and a rather bland cut-off rear end with a very subtle built-in spoiler on the rear top of the boot lid; below this were rectangular rear lights flanking the number-plate recess. At the front the bonnet line was low, thanks in part to the slim rectangular headlamps that flanked the classic Aston Martin grille.

## Virage Technical Description

### *Chassis and Bodywork*

The Virage platform chassis was a refined version of the Lagonda's box-section platform chassis, a decision taken in order to minimize the time taken to build it, as well as reducing parts differences within the range, as the intention was originally to have the Lagonda and Virage making up the model range until a new base model was introduced. In comparison to the outgoing V8, the Virage was significantly larger, with the width and length both increased by 3in (7.5cm); however, the company claimed that the revised chassis was both lighter, easier to manufacture and stiffer than that of the V8.

The exterior bodywork was all aluminium, with the panels hand finished and fitted to steel mounts on the chassis in the best Aston Martin tradition. New press tools were bought to produce the body panels, rather than using traditional hand forming – while it was hardly mass production, the use of pre-pressed panels would again reduce the labour needed to produce the cars. But despite the cost cutting, the cars were still hand-made, with much fettling needed to perfect the fit and finish of the panels.

### *The Engine*

The Virage was fitted with an extensively developed version of the Tadek Marek V8. In the Virage the capacity remained at 5340cc, but the heads were new and were fitted with 4 valves per cylinder to improve breathing. The US race shop Callaway Engineering was responsible for the work, and the new engine, still 5.3 litres in capacity, gave 330bhp and 340lb ft of torque.

**From the rear the Virage's sleek lines and clean design can be appreciated.**

**The final iteration of the Aston Martin V8 was the twin-supercharged, 4 valves per cylinder, 6.3-litre unit seen on the V600.**

In 1992 the engine's capacity was raised to 6.3 litres, when Aston Works Services could bore and stroke an existing owner's V8 to have a capacity of 6347cc. The fuel and sparks were provided by a Weber-Marelli electronic fuel-injection and engine-management system, with new inlet manifolding designed to fit the new cylinder heads.

*Steering and Suspension*

The Virage was initially offered with either a ZF five-speed manual or a three-speed automatic, which was replaced with a four-speed automatic box in 1993. The Virage's suspension followed that of the Lagonda, with unequal-length wishbones at the front and a de-Dion set-up at the rear. The brakes were discs all round, with solid rotors at the rear, and ventilated up front. Unlike the outgoing V8, the rear discs were moved outboard, giving more passenger space, and the car was designed to have anti-lock brakes from the start.

*The Interior*

The Virage's interior continued in the classic 1980s Aston Martin GT car style, with the driver swaddled in leather trim that covered the seats, door panels and dashboard, his feet luxuriating in high quality Wilton wool carpeting, and his eyes seduced by walnut trim laid out on the dashboard and doors. The car did have some concessions to the 1990s: the full set of instruments were integrated into a single binnacle, with the large speedometer and tachometer in the centre, above which sat the smaller but all-important oil-pressure gauge. Outboard of the speedo and tacho were the other four minor gauges, two each side, monitoring oil and water temperature, fuel level and voltage.

## Developments: Virage to V600

Once the Virage was established, the next development of the basic car was the Volante, launched in 1990. The original Volante did not follow the format of the preceding V8 Volante, as it was a strict two-seater with a small luggage platform behind the front seats and a somewhat ungainly hood design, which when folded, sat high above the boot line. The model was revised for 1992, when the hood design was improved so it looked a lot neater when down, and a pair of vestigial rear seats were fitted.

The Virage Shooting Brake continued the Aston Martin tradition of offering estate-car versions of the saloons, and was offered from 1992. The cars were produced by Works Services, and it is believed that six were built.

The range was further modified in 1993 with minor improvements, which included the introduction of the classic Aston Martin front-wing air vents, and an improved interior. There was a new instrument binnacle with walnut veneer surrounding the individual instruments, an improved security alarm and immobilizer, and an upgraded in-car entertainment system. Mechanically the main change was the adoption of a

**Aston Martin works produced up to six shooting brakes based on the Virage.**

new, four-speed, electronically controlled automatic gearbox option. Special options, including a 6.3-litre engine, were also offered, but were only available as after-market modifications to existing cars to avoid having to homologate them.

## The Vantage (the V550)

The Vantage (also known as the V550) appeared in 1993, and was the high performance development of the Virage – although it shared virtually no parts with the original car. It had a twin supercharged, 5.3-litre version of the venerable 48-valve V8 that produced 550bhp and 550lb ft of torque. The bodyshell was extensively modified and all panels, apart from the door skins and roof, changed to reflect the wider and more muscular style of the car. Front and rear wings were extended by some 4in (10cm) to accommodate wider wheels, bigger brakes and revised suspension, while the front and rear panels were aerodynamically tweaked.

The front wings also regained the Aston Martin trade-mark vents to help keep the engine bay cool, and the bonnet grew new bulges and grilles to fit the twin Eaton superchargers. At the rear the VW Scirocco rear lights were replaced with individual round units, and the rear deck was reshaped.

Alongside the V550, Aston Martin produced a further two Virage-based models, the V8 Coupé and the Volante.

The V8 Vantage Le Mans edition, produced in 1999, was intended to be the last of the line that started with the Virage, as Newport Pagnell was rejigged to start to produce the all-new Vanquish.

In the late 1990s Aston Martin formalized their tuning offerings for the Virage family of cars, which resulted in the Vantage 600. Never an actual factory-produced model, and avoiding the need to homologate a revised model, the V600 was basically a number of modifications made to a 'standard' Virage, V8 Coupé or Vantage, which were fitted to an existing car at the Newport Pagnell factory. This resulted in the ultimate car in the line that started with the DB4, the V600, described in the contemporary press as the car for 'current Vantage owners for whom too much is not enough'. The 600 in the name reflected the claimed bhp and torque of the twin supercharged, 48-valve, V8 engine.

**A good-looking Virage with clean lines and that indefinable Aston Martin look. This car has the air scoops and wider wings of the Vantage.**

**Rodney McMahon's superb Vantage Volante long wheelbase. He finds it a fine cruiser, perfect for sunny weather driving.**

The V600 specification was also given as an option on the last of the line, the Vantage Le Mans, offered as a limited edition of forty cars in 1999, commemorating Aston Martin's 1959 Le Mans win.

The last of the Virage line was created during 2000 with a run of nine V8 Vantage Volantes built, many of which were fitted with the full V600 range of performance goodies at the Works Service after they were produced. Unlike the previous Volante, these final cars were built on the short chassis used on the V8 Coupé. The Vantage Le Mans was replaced by the all-new Vanquish, which was the last coachbuilt car produced at Newport Pagnell.

**The DB7 is a fine-looking car. Designed by Ian Callum, it has timeless lines that reflect past designs. This is an early DB7 Coupé.**

### The DB4GT Zagato Sanction II

In 1987 Aston Martin, seeing how the price of classic cars, and especially Aston Martins, had risen, decided to cash in on their heritage and build four all-new DB4GT Zagatos, using the four chassis numbers from the original sequence that had not been built. Using four new platform chassis built by independent Aston Martin specialist Richard Williams, and bodies based on an original DB4GT Zagato, the Italian coach works added the all-alloy lightweight bodies to the four chassis units at their plant in Milan, and these were then shipped back to Newport Pagnell for completion.

## THE DB7 – THE CAR THAT SAVED ASTON MARTIN

As has often been said, the DB7 was the car that saved Aston Martin. By the 1990s the company's product range was reduced to the expensive and anachronistic Virage. While clothed in a reasonably modern body designed in the 1980s – which was doing a good job of disguising the 1960s developed V8 and 1950s platform – the car was only selling in minute quantities to a very small but discerning and rich clientèle. The car was generally liked by the press and the public, but was also considered to be rather a dinosaur: its fuel consumption was out of tune with the emerging 'green' lobby, its weight and bulk made its undeniably high performance hard to exploit in the real world, and its price placed it out of reach of all but the mega rich, a limited market at the best of times.

So Aston Martin, in the shape of long-term Ford man Walter Hayes, recognized that the company desperately needed a second model line that sat below the expensive, hand-built Virage and was attractive to a much wider range of customers – and that meant the car had to be cheaper than the Virage. The Aston Martin press release for the DB7 described it as being designed and developed as a successor to the DB6, but arguably the Virage was that car. The DB7 was in fact entering a new market segment for Aston Martin: a cheaper car that would be built in much greater numbers than any of the Aston Martins that came before it.

### DB7 Overview

The DB7 was launched in March 1993 at the Geneva Motor Show, and the first production cars were produced in June 1994. A two-door coupé with stunning traditional styling, it was exactly what Aston Martin needed to expand their product range and provide customers with a stylish, economical and practical Grand Touring car that slotted neatly into the bottom of the range. It is no exaggeration to say that the DB7 was the car that saved Aston Martin. The car was greeted with enthusiasm from the press and owners; it was fundamentally sound, very well developed and lived up to all their expectations. Thanks to Ford's input of money and facilities the car went through an exceedingly rigorous development and test process, and Aston Martin, probably for the first time in their recent history, was not relying on their customers to carry out the final stages of product testing!

Initially the DB7 was offered as a two-door coupé, with a 3239cc straight-six engine that was supercharged and produced a healthy 335bhp at 5,750rpm, along with 361lb ft of torque at 3,000rpm. Later developments would result in a soft-top version, named, as tradition demanded, the Volante, and the car was later fitted with the new Aston Martin 5935cc V12 engine to create a Vantage model: this had a healthy 476bhp at 6,000rpm, along with 470lb ft of torque at 4,500rpm.

### The DB7's Ancestry

The DB7's ancestry can be traced from the XJS, Jaguar's Grand Touring car launched in 1976, through to the cancelled

Jaguar 'E-Type replacement' named the F-type and coded XJ41 (coupé) and XJ42 (soft top), and on to the TWR 'XX' project for a new sports car based on the XJS/XJ41.

The first element of the DB7's gestation lies firmly at Jaguar, and the company's desire to replace the E-Type with a 'proper' sports car. This had resulted in a long-running, stop-start project that began in 1980, and resulted in the design of two similar cars based on the XJS platform: the XJ41 coupé and the XJ42 soft top. This pair of cars, often referred to as the 'F-Type' at the time, were intended to be smaller, sports-oriented cars that would complement the Grand Tourer XJS in the Jaguar range; but the project was slow moving, with Jaguar concentrating its engineering resources on the much-needed XJ saloon replacement, the XJ40.

The F-Type project was finally cancelled in 1990 after significant project creep, which resulted in the car's weight and complexity growing out of hand when four-wheel drive, a hatchback, and widening the body to improve cooling were suggested. Jaguar would eventually end up producing a new sports car, codenamed the X100 and launched and put into production as the XK8 in 1996 – and although it was also based on a heavily modified XJS platform, it had all-new suspension and a brand new V8 engine.

**The cover of April 1983 *Car* magazine, showing how the supposed 'F-Type' Jaguar has a close resemblance to the DB7, while luckily the proposed V8 replacement was well off the mark.**

The second important element of the DB7 story rested with TWR. Originally known as 'Tom Walkinshaw Racing', TWR had been in partnership with Jaguar since the early 1980s to successfully build and race the XJS in Touring Car championships, and to produce purpose-built sports racers, the XJR-6 Group C cars for endurance racing. TWR also had a joint company with Jaguar, JaguarSport: this enterprise concentrated on road cars, and engineered the high performance versions of the XJ40 saloon and the XJS, resulting in the popular and successful XJR 4.0 and the XJR-S. It also re-engineered and productionized the XJ220 supercar, putting it into production at a new factory at Wykham Mill, near Blockley in Oxfordshire.

TWR had been aware of the XJ41/42 project and realized they could potentially do something with it by going back to the initial simpler design. However, Jaguar had their X100 project for their sports car, and there was no place in the model range for the TWR 'XX' project. But this all changed when Ford purchased Jaguar in 1990 and Aston Martin appeared on the scene. The TWR 'XX' was the ideal basis for the relatively low volume, high performance car that the Aston Martin range needed – and Project NPX (standing for Newport Pagnell Experimental) was born.

Artists' impressions of the Jaguar F-Type and a 'new' Towns-designed V8 appeared on the cover of the April 1983 issue of *Car* magazine. The F-Type rendering shows unmistakable resemblance to both the DB7 and the Jaguar XK8, while the angular Towns car bears a more than passing resemblance to the second generation Toyota Supra – though this was probably not a look that Aston Martin would want, and was also a style that has aged rapidly. The *Car* article relates that it was intended to be powered by a Jaguar straight-six engine, and that the overall concept was that it should hold the same market niche as the original DB4 – an expensive and exotic two-plus-two sports GT car, available in both coupé and soft top. So while the article described exactly in fact what the DB7 turned out to be, the new Aston Martin actually had styling that moved away from the Towns-inspired wedge look, and was very similar to the Jaguar F-type described alongside the new V8.

## DB7 Design and Development

The DB7's styling was done by Ian Callum, and was intended to reflect the style of the Astons from the highlight of the DB era – the DB4, 5 and 6 – but with an added touch of

**The Aston Martin cutaway shows the bones of the DB7. Note the straight-six engine and the front engine and gearbox, and the rear-wheel-drive layout.**

modernity. Callum was also responsible for the styling of the later Jaguar XK8 coupé and inevitably there are similarities to be seen between the two cars. The DB7 was the first complete car styled by Callum, who would go on to head up Jaguar's styling department, and the DB7 was without doubt a masterpiece. Bearing in mind that the basic layout of the car – the wheelbase, passenger placement and mechanical component placement – was already all but fixed by the decision to use the XJS platform, Callum's design managed to be both practical and beautiful.

The first stage of the DB7 project was to build a prototype to present to Ford management so they would sign off the costs needed to take the car into production. This was the sort of work TWR excelled at, and the result was a car that was remarkably close to the actual production models. TWR gambled that a running car would be a better bet than a styling mule, and within three months had assembled a working car that could be driven into Aston Martin's Knightsbridge showroom where the great and the good of Ford's management would be assembled in order to decide whether to take the project forwards. Obviously the use of Jaguar underpinnings and the XJS monocoque helped to speed up the development of the prototype, but it was still an impressive achievement, and the project got the go ahead, with a budget approved that was sufficient to finance the prototype cars needed to make the DB7 project a reality.

### *The Chassis and Bodywork*

The DB7's monocoque was not identical to the XJS unit, but was subtly modified in various areas. It retained the XJS suspension subframe pick-up points and its wheelbase, but the original Jaguar structure was reworked, with subtly modified 'A' pillars and scuttle to give a more sharply raked windscreen line, and the structure in front of the front wheels and behind the rear wheels was shortened as much as possible to reduce the overhangs. While the first prototype had a clamshell-style bonnet, a style last seen on the DB2 Mark III, production models had a conventional bonnet and front wings, as it proved too difficult to produce an accurate composite moulding in practice.

The result was a steel structure made from individual panels welded together. The main structure incorporated the rear wings and roof, and provided pick-up points at the front and rear. At the front there were mounting points for a separate steel subframe that carried the front suspension and the engine, and at the rear a second subframe carried the differential and independent rear suspension in a pressed steel cage

**The DB7 had a Jaguar-derived, independent rear suspension set-up mounted in a separate steel subframe.**

similar to that used by Jaguar since the Mark X and E-Type, albeit with outboard rear disc brakes.

While the DB7's outer panels from the windscreen back were steel and formed part of the monocoque shell, the front wings, bonnet, boot lid and front and rear bumpers were all made from lightweight composite material. The body incorporated some zinc-coated panels, the closed box sections were wax injected, and the complete body structure was subjected to a full electrocoating treatment for further corrosion protection.

One major alteration to the XJS structure was the design and adoption of a modified front subframe. The front subframe carries both the front suspension and the engine. One of the design criteria was to have a low bonnet line without any bulges in the bonnet, as the bulge was considered to be too 'Jaguar' – just look at the bulge in the E-Type's bonnet for confirmation of this! Even though the AJ6 engine was laid over at 15 degrees to the right, the front of the engine, thanks to its cam drive gear, was still too high for the proposed smooth bonnet, necessitating a redesigned subframe to drop to engine height.

### *The Interior*

The DB7's interior, designed by Neil Simpson, was very much a take on the 1990s impression of what a classic British GT car should be, with a feast of leather and woodwork, apparently a stipulation of Walter Hayes. Often described as 'cocoon like', the interior wrapped around the driver and passenger, surrounding them with high quality natural materials with very little plastic in evidence. The specification for the interior equipment was also very high, with electrically operated seats, climate control, and a comprehensive set of instruments to complement the plentitude of leather, plush carpets, and of course wood facings on the dash and doors.

Like all post-war Aston Martins, many fixtures and fittings were sourced from other manufacturers, and in the DB7's case this was almost exclusively from the Ford family of companies.

**The DB7 interior was as traditional as it gets, with leather and wood in abundance. This is a Volante, and shows the heavily padded dashboard.**

While this led to some criticism at the time, as the use of such components was considered inappropriate on an up-market car, without them the DB7 would probably never have been built. The Mazda parts bins supplied the most obvious parts. The door handles were chromed, again apparently at the instance of Hayes, and as the only units from the Ford parts bin that were chromed at the time were from the Mazda 323 Estate, so they were chosen. The interior door-release handles and the front indicator and side-light clusters came from the MX-5. Slightly less recognizable were the rear-light clusters, which also came from the 323, but these were recessed into a frame, which helped to disguise their humble origins. Other parts included Ford switchgear and a Jaguar instrument panel.

### *Steering, Suspension and Brakes*

As would be expected from the use of the XJS monocoque and (albeit modified) front subframe, the DB7's front and rear suspension was Jaguar derived, but with spring and damping rates set up to suit the new car.

The front suspension was a double wishbone system, and used the bottom wishbone as a mounting pan for the bottom of the single large-diameter coil spring, the top of which butted up to the subframe. The anti-roll bar was taken off the lower wishbone using drop links, and was mounted forwards on the subframe. There was a single telescopic damper on each side.

At the rear the classic Jaguar independent rear suspension set-up, encased with the differential in its dedicated subframe, was used. This was based on the dual wishbone set-up, but using the driveshaft as the top link, while the bottom link was really a tubular forked arm rather than a 'traditional' wishbone. Fore and aft location was achieved using a trailing arm, which ran back from a rubber mount on the floor of the monocoque to the bottom link. There were two combined spring damper units on each side, positioned either side of the lower wishbone and with the top mount incorporated in the subframe. The hubs were carried on large cast-alloy carriers, and ran on large diameter roller bearings. The driveshafts had a universal joint at each end – as they formed the top 'wishbone' of the suspension, their length was fixed.

The brakes were, unsurprisingly, discs all round. At the front there were 11.2in (28.4cm) ventilated discs, and the calipers were four piston types made from lightweight alloy. At the rear there were 12in (305mm) diameter ventilated discs mounted outboard on the hubs, which were gripped by four piston alloy calipers. A Teves anti-lock braking system was fitted as standard.

### *The Engine and Transmission*

Paying homage to the tradition originated by the DB2, the DB7 was fitted with a double overhead camshaft straight-six engine. This engine was based on the AJ6 3.6 unit first seen in

**The DB7's straight-six, dohc, 4-valve per cylinder engine was based on the Jaguar AJ6 unit, but was fitted with an Eaton supercharger. It is a tight fit under the DB7's low bonnet.**

the XJS in 1986, which was fitted to the XJS with a 15-degree slant to the right to allow for the XJS's low bonnet line, a trait that was preserved in the DB7. Production XJS 3.6 models were all normally aspirated, although the F-Type project was to have had a twin turbocharger installation. However, in the DB7 the engine was equipped with an Eaton supercharger. This was to ensure that the DB7 engine was different to any other Jaguar unit, as well as Walter Hayes wanting it! In addition a supercharged engine tends to have a much more linear power delivery than a turbo, with none of the problems caused by the turbocharger having to 'spool up', causing lag in the power delivery; this property also made it easier to meet emissions standards, especially when the engine was first started.

As described above, the DB7 unit was a straight-six, double overhead camshaft unit with 4 valves per cylinder. The block and head were made from cast aluminium, and the crankshaft was supported on seven shell-type main bearings. It was derived from the Jaguar AJ6 (Advanced Jaguar 6-cylinder) unit, designed to replace the venerable XK6 unit and which was first used in the 1984 Jaguar XJS; it then went on to power the XK40, the four-door saloon that replaced the Series 3 XJ6 in 1986. The DB7 unit had a new cylinder head, and a bore and stroke of 91 × 83mm, giving a capacity of 3239cc, and unlike any of the Jaguar engines was fitted with a supercharger. The Eaton supercharger was designed to operate at a maximum boost of 1 bar (14 psi), and the engine gave a healthy 335bhp at 5,600rpm, and 368lb ft of torque at 3,000rpm.

## The DB7 Volante

Some eighteen months after the start of production of the DB7, the soft-top version was launched at the Detroit and Los Angeles motor shows in January 1996. Oddly, the design of the Volante had only started once the original coupé version of the DB7 was completed, the explanation for this being that designer Ian Callum did not want to compromise the original coupé design. Cutting the roof off any car usually means there is a reduction in rigidity, and the DB7 was no exception. Building on the experience of producing the soft-top Jaguar XJS, the DB7 Volonte's monocoque was reinforced in the same way, with reinforcing tubes added inside the sills and a cross-brace structure under the floor.

Additional gusseting was also applied to the bottom of the 'A' and 'B' pillars around the new structural elements and elsewhere. Finally the windscreen frame received extensive internal bracing, both to help stiffen the overall structure and to ensure that roll-over protection was maintained.

**The DB7 Volante came out in 1994 and retains the closed car's good looks. While the hood does not fold down fully flush, the tonneau cover keeps things neat.**

**The DB7 Vantage came out in 1999 and was fitted with the new Aston Martin V12 engine. While very similar in looks to the straight six, the main external distinguishing feature are the large driving lights set in the front bumper.**

## The DB7 Vantage

In the middle of 1999 the DB7 became the first Aston Martin to be fitted with the company's new 5935cc V12 engine, and the model was given a new name – the DB7 Vantage. In order to fit the V12 there were modifications to the monocoque, mainly around the transmission tunnel, which had to be enlarged, and the whole understructure was reassessed and stiffened with extra bracing. The interior was updated, with new seats, switchgear and instrument graphics. The car was offered with the V12 in 420bhp tune, with a six-speed manual or optional five-speed automatic gearbox.

The extra airflow needed to cool the larger engine was achieved by making the grille larger, and this also gave the designers the chance to make another nod to Aston Martin's heritage: the new twin round driving lamps mounted below the main headlamps on the front bumper alluded to the DP 212/214/215 works cars of the mid-1960s. In 2000 Aston Martin offered a 'Touchtronic' version of the automatic gearbox, with controls mounted on the steering wheel.

**Under the bonnet of the DB7 Vantage the V12 fills the engine bay.**

## The DB7GT, GTA, Zagato and the DB7-AR1

There were a number of DB7 developments that were produced in small numbers. The DB7GT was a V12-engined coupé introduced in 2002 as a car that offered a little more sports-car DNA than the standard models, which tended towards the GT and 'cruising' end of the market. The new sporting appeal was achieved by fitting a new version of the V12 engine, which was tuned to produce 435bhp and 410lb ft of torque, up 15bhp and 10lb ft from the unit fitted in the DB7 Vantage, but 25bhp less than that produced by the V12 in the newly introduced Vanquish. A stronger clutch was also fitted, and the differential ratio was lower than the standard cars. This gave the car a useful performance boost while not impinging on the Vanquish. The GT's suspension was reworked by ex-Lotus chassis engineer John Miles. The front suspension was rebushed, the bump stops revised to increase wheel travel, and damper fixing points revised.

At the rear the suspension geometry was modified to reduce 'toe out' under heavy braking. All the dampers were modified to provide what was described as 'digressive damping', meaning that the damper effect was reduced the faster a wheel moved. This meant that the base damper setting could be much stiffer than the standard setting, which in turn gave a very compliant ride without the harshness that stiffer springs would give. The steering-rack mounts were stiffened to give a better feel to the steering.

The exterior was also lightly modified: a small GT badge was fitted to the rear, along with a large boot-lid spoiler, while at the front anodized wire-mesh grilles were fitted, along with a pair of bonnet-top grilles to allow hot air to escape from the engine bay. The most obvious modification was the fitment of five-spoke alloy wheels, which, while the same size as before at 8 × 18in front and 9 × 18in rear, were fitted with larger 245/35 × 18 (front) and 265 × 18 (rear) tyres. The brake discs were grooved rather than drilled, and different pads and an uprated servo finished off the changes.

### *The DB7GTA*

The GTA was an automatic version of the GT, fitted with the standard 420bhp engine but which retained all the cosmetic and chassis modifications of the GT. The GT and GTA were only offered in coupé form. Some 190 GTs and 112 GTAs were produced.

### *The DB7 Zagato*

The DB7 Zagato was designed to be a super sports version of the DB7, with increased performance given by lighter weight, enhanced aerodynamics and tuned engine in true Zagato fashion. Work started on the car during 2001, and the project was officially unveiled at the Geneva Motor Show in March 2002. Zagato worked closely with Aston Martin's new design director Helmet Fisker to quickly produce a design that was production ready by June 2002. The car was based on the DB7 Vantage Volante monocoque, mechanics and suspension, but all the aluminium external panels were new, and the wheelbase was reduced from the standard 102in (2,591mm) to 99.6in (2,531mm); also the weight of the car was significantly less than the standard Volante at 3,828lb (1,740kg) – the Volante being 4,125lb (1,875kg) – but only 22lb (10kg) lighter than the standard Vantage Coupé's 3,850lb (1,750kg) thanks to the weightier Volante underpinning.

Sporting the Zagato trademark double-bubble roof, a massive but attractive Aston Martin grilled front end, muscular Vanquish-style flanks, and an all-new style tail with a small drop-down hatch to access the boot space, the DB7 Zagato

**The DB7 Zagato marked Aston Martin's return to the limited edition market with a distinctive and comprehensive rejig of the DB7 by Italian coachbuilders Zagato.**

**The trademark double bubble roof on the DB7 Zagato is apparent from this angle.**

was a handsome car – and also rare. The Zagato's V12 was in GT tune, with 425bhp and 410lb ft of torque, and a manual six-speed gearbox, giving a top speed of around 185mph (298km/h) and a 0–60 time of 4.8sec. In all, ninety-nine DB7 Zagatos were sold, with one car (chassis no. 100) retained by Aston Martin.

### *The DB7-AR1*

The DB7-AR1 was a 'roadster', a roofless two-seater produced for the American market. The cars were intended for a dry climate as they had no roof at all. The car was designed by Zagato, but unlike the DB7 Zagato, was based on the standard wheelbase DB7 Volante chassis and mechanicals. There were no real issues in removing the roof, and the car featured a front end broadly the same as the DB7 Zagato, but it had a completely new 'double bubble' rear deck that mirrored the traditional Zagato roof treatment, and a conventional boot lid. Longer doors meant changes to the front and rear wings, and there were three small air ducts added under the large main grille. Mechanically the car could be specified with either the Zagato/GT specification V12 with six-speed manual gearbox, or the Volante's 420bhp V12 with five-speed ZF touchtronic gearbox. Like the DB7 Zagato, the DB7-AR1 had a production run of only 100 cars, with the final car retained by Aston Martin.

## In Conclusion: The DB7 Game Changer

The DB7 was undoubtedly the car that saved Aston Martin in the 1990s. It changed the company from being an anachronism producing very small numbers of very expensive cars for a few very, very wealthy customers, to a company that, while still being an aspirational brand, could supply relatively reasonably priced cars in relatively reasonable numbers to relatively wealthy customers. On its introduction the 'basic' DB7 Coupé cost around £65,000 in the UK, while the other Aston Martin product, the then current Vantage version of the Virage, was an eye-watering £177,000.

The DB7 put Aston Martin back into the market competing against the top end Mercedes and BMW coupés, and Porsche with its 928. It meant that people could aspire to owning an Aston, rather than just dreaming about them, and sent a strong message to the market that Aston Martin meant business. As an aside, the introduction of Jaguar's 'E-Type replacement', the 1986 XK8, was also based on the XJS platform but was powered by a new V8 engine, and actually served to neatly mirror the relationship between the DB4 and the E-Type back in the 1960s. The cars were quite close in size and performance, but the Jaguar was cheaper to buy (under £50,000 when introduced, as compared to the DB7's £65,000), and was made in greater numbers than the DB7. Thus the two cars were not, strictly speaking, competitors, rather they complemented each other in the overall Ford PAC range of cars. While the DB7 probably looked a little nicer than the XK8, both cars were impressive examples of a traditional British GT coupé.

The DB7 also took Aston Martin back into the coachbuilt market, the DB7 Zagato and DB7-AR1 harking back to Aston Martin glory days, and other coachbuilders, such as Giorgetto Giugariaro's Twenty Twenty concept car by Italdesign, and Pininfarina's AM3 and AM4, which were rebodied DB7 Vantages built for the Brunei Royal collection.

**Walter Hayes shows Fiona Fullerton around the Aston Martin Vantage at the 1992 Motor Show at the NEC Birmingham, UK.**

## KEY FIGURES

### Walter Hayes, Chairman from 1991

Walter Hayes was born in 1924 and initially went into journalism, progressing to be editor of the *Sunday Despatch* newspaper in 1956. In this role he met Lotus founder Colin Chapman, who wrote a motoring column for the paper. Hayes then went on to join Ford as Director of Public Affairs in January 1962. While at Ford, Hayes had a long history of promoting motor sport: he worked with Lotus in the 1960s to create the Lotus Cortina, and promoted sports models in the Ford range throughout the 1960s and 1970s – this included being involved in the Shelby/AC relationship that resulted in the Cobra. He also had a great deal of influence in the creation of Ford Advanced Vehicles, builders of the GT40 under ex-Aston Martin competition manager John Wyer. He was an advocate of the Ford Advanced Vehicle Operation, based at Aveley in Essex, that built Ford's 'RS' cars, and was also involved with Ford's buying into AC in 1986.

Hayes retired as vice chairman of Ford Europe in 1989, but retained a close relationship with the Ford company through his friendship with Henry Ford II. This relationship both influenced Ford when Aston Martin was bought, and resulted in Hayes being brought in as a director of Aston Martin in 1988; he became chairman of Aston Martin in 1991 when Gauntlett stepped down as chairman, and sold his remaining shareholding to Ford. He eventually retired in 1994, once the DB7 project was firmly under way. In 1982 Hayes was awarded a CBE for services to the motor industry. He died on 26 December 2000.

### Ian Callum, Designer

Ian Callum was born in Dumfries, Scotland, in 1954. He studied at Lancaster Polytechnic's School of Transportation Design, and then gained a degree in Industrial Design at the Glasgow School of Art, followed by a Masters in Automotive Design at the Royal College of Art. He joined Ford in 1979, where he worked on the design of various car parts – to quote him: 'bits of cars, mainly steering wheels' – but he also contributed to iconic cars such as the RS200 and the RS Cosworth. His final role at Ford was in Italy, where he headed up the Ghia Design Studio, working on the Via, Zig, and Zag concept cars.

In 1990 Callum left Ford to form TWR with Peter Stevens and Tom Walkinshaw, and in 1991 he was appointed chief designer and general manager of TWR Design. He was involved in the design of the DB7 and the Vanquish, and continued to oversee design at Aston Martin, where he worked on the DB9 and the Vantage. In 1999 he moved to Jaguar (then owned by Ford) while still looking after Aston Martin. In 2019 Callum left Jaguar in order to set up his own Warwick-based automotive product design agency, called simply 'Callum'. He was retained by Jaguar as a design consultant.

## DB7 TECHNICAL DESCRIPTION

The DB7, introduced as a Coupé in 1993, and in 1996 in open-topped Volante form, was arguably the car that saved Aston Martin. Based on a modified Jaguar XJS steel monocoque and styled by Ian Callum, the DB7 was a beautiful looking and very competent GT car. Front-engined and with rear-wheel drive, the car was powered by a supercharged straight-six engine that was based on Jaguar's AJ6 unit. Coupled to a manual five-speed or a four-speed automatic gearbox, the car had a top speed of 165mph (265km/h) and a 0–60 time of 5.7sec. The suspension was also Jaguar derived, independent all round with double wishbones front and rear, with coil springs and telescopic dampers all round.

## SPECIFICATION TABLE: ASTON MARTIN DB7

| | | |
|---|---|---|
| **Layout and chassis** | Front-engined, rear-drive two-plus-two sports car. Closed two-door body, steel monocoque body structure, composite front wings, bonnet, boot lid, sill panels | |
| **Engine** | | |
| Type | Straight six, twin overhead camshaft, 4 valves per cylinder | |
| Block material | Aluminium alloy | |
| Head material | Aluminium alloy | |
| Cylinders | 6 in-line | |
| Cooling | Centrifugal pump with water/antifreeze mix | |
| Bore and stroke | 91 × 83mm | |
| Capacity | 3228cc | |
| Valves | 4 valves per cylinder, operated directly via bucket tappets from chain-driven double overhead camshafts | |
| Compression ratio | 8.3:1 | |
| Induction system | Eaton M90 supercharger, Rootes type with bypass air system | |
| Fuel system | Twin pump electronic sequential fuel injection | |
| Max. power | 335bhp @ 5,600rpm | |
| Max. torque | 368lb/ft @ 3,000rpm | |
| **Transmission** | | |
| Gearbox | (5-speed manual) | |
| Overall ratios | 1st: | 3.55:1 |
| | 2nd: | 2.04:1 |
| | 3rd: | 1.40:1 |
| | 4th: | 1.00:1 |
| | 5th: | 0.74:1 |
| Final drive | Limited slip, 3.5:1 | |
| Gearbox (4-speed auto) | | |
| Overall ratios | 1st: | 2.48:1 |
| | 2nd: | 1.48:1 |
| | 3rd: | 1.00:1 |
| | 4th: | 0.75:1 |
| Final drive | Limited slip, 3.54:1 | |
| **Suspension and steering** | | |
| Front | Independent, double wishbone with coil over dampers. Anti-roll bar | |
| Rear | Independent, double wishbone. Coil springs with dual dampers on each side | |
| Steering | Rack-and-pinion, power assisted, 2.54 turns lock to lock | |
| Wheels | 18in diameter 8in wide alloy wheels | |
| Tyres | 245/40 ZR 18in | |
| **Brakes** | | |
| Type | Front and rear hydraulically operated discs. Teves anti-lock system | |
| Size (front) | 11.18in (28.4cm) diameter ventilated steel disc, four piston calipers | |
| Size (rear) | 12in (30.5cm) diameter ventilated steel disc, sliding aluminium calipers with drum handbrake | |
| **Capacities** | | |
| Fuel capacity | 19.6gal (89.1ltr) | |
| **Dimensions** | | |
| Track | | |
| Front: | 60in (1,524mm) | |
| Rear: | 60.25in (1,530mm) | |
| Wheelbase | 102in (2,591mm) | |
| Overall length | 182.25in (4,631mm) | |
| Overall width | 71.5in (1,820mm) | |
| Overall height | 50in (1,268mm) | |
| Weight | 3,804lb (1,725kg) | |
| **Performance** | | |
| Top speed | 165mph (266km/h) | |
| 0–60 | 5.7sec | |

CHAPTER 9

# THE START OF THE GAYDON ERA: 2000–2014

After Ford's purchase of the company in 1987, Aston Martin had the financial backing and management expertise to embark on a long-term plan to bring the company back into profit. This would not be an easy task – Aston Martin would need to design a new and attractive model range, which, while building on the good will and customer acceptance of the DB7, would need to be produced in larger numbers in order to make the company viable. The company would also need to be careful to preserve its core values: producing good-looking, high performance cars powered by an Aston Martin engine, which would appeal to and actually sell to a wider audience than the current range.

To achieve these aims the company saw the need not only to plan for an all-new GT car to replace the DB7, but also to produce a more sports-oriented car to compete in the two-seat sports-car market, which had for so long been dominated by the Porsche 911, as well as a traditional hand-built supercar to replace the Virage-derived models. The hand-built flagship model would be expected to sell in smaller numbers, and would be much more expensive than the GT and sports cars.

**The DB9 was the first of the Gaydon-era cars. With its VH-architecture chassis, the Aston Martin V12 engine, and a combination of alloy and composite body panels, it is all Aston Martin.**

## THE COMPANY

A very significant event occurred in 2000, with the appointment of Dr Ulrich Bez as CEO. The experienced automotive engineer had a clear and unambiguous aim for Aston Martin, and in contrast to the previous Ford-appointed CEOs who tended to move on after a year or so, Bez asked for a term of a minimum of five years so he could take a long-term strategic approach to running Aston Martin. After a few months at the helm, in August 2001 Bez gave Ford three options for their continuing stewardship of Aston Martin. These were to shut the company down, to allow the company to be bought by Bez himself, or to invest 300 million dollars in Aston Martin and give Bez four years to turn the company around.

Luckily for Aston Martin Ford took the third option, giving the company a firm base on which to move forwards on its own terms under Bez's leadership. Bez realized that if Aston Martin were to survive as a maker of fine automobiles, it would need to follow its own path and not rely on platforms and engines from other manufacturers. The injection of cash and time by Ford also meant that Aston Martin at last had the resources to acquire a new, purpose-built home.

In 2003 Aston Martin opened its new factory on a 55-acre (22ha) site at Gaydon in Warwickshire, which was next to Jaguar's research and development centre. The Aston Martin site was the first purpose-built factory in Aston Martin's history, and comprised an 8,000sq m front building and a 35,000sq m production building, where production of the DB9 coupé commenced in that year. In 2007 the Design Centre was added to the side of the main Gaydon building: this included a design studio in which the creative teams of designers tasked with designing all-new Aston Martins would work. Having the design studio on site was a major boost to the design process,

**The author's DB9. Looking from above, the clean lines and great styling are obvious.**

and enabled Bez to adopt a hands-on approach to the cars' designs.

In 2001, Bez appointed ex-BMW Tecknic and BMW's California-based industrial design studio Designworks Hendrick Fisker as head of design at Aston Martin. Fisker's first task was to bring the DB9 and Vantage concepts – already mostly

**The Gaydon facility is a modern, built-for-purpose building, the first time Aston Martin has had its own purpose-built factory.**

**The Vantage was the sports car of the range. A two-seater, the car had a hatchback to give it a modicum of practicality. It shares the good looks of the DB9 with some subtle differences. This is Jeff Sear's 2017 V12-powered Vantage S.**

complete designs by Ian Callum – into a production-ready form. Fisker left Aston Martin in 2005 to form his own company, 'Fisker Coachbuild'. He was replaced with Englishman Marek Reichman, whose CV included stints at Rover and BMW Designworks, and who designed the 2003 Range Rover. At the time of writing, Reichman was still Aston Martin's chief designer, and had overseen the design of all Aston Martin models after the Callum/Fisker-designed DB9 and Vantage.

Finally the last part of the Aston Martin production jigsaw was placed, with the official opening of the Aston Martin Engine Plant in October 2004, which would be used to produce the engines for the DB9 and Vantage. The plant was sited in Ford Germany's Neihl plant on Cologne, and comprised a 12,500sq m area dedicated to Aston Martin production. With 100 technicians in place, the plant was designed to produce up to 5,000 engines per year – V8s and V12s, and, in the Aston Martin tradition, a single technician was responsible for building up each engine.

**The Vantage was originally powered by a V8 engine. Although derived from the Jaguar AJ-V8, the Aston Martin unit shares only the cam covers, and is hand built at the Aston Martin engine plant.**

## THE ENGINES: THE NEW ASTON MARTIN V8

The Vantage's all-alloy, quad-cam, 32-valve V8 is loosely based on the Jaguar AJ-V8 unit, and while it uses the Jaguar block casting, the only common parts between the two makes are the rocker covers. With all-new machining on the main block casting and all-new internals, the engine can rightly be claimed to be an Aston Martin unit. The bore and stroke of 89 × 86mm give a capacity of 4280cc (generally referred to as 4.2-litre), and with a compression ratio of 11.3:1, the unit gives maximum power of 380bhp.

A further refinement is the use of variable inlet cam timing, designed to give improved end throttle response and improved mid-range torque. Power was a healthy 380bhp at 7,000rpm, and torque was 302lb ft at 5,000rpm. The twin overhead camshafts were driven from the crankshaft with y-Vo inverted teeth chains, and the valves were operated directly from the cams using bucket tappets. The exhaust system featured an active valve system that opens above 4,500rpm, giving a slight power boost and an aural reward for the driver. The smaller size, both in capacity and physical dimensions, means that the V8 is some 100kg lighter than the V12 unit.

The engine was fitted with a dry-sump oil system, giving the unit a very shallow sump, which enabled the unit to fit very low down and far back in the Vantage's chassis. Post-2008, 4.3 units have revised engine-management programming, which gave an improvement in fuel consumption and a corresponding drop in $CO_2$ emissions.

The V8 was upgraded in 2009. While the overall architecture of the engine remained the same, the new version of the engine featured a revised bore and stroke of 91 × 91mm, giving a capacity of 4735cc; it is generally referred to as the 4.7-litre unit. The block, still based on the Jaguar AJ-V8 component, featured pressed-in cylinder liners rather than the original 4.3 unit's cast-in liners. One important element of the redesign was to minimize the effects of local air movement within the engine as the pistons went up and down. Inter-bay drillings were made between cylinder walls, allowing the air pushed down by descending pistons to be quickly dissipated into the spaces left by adjoining pistons, and sump design was changed to allow for better air flow within the crankcases. These changes alone were believed to give an additional 5bhp, thanks to reduced resistance from air pressure within the engine.

The engine was fitted with a crankshaft, which as well as catering for the longer stroke, had revised drillings in the

**The Vantage engine sits further back in the car than the DB9's longer V12 unit, improving weight distribution and giving the Vantage quicker handling.**

rotating balance masses to lighten it and give better throttle response. The con rods and pistons were both changed to reflect the larger bore and stroke, the heads had revised inlet manifolds and 1mm larger diameter valves for better breathing, and the timing gear had stronger chains to drive the camshafts. With these modifications the 4.7-litre unit offered a significant increase in power and torque over the 4.3-litre unit, with 420bhp at 7,000rpm and 347lb ft at 5,000rpm.

The unit fitted in the Vantage 4.7S was built to a similar internal specification, but the combination of revised and improved intake plumbing, a new, less restrictive exhaust with revised times for the bypass valves, and revised ignition programming, upped the power by 10bhp and the torque by 15lb ft.

## THE CARS

The cars produced by Aston Martin from 2005 shared the VH platform, which, although similar in concept to the carbon-fibre and aluminium chassis used on the Vanquish, was an all-new structure, made from extruded aluminium and bonded together. The VH1 platform sat under the DB9, and a shortened version, named VH2, was used on the Vantage. The platform underwent some minor revisions in 2009, and the next generation, VH3 or VH300, appeared in 2011 with additional carbon-fibre elements. The final version of the VH platform, VH4 or VH310, was developed from VH3 to give the longer wheelbase needed for the Rapide, introduced in 2009.

Thanks to the use of the VH platform, Aston Martin was able to produce a large number of different models, which, apart from the mainstream DB9, Vantage and Rapide, tended to be made in very small numbers. Hence there are a bewildering number of Aston Martin models made at this time, which are not only very similar visually, but also share their underpinnings – which can, and does, confuse many observers!

### The VH Platform

The introduction of the DB9 in 2004 marked two important milestones for Aston Martin: it was the first car to be produced at the all-new production plant at Gaydon, Warwickshire, and it was the first to be based on the company's new 'Vertical Horizontal', or 'VH' architecture to form the underlying structure of the vehicle. Prior to the Gaydon plant's opening, the Virage family produced at Aston Martin's original post-war home at Newport Pagnell had used the final development of Harold Beach's original steel DB4 platform chassis, while the

**The Rapide had the longest wheelbase of the Gaydon-era cars. A four-door, four-seat saloon, it was introduced in 2009.**

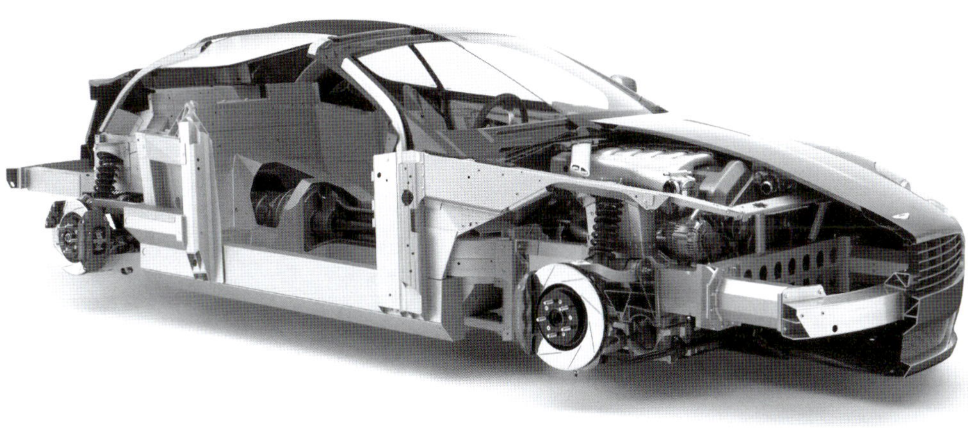

**The VH platform was made from extruded aluminium members and pressings, which were bonded together to form a rigid body tub.**

**The drivetrain and suspension of a VH platform Aston Martin forms a separate sub assembly which bolts onto the VH chassis. Front and rear subframes are joined by a torque tube, inside which runs the propellor shaft.**

Bloxham-produced DB7 had used a development of the Jaguar XJS platform. The Newport Pagnell-produced Vanquish of the 2000s used the forerunner to the VH platform, in the shape of a chassis (or platform) designed with the help of Lotus, who used their experience to produce the Lotus Elise platform.

The Elise platform was made from extruded aluminium sections, aluminium sheet and carbon-fibre structures bonded and riveted together to form a rigid and stiff platform or chassis, on to which were affixed composite non load-bearing body panels. The Elise's design was fairly simple, catering for the rear-engine, rear-wheel-drive layout of the Elise, which, combined with the car's low weight, meant the front element only had to support the suspension and steering loads, while the one-piece engine and transmission was a compact unit located just behind the cabin. In the Vanquish's case its front/mid-engine, rear-wheel-drive configuration required a complete redesign as the chassis was doing a very different job to that of the Elise.

So while the Vanquish chassis used the principles of the Elise chassis design, the execution was very different. One of the major changes was to the chassis layout, with the adoption of a carbon-fibre transmission tunnel that formed the structural basis of the whole structure, as well as redesigning the Elise's side sills to allow for the Aston's substantial door openings. The Vanquish platform's aluminium and carbon-fibre components were glued together using a heat-cured epoxy resin glue, and a feature carried over from the Lotus platform was the use of micro-ribs on the surfaces of each glued joint: these served to set the exact gap for the glue, and stopped the glue being extruded when the parts were assembled in the jig.

The design of the structure of the Vanquish platform was a step towards the design of the platform used on the mainstream Gaydon-produced Aston Martins, the VH platform. These cars, primarily the DB9 and the Vantage, would form the majority of the cars produced by the company between 2004 and 2015. The Vanquish platforms were produced by external firm Hydro Aluminium, who also produced a few DB9 VH platforms before production was taken in-house at Gaydon.

The purpose of the VH platform was to provide a flexible and configurable base on which to base future Aston Martin models. The 'Vertical', or 'V', refers to the body construction techniques, while the 'Horizontal', or 'H', refers to the systems, including components such as the engine, from the drivetrain, the suspension, interior trim and dashboards. The prime objective of the 'VH' platform was to give the company the ability to roll out changes quickly and easily across the project range, as well as making it easier to introduce new models with less engineering effort.

The need for flexibility meant that the components used to construct the platform were mainly extruded aluminium members and aluminium sheet. The all-aluminium core tub design had a standard bulkhead, and the addition of different length aluminium extrusions running longitudinally or transversely meant that the length and width of the bodyshell could be altered to suit the car's requirements. The extrusions were bonded and riveted in place, and front and rear subframes were fitted to fixed points to carry the engine, transmission and suspension. While the body panels were mainly aluminium, the front wings, sill and boot lids were usually formed in composite material, and the Vantage and Rapide used steel rear quarter panels. The original VH bodyshells built at Gaydon were assembled and glued together by Aston Martin's first robot, nicknamed 'James Bonder'.

The first fruit of the VH platform, designated VH1, was the DB9. The second generation, or VH2, came with the introduction of the DBS of 2008 and was shared with the V12 Vantage. The 'V' elements introduced carbon-fibre elements of the body, while the 'H' elements included adaptive damping and carbon-fibre brakes. VH3 was introduced by the Rapide, with its longer wheelbase and isolated front and rear subframes, while VH4 was the all carbon-fibre Vanquish.

**The Vanquish was Aston Martin's flagship from 2001, pre-dating the DB9 and replacing the Virage/Vantage. Hand built at Newport Pagnell, the Vanquish used an all-new chassis that would evolve into the VH platform.**

## The Vanquish

The Vanquish replaced the line of Virage-derived cars as the flagship of the Aston Martin range, and while still hand built at Newport Pagnell, was an all-new design. Unveiled at the Geneva Motor Show of 2001, the Vanquish was powered by the V12 engine first seen in the DB7 Vantage, and was very similar in appearance to the 'Project Vantage Concept' seen at the North American International Motor Show at Detroit in January 1998.

The car was styled by Ian Callum and offered a glimpse of the future of Aston Martin with its revolutionary bonded aluminium and carbon-fibre chassis, the development of which led to the 'VH' platform (*see above* for details). The body panels were aluminium, and were hand finished after being pressed, rather than formed fully by hand. Styling was an evolution of the DB7, with elements of the DB7 Zagato, including the muscular haunches, and was a signpost to the appearance of the DB9.

The interior also moved away from the traditional 'wood and leather' seen on the DB7 and the last V8 Coupés, with aluminium trim replacing the walnut and a much more modern feel to the cabin, with its prominent 'waterfall' centre console, which would next be seen on the DB9.

The Vanquish was powered by the company's V12 engine first seen in the DB7 Vantage, but in a different state of tune, giving 466bhp and 400lb ft of torque; it was front-engined, with the engine linked to the transaxle via a short propshaft.

**The trademark styling feature of the Vanquish is the muscular haunches that cover the rear wheels and extend into the door.**

The interior of Rob Smith's Vanquish, showing how it set the design cues for the interiors of the DB9 and Vantage models that would follow.

Under the bonnet of the Vanquish sits the Aston Martin V12 engine. The use of carbon fibre in the car is emphasized by the sculptured brace between the front suspension turrets.

The car was fitted with a six-speed automated manual transmission derived from that used in manual form in the DB7 and Chrysler Viper. The box was modified by Italian company Magneti-Marelli and Ford so switches on the steering wheel could be used to operate the gear change and clutch mechanisms manually, or it could be switched into automatic mode. The press at the time reported that the box was superb when driving fast, with very fast changes and great gear choice, giving the car an excellent performance. The downside was that the box could cook the clutch at low speeds in heavy traffic, when the changes could also be jerky.

Front suspension was by double wishbones, and at the rear the independent suspension was also double aluminium wishbones; the stiffness of the underlying chassis meant that the springs and dampers could be soft and compliant, giving the car a good ride as well as excellent handling and roadholding.

With a coefficient of drag of 0.33 and power output of 460bhp, coupled to a six-speed automated manual transmission, the Vanquish could do 0–60mph in under 5sec, and had a top speed of 190mph (305km/h).

Made from 2004 through to 2007, the Vanquish S was an updated version of the original Vanquish, with new wheels, a revised nose, a small lip spoiler on the boot lid that incorporated the high level rear brake light, a Vanquish S badge on the rear, along with a lower rear splitter in the rear bumper. The aerodynamic tweaks reduced the car's coefficient of drag to 0.32. In addition the car received as standard the elements of the 2004 Vanquish Sports Dynamic package, namely stiffer suspension, revised steering ratio and larger brakes. The most important modification was to the engine, which now gave a claimed 520bhp; along with the aerodynamic tweaks, this gave the car a top speed of 200mph (322km/h).

The Vanquish was a long-lasting model, always hand built but sold in relatively large numbers for a flagship model, with 656 sold in its best year, 2003, and then production running at a little over 300 per year until 2007. The flagship of the range then passed over to the DBS, until the second generation Vanquish was introduced in 2012. This was based on the DBS, retaining the front-engine, rear-transmission layout, and was built around a variant of the VH platform rather than the original Vanquish's chassis design. The platform is described by Aston Martin as the fourth generation of the VH platform, with extensive modifications to take into account newer crash legislation, including the use of carbon-fibre panels behind the bulkhead and carbon-fibre outer panels.

Under the skin of the second generation Vanquish is its light alloy and composite structure, which was evolved from the VH platform. This is the AMHT's cutaway of the 2012 Vanquish S, with a carbon-fibre body rather than the alloy panels of the first-generation cars.

**The Vanquish was used as the basis of a range of Zagato-styled cars – this is the Shooting Brake from 2016.**

The second generation Vanquish was another evolution of the Vanquish/DBS style, with a large carbon-fibre front spoiler and LED light blades embedded in the headlights, along with carbon-fibre sill trims and rear splitter. The body panels were all made from carbon fibre covered in an epoxy layer to provide a good paint key. The car was powered by a 565bhp version of the V12, and a Volante version was added in 2013. In 2014 the cars gained an eight-speed gearbox, and in 2016 the engine was uprated to give 592bhp. Zagato versions were launched in late 2016, with a coupé, shooting brake, convertible or speedster models. Only ninety-nine coupés, shooting brakes and convertibles were made, along with twenty-eight speedsters.

## The DB9

The first car to come out of the new Gaydon factory, and the first to use the new VH chassis, was the DB9. The car was the logical successor for the DB7, and because the DB7 was the most successful Aston Martin model in terms of numbers sold, the DB9 had big boots to fill. And it did so with unqualified success. The car's structure, running gear and transmission were all new, and only the V12 motor was shared with the outgoing DB7. The car immediately dispelled the 'Jag in drag' connotations of the DB7: with its superb styling, and underpinnings that were exclusive to Aston Martin, the DB9 was exactly what Aston Martin needed, and made a bold statement as to the direction the company would take in the 2000s and beyond.

### *Structure*

The DB9's structure took the Vanquish's design a further step forwards. It was designed in a direct collaboration with Worcester-based company Hydro Aluminium/Raufoss, who

**From any angle the DB9 is a good-looking car. This view of the author's black 2007 DB9 alongside Roland Long's 2005 example shows the lines of the car.**

also manufacture the Vanquish and DB9 tubs. The DB9 VH frames were constructed using the same gluing techniques as the Vanquish, but with the addition of self-piercing rivets in some areas. Another important technological innovation on the DB9 was the use of ultrasonic welding to join the aluminium panels that make up the upper and lower 'C' pillars of the body. The welding uses a sonic electrode, or 'sonotrode', to generate high frequency (20kHz) vibration to fuse the panels together at a molecular level. As the process uses no heat there is no possibility of creating oxides to contaminate the join, and there is no risk of heat distortion to the panels. The overall VH platform used for the DB9 was designated 'VH1' by the factory.

*Exterior*

The DB9's windscreen frame was made from cast aluminium, and the steering column and inner door frames were constructed from lightweight magnesium alloy. The bonnet, roof and rear wing panels were 'superformed' – a process of pressing the panel's basic shape using dies – before they were hand finished. The front wings and the boot lid were moulded in composite material. The complete bodyshell was assembled in the Gaydon factory, when the body panels were glued in position on the base VH platform. Aston Martin's first robot, nicknamed 'James Bonder', was used to apply the glue to the shell and place the panels in position ready for curing. When assembled, the body's torsional strength was measured at 27kN per degree – around twice that of the outgoing DB7.

Front and rear suspension followed the example set in the Vanquish, with double wishbones all round. Ventilated brakes were outboard discs, with 355mm-diameter units up front complemented by 330mm units on the rear. The multi-spoke alloy wheels were 8J × 19in front and 9.0J × 19in rear.

*Interior*

The DB9's interior was a step forwards from the DB7. The waterfall dash centre, first seen on the Vanquish, was refined, with the upper part clad in a choice of polished wood – mahogany, piano black or bamboo; the sat nav was concealed under a rotating flap at the top, above five round buttons sitting below a pair of air vents. These buttons were four gearbox controls (P, R, N and D) with a backlit 'Start' button sitting in the middle. Below this were the stereo controls with a small screen, and ancillary and somewhat small, fiddly and indistinctly marked rectangular push buttons sitting above three rotary switches that control the heating and ventilation.

The centre console then flattens out between the seats, with a small cubbyhole and four further buttons at its rear for sport mode, heated front and rear screens, and front park mode buzzer (when fitted). The sides of the console are trimmed in leather, as is the plain passenger side dash; the top of the instrument cluster faces the driver. In the cluster is the speedometer and tachometer, along with fuel and temperature gauges, and a number of electrofluorescent warning lights and a small digital display. The display can be set to display the speed, which is a useful function as the 220mph (350km/h) speedometer has small and hard-to-read graphics, making it easy to go faster than the speed limit.

The rest of the cabin is trimmed in leather, including the door cards and the seats, which are electrically adjustable

**The DB9 is also a true driver's car. As a Grand Tourer it is capable of travelling fast and far.**

The DB9's interior is an evolution of that first seen on the Vanquish. The 'waterfall'-style dash centre could be had in walnut, bamboo or piano black wood, as could the door tops; the rear is trimmed in leather.

using Ford controls mounted on the side of the centre console. While the rear seats are small they can seat an adult, but the front seat needs to be positioned fairly far forwards. All in all the interior is a very attractive and modern design, and importantly is very comfortable, making it the ideal place for a couple of hundred miles of fast travel for two people.

### *The DB9 Volante*

The soft-top DB9 Volante was released in 2005, the power-operated hood giving the car a notchback appearance with a separate boot. The hood fitted flush under an opening panel between the boot lid and the cabin, leaving a flush rear deck making for a good-looking car which retained the rear seats.

### *The Engine*

The DB9 was powered by the AE28 V12 unit. Fitted well back behind the front axle line, the car is arguably a mid/

The DB9 Volante was introduced in 2005; the top folds down flush with the rear deck, making it a cleaner design than the DB7.

With the hood up the DB9 Volante is a pleasing and sleek looker.

Under the bonnet the DB9's V12 fills the engine bay. The view is dominated by the inlet manifold's air tubes, and the strut brace bisects the bay.

front engine configuration. In the DB9 the V12 is tuned to give 450bhp at 6,000rpm along with 420lb ft of torque at 5,000rpm. In the DB9 it pulls the car along effortlessly and discreetly, with more than ample power and torque to give the car an impressive performance.

### Gearbox and Steering

The DB9 was fitted with a ZF HP26 six-speed automatic gearbox, operated through a torque converter and fitted in a transaxle casing located in the rear of the car. While the transmission was a traditional automatic, a sport mode was also available, with the gearbox change up and down at higher revs than the default mode. In addition, a semi-manual 'Touchtronic' mode was available, so the driver could make manual gear changes using the pair of cast-alloy 'flappy paddles' mounted on the steering column.

A manual option was also offered, in which case a new rear-mounted transaxle was fitted, with a six-speed plus reverse, Italian-sourced Graziano gearbox, combined with a plate-type limited slip differential. The interior of the manual car featured a gear lever mounted on the centre console, which operated the gearbox directly using cables. The clutch was a hydraulically operated, twin-plate unit, which, along with the flywheel, replaced the torque converter fitted to the automatic cars and was fitted to the end of the engine.

### The DB9 Going Forwards

The DB9 was given a facelift in 2008, the main change being an increase in engine power to 470bhp and 443lb ft of torque, giving a small performance boost. In 2013 the car was given a refresh, with some changes to the front bumper, and clear and rear tail lights; the suspension was updated by fitting

Roland Long's DB9 complements the background at Poole Harbour. Roland thinks the DB9 is probably the best-looking car Aston Martin have produced to date.

adaptive dampers, which rendered the original model's optional sport pack obsolete. The final version of the DB9 was the DB9GT introduced in 2015. The engine power was increased to 540bhp at 6,750rpm, and torque was 457lb ft at 5,500rpm.

## The Aston Martin Vantage V8 (2005–2018)

While the 2004 DB9 heralded Aston Martin's new range of cars produced at Gaydon on the VH platform, the Vantage was the car that successfully repositioned Aston Martin back into the sports car class, which it arguably last occupied with the DB4GT. Intended to be a competitor for the Porsche 911, the Vantage was a strict two-seater, and was equipped with a hatchback for increased flexibility.

Introduced in 2005, the VH underpinnings of the Vantage were similar to that of the DB9, but with detailed differences to accommodate the shorter wheelbase and V8 engine: it was designated VH2.

Otherwise the Vantage was very much a mini DB9 – the interior was very similar, apart from having a shorter cabin with no rear seats, and a hatchback for slightly more practicality when carrying luggage. Also the shorter wheelbase and

**The Vantage has a shorter wheelbase than the DB9, but is otherwise very similar as regards styling. The giveaway is the traditional wing strake ends at the door line.**

**The Vantage is a strict two-seater but does have a hatchback for a minimum of practicality. There is plenty of room for luggage for two, with a low lip to aid loading.**

different suspension settings gave the car a more sporting feel as compared to the DB9's Grand Touring approach, with stiffer suspension giving the car sharper handling.

The 4.3-litre V8 produced 380bhp at 7,300rpm and 308lb ft of torque at 5,000rpm, so it needed to be revved to give its best, and the six-speed manual Graziano transaxle needed to be used to get the best out of the car. The main downside to the set-up was that the clutch could took only 25,000 miles (40,000km) and it was a big job to change it. However, the car received excellent reviews, and proved to be extremely popular with the buying public. The press generally considered it to be a plausible competitor to the class benchmark, the Porsche 911, and sales reflected this, with twice as many Vantages selling as compared to DB9s in the first couple of years of production; but then it was some 20 per cent cheaper than the larger car.

The Vantage Roadster appeared in 2007, with the hood giving the car a notchback appearance with a separate boot.

The N400 was a special edition launched in 2007 to celebrate the V8 production racer beating the 8min lap on the Nürburgring. A total of 480 was produced, split between coupés and roadsters, and these had modified sills, clear rear lights, silver mesh behind the bonnet and wing vents, and a choice of three colours – black, silver or orange.

In 2007 the Vantage was given a mid-life update with the 4.7-litre version of the V8, which gave 420bhp; then in 2010 the special edition N420 was launched. In 2011 a new top model was added to the range: the Vantage 'S', which had an extra 10bhp and a top speed of 190mph (305km/h), thanks to the engine's ability to rev slightly higher, at 7,450rpm.

## Aston Martin Vantage V12 (2009–2018)

Thanks to the flexibility of the VH platform, it was possible to fit the DB9's V12 into the Vantage, but it needed some lateral thinking. Bez describes how the engineers initially struggled to physically fit the V12 into the existing Vantage V8's engine bay. However, the VH architecture meant that it was perfectly feasible to graft the DB9's engine bay (along with the V12) on to the Vantage's passenger compartment, and then add the Vantage's shorter front module on the nose of the car. The V12 did have a shallower sump to allow for the greater cornering forces the Vantage could generate. The homologation of the car for the US regulations also caused some headaches, but by first producing a European market car and doing some light modifications, the car passed its US track tests. The V12 Vantage was fitted with DBS carbon ceramic brakes and lightweight 19in wheels.

## Aston Martin Rapide (2009–2020)

Design of the four-door, four-seater Rapide was started in 2005, with newly appointed design director Marek Reichman at the helm. The initial concept was fleshed out in some five weeks, and thanks to the flexibility of the VH platform and the use of the DB9 engine, transmission and running gear, the first prototype was built up in only four months by a dedicated team of twenty-six engineers. This fully functional car made its public debut at the January 2006 Detroit Motor Show, where it was presented as a concept car to compete against other four-door rivals such as the Porsche Panamera and the

**The Vantage Roadster has a very neat and tidy soft top. When down it is concealed by a hatch that has neat little styling bumps behind the driver and passenger.**

**The Rapide was a five-door hatch, with just about enough room for four adults. It had a longer wheelbase than the DB9 and sold well.**

Maserati Quattroporte. Production of the Rapide started in 2010 and was outsourced to Magna Steyr in Austria. Rapide production returned to Gaydon in 2012.

The second version of the Rapide, the Rapide S, replaced the original Rapide and was produced between 2013 and 2020. It was powered by a 550bhp AE28 V12.

## The Aston Martin DBS (2007–2012)

The DBS used the VH2 platform used on the Vantage and One-77, but was largely based on the DB9. The DBS was the hand-built supercar in the range, replacing the Vanquish. The car was fitted with a 510bhp version of the V12, achieved by increasing the compression ratio and fitting a new air-intake system, and came in coupé or Volante specification. Based on the production VH platform rather than the Vanquish's unique chassis, the car was still hand built and with superior performance to the DB9. Fitted with adaptive suspension and carbon-fibre brake discs, the DBS handled as well as it went and was a fitting flagship.

The DBS Volante was launched in 2009, and was similar mechanically to the Coupé. The main differences were in the bodyshell, with a carbon-fibre rear deck to accommodate the power hood and its mechanism, and a separate boot behind it. However, the DBS suffered from not being different enough from the DB9 to justify the greatly increased cost, and it was replaced with the 2012 model Vanquish.

## Aston Martin Cygnet (2010–2013)

The Cygnet was a reworked Toyota IQ, and was designed on the behest of Ulrich Bez to give the Aston Martin range a 'city' car. It was not, as rumour says, designed to reduce Aston Martin's overall emissions targets. Nearly every body panel was changed to give the car a number of Aston Martin styling cues – most notably the traditional air ducts on the front wings – and the cars were repainted and retrimmed to Aston Martin standards. Mechanically the cars were not modified, avoiding homologation issues, and the interior was very sumptuous, with leather throughout.

Sales of the Cygnet were slow: worldwide figures were 593 produced, with about 150 staying in the UK. A single V8-powered Cygnet was made by Aston Martin's 'Q' division in 2018. The car was unusual, with Vantage mechanicals mounted on new subframes, along with a new front bulkhead, transmission tunnel, and wider wheel arches added to the standard monocoque – it must also have been quite a handful!

## Aston Martin DB10 Concept Car (2014)

The DB10 was developed specifically to appear in the James Bond film *Spectre*, and was billed as a bespoke Grand Tourer. The car's design was led by Aston Martin's chief creative officer, Marek Reichman, and the design was based on a concept by Sam Holgate. Ten cars were produced, all hand built by the design and engineering team based at Gaydon, and of those, eight appeared in the film and two were used for promotional tasks. The DB10 was based on the then current V8 Vantage VH2 chassis and running gear, including that car's 4.7-litre V8 and six-speed Graziano transaxle. However, the Vantage platform was both lengthened and widened to give the DB10 a wheelbase of 106in (2,692mm) and a width of 87in (2,210mm). Overall the car was a headline-gathering concept, which usefully piggybacked on the relationship between Aston Martin and Eon Productions, owners of the Bond franchise. However, it was rather more than a simple exercise in building a Bond car. Aston Martin stated at the time

**Here, Rob Smith's Cygnet is parked next to the author's DB9. Although it is based on a Toyota IQ, the Cygnet is very much a mini Aston Martin.**

**The Cygnet's interior is trimmed in leather with metal highlights to the highest standard.**

that 'the DB10 gives a glimpse of the future design direction for the next generation of Aston Martins'. This it did, and the family lineage is clearly visible in the DB11 released in 2011.

## Aston Martin One-77 (2010–2012)

The One-77 was Aston Martin's first foray into the hypercar market. Designed to go head to head with cars such as the Bugatti Veyron and Pagoni Zonda, the £1.1 million One-77 was a two-seat coupé with unmistakably Aston Martin lines. It was completely hand built and based on an all carbon-fibre tub, to give both lightness and strength, over which was wrapped a hand-built aluminium body. The front-engine, rear-transaxle car was powered by the Aston Martin V12 engine, with a capacity increase to 7312cc, which gave 750bhp at 7,500rpm and 553lb ft of torque at 5,000rpm – this was claimed at the time to be the most powerful normally aspirated engine in the world.

Only seventy-seven cars were made, although one development car was completely refurbished by Aston Martin and sold in the USA. Produced between 2010 and 2012, the One-77 had a claimed top speed in excess of 220mph (352km/h).

## Aston Martin Virage 2011–2012

The Virage was a short-lived model designed to slot into the range between the DB9 and the DBS. It was based on the DB9/DBS platform, with subtly restyled bodywork and 20bhp more than the DB9. However, the gap in the range was rather narrow, and few buyers emerged. It was only in production for a year, and was effectively reintroduced as the updated DB9 in 2013.

## COMPETITION

In 2003 Aston Martin announced it would return to motor sport, and set up a new division, Aston Martin Racing, to develop, with Prodrive, the DBR9 in order to compete in the GT classes – including Le Mans. The Prodrive DBR9 won at its debut race, the Sebring 12 Hours in 2005, and went on to win two Le Mans races in the GT1 class, in 2007 and 2008. The team then unveiled the Aston Martin LMP1, which had a Lola chassis and was powered by a DBR1 V12 engine, winning the Le Mans series in 2009, and finishing fourth as the highest placed petrol-powered car at Le Mans. The team went on to compete in the FIA World Endurance Championship (WEC) from 2015, competing in a car based on the production Vantage, the Vantage GTE.

## KEY FIGURES

### Ulrich Bez

Born in Bad Cannstatt, Germany, on November 1943, Ulrich Bez was Aston Martin's CEO and chairman from July 2000 until November 2013. Bez started work at Porsche when he left school, initially as an apprentice and working on the production line, before starting to study mechanical engineering at the University of Stuttgart. He joined Porsche full time when he graduated, and for the next ten years he was involved in many aspects of manufacturing and testing; during this time he was also studying for his Doctorate at the Technical University of Berlin.

In 1986 Bez left Porsche to join BMW, where he headed up vehicle pre-development before being asked to set up BMW's Research and Development spin-up: BMW Technic GMBH. Here Bez developed BMW's V8 and the Z1 sports car. This success did not go unnoticed, and in 1988 Bez was asked to rejoin Porsche as head of development, research and motor sport. The first job in this post was to look at a replacement for the soon-to-be-introduced 964 variant of the classic 911. Alongside this Bez also had to look at Porsche's motor-sport commitments, the increasingly urgent need for cost reductions within production, and the need to expand the company's model range.

One area in which motor sport was a success was in the setting up of the 911 cup One Make race series, which turned into one of the most successful race series in the world.

Cost reduction measures inevitably brought Bez into conflict with other board members, and in September 1991 he left Porsche. In March 1993 he joined Daewoo, where he oversaw the introduction of four new indigenous models, including the Matiz and Nubira, as well as establishing design and development centres in Munich, Worthing and Seoul.

Bez left Daewoo in 1998, going back to Germany and taking the post of CEO for the Flender Gearbox and Transmission factory in Bolcholt, Germany. He then acted as a consultant to Ford to help with Ford's ultimately unsuccessful bid for Daewoo. By 2000 Bez was a business adviser to Ford, and this role led to him being appointed the Chief Executive Officer and Chairman of Aston Martin in July of that year.

### David Richards – Aston Martin Chairman 2007–2013

David Richards was born in 1952, and at the time of writing was the chairman of both Prodrive, and the Royal Automobile Club Motor Sports Association Motorsport UK. In the context of this book it is his chairmanship of Aston Martin from 2007 to 2013 that is of interest. After leaving school and five years of study, Richards became a chartered accountant; at this time he was also competing as a professional rally co-driver, winning his first national rally championship alongside Tony Drummond in 1974.

There followed a successful career in rallying and rally team managing, which included being team manager for Fiat and then joining the Ford rally team and teaming up with Ari Vatanen, where they won both the British and Scandinavian championships in 1980, and the World Rally Championship in 1981. After this win Richards retired from active participation in rallying, and concentrated on organizing rallies for Rothmans, and setting up and managing his own rally team. This led to him setting up Prodrive to manage his Rothmans Porsche rally team in 1984.

As well as supporting the Rothmans Porsche team, Prodrive ran their own MG/Rover Metro 6R4 in the British and Irish rally championships, and entered into a partnership with BMW in 1987 to manage their rally and British Touring Car Championship teams; this relationship resulted in BMW winning the BTCC in 1988, 1989 and 1990. In 1989 Prodrive and Fuji Heavy Industries set up the Subaru World Rally Team, which won the British titles in 1991, 1992 and 1993. Further success came with the team winning the Manufacturers and Drivers World Rally titles in 1995, with two more Manufacturers' titles in 1997 and 1998.

Prodrive entered the sports-car racing arena in 2001 with a team running modified Ferrari 550 GTS cars to enter the FIA GT championship. The team was independent of Ferrari, and in 2003 won the GT1 class at Le Mans. In 2003 Prodrive signed an agreement with Aston Martin to take Aston Martin back into racing: this led to the creation of Aston Martin Racing, and the new team unveiled the DBR9 in November 2004.

Richards also has a great track record in Formula 1. He was director of the Benetton F1 team for the 1997 season, and went on to become Team Principal of the BAR team in 2001, with Prodrive running the team. BAR took second place in the F1 Constructors Championship in 2004, but Prodrive and Richards stood down at the end of 2004 when BAR sold a 45 per cent share of the team to Honda. While F1 granted Prodrive entry to run a F1 team for the 2008 season, Prodrive did not enter due to uncertainty around certain contractual matters.

In 2007 Richards led the consortium comprising Investment Dar and Adeem Investment, which bought Aston Martin from Ford. Richards became chairman of the company from 2007, finally stepping down at the end of 2013.

## TECHNICAL DESCRIPTION

The DB9 is a two-door 2+2 coupé, and was the first production Aston Martin to use the VH platform. The VH platform is an aluminium chassis that accepts front and rear subframes that carry the suspension as well as the drive train, which uses a torque tube to join the front engine and rear transmission and axle in a single rigid assembly. Body panels were made from a mixture of aluminium and composite. The DB9 was powered by Aston Martin's dohc 48-valve V12 engine, and had a six-speed ZF automatic transmission or a Graziano six-speed manual system. The front and rear suspension were both independent dual aluminium wishbone systems, with the rear fitted with longitudinal control arms. Both front and rear systems used coil springs and alloy 'monotube' dampers. Ventilated disc brakes were fitted all round.

## 2008 DB9 SPECIFICATION TABLE

| | | |
|---|---|---|
| **Layout and chassis** | Front engine, rear transaxle two-plus-two GT car. Closed two-door body, VH platform chassis, alloy and composite body | |
| **Engine** | | |
| Type | Aston Martin twin overhead camshaft V12 | |
| Block material | Aluminium alloy | |
| Head material | Aluminium alloy | |
| Cylinders | V12 | |
| Cooling | Centrifugal pump with water/antifreeze mix | |
| Bore and stroke | 89 × 79.5mm | |
| Capacity | 5935cc | |
| Valves | 4 valves per cylinder, operated directly via bucket tappets from chain-driven double overhead camshafts | |
| Compression ratio | 10.2:1 | |
| Fuel injection | Multi-point sequential fuel injection | |
| Max. power | 450bhp @ 5,750rpm | |
| Max. torque | 420lb ft @ 5,000rpm | |
| **Transmission** | | |
| Gearbox (auto) | ZF six-speed | |
| Overall ratios | 1st | 4.17:1 |
| | 2nd | 2.34:1 |
| | 3rd | 1.52:1 |
| | 4th | 1.14:1 |
| | 5th | 0.87:1 |
| | 6th | 0.69:1 |
| Reverse | 3.31:1 | |
| Final drive | Hypoid bevel, 3.15:1 | |
| Gearbox (manual) | Graziano six-speed | |
| Overall ratios | 1st | 3.15:1 |
| | 2nd | 1.97:1 |
| | 3rd | 1.44:1 |
| | 4th | 1.15:1 |
| | 5th | 0.94:1 |
| | 6th | 0.76:1 |
| Reverse | 2.39:1 | |
| Final drive | Hypoid bevel, 3.54:1 | |
| **Suspension and steering** | | |
| Front | Aluminium double wishbone with coil over aluminium monotube dampers. Anti-roll bar | |
| Rear | Aluminium double wishbone with longitudinal control arms, coil over monotube dampers, anti-roll bar | |
| Steering | Speed-sensitive power-assisted rack-and-pinion | |
| Wheels | Front: 8.5J × 19 alloy | |
| | Rear: 9.5J × 19 alloy | |

**Brakes**

| | |
|---|---|
| Type | Hydraulic front and rear discs, incorporating anti-lock system, electronic brake force distribution, emergency brake assist, dynamic stability control and traction control |
| Size (front) | 14in (35.5cm) diameter disc |
| Size (rear) | 11.125in (33.0cm) diameter disc |

**Capacities**

| | |
|---|---|
| Fuel capacity | 18.6gal (85ltr) |
| Oil capacity | 19.4 pints (11ltr) |

**Dimensions**

| | |
|---|---|
| Track | |
| Front: | 62in (1,586mm) |
| Rear: | 62in (1,568mm) |
| Wheelbase | 108in (2,740mm) |
| Overall length | 185.5in (4,710mm) |
| Overall width | 74in (1,875mm) |
| Overall height | 50in (1,263mm) |
| Weight (Coupé) | 3,970lb (1,800kg) |

**Performance**

| | |
|---|---|
| Top speed | 186mph (299km/h) |
| 0–60 | 5.4sec |

CHAPTER 10

# ASTON MARTIN 2014–2021

## THE COMPANY

In 2013 the company signed an agreement with Mercedes Benz to supply engines and electrical systems. In this year Ulrich Bez left, and was replaced as CEO in October 2014 by ex-Nissan Chief Planning Officer Andy Palmer. Palmer introduced his vision for Aston Martin at the 2015 Geneva Motor Show, called the 'Second Century Plan'. This was intended to take Aston Martin forwards into its second century of car production, by boosting car production by diversifying into new vehicle categories, while not compromising Aston Martin's reputation for style and engineering. His main achievements were overseeing the design and development of the DBX SUV, and setting up the new factory at St Athen to produce the car. In 2018, Palmer set up the Palmer Foundation, a charity that would fund apprenticeships in the automotive industry for disadvantaged young people.

In 2018, the company was floated on the London stock exchange, with the initial public offering (IPO) with original investors Investindustral and Investment Dar selling 25 per cent of their stake in the company for £1.1 billion. However, the IPO did not generate any new capital for the company, leaving it with the existing debt.

Palmer's efforts increased sales and moved Aston Martin into profitability, but despite this he still suffered from a shortage of cash in the company, and during 2019 he had to raise some £536 million through a rights issue and a private placement, resulting in a further significant debt burden.

The final act in the Palmer tenure occurred in 2020. This was the purchase for £182 million of a 16.7 per cent stake in

**The DBX and the DB11 were two of the main new models introduced between 2016 and 2021. The DB11 was the grand tourer to replace the DB9, while the DBX was Aston Martin's first SUV.**

the company by a consortia led by Lawrence Stroll, a Canadian billionaire businessman and owner of the Racing Point (formerly Force India) Formula 1 team. Palmer's departure from Aston Martin was announced by the company on 26 May 2020; his replacement was the former CEO of Mercedes AMG, Tobias Moers.

In his six years at Aston Martin, Palmer had built on the great work done by Ulrich Bez, and left the company in an arguably better state that when he arrived, with the new DBX just getting into production.

Palmer's legacy can be summarized as the introduction of four new models: the DB11 replacing the DB9, the new Vantage in 2016, the DBX SUV in 2020, and the DBS Superleggera to replace the Vanquish. Alongside these models Palmer resurrected the Lagonda name with the Lagonda Taraf, a very expensive four-door saloon. Finally Palmer put in place the development of the mid-engined Valkyrie model. In order to produce the DBX a new factory in South Wales was commissioned, utilizing one of the 'super hangers' built on the old RAF station at St Athen.

## THE CARS

### The Second Century Architecture

With the VH architecture approaching fourteen years of age, and Aston Martin's increasing experience of creating bonded and riveted aluminium structures, it was no surprise to see the VH architecture evolving into a new structure that offered significant advantages over the VH chassis. The new Second Century underframe uses a combination of aluminium extrusions, die castings, flat or curved sheet and complex shaped panels to produce a bonded and riveted aluminium tub or chassis. By stepping back and reviewing the VH architecture's strengths and weaknesses, the Aston Martin engineers devised the new platform, which in the DB11's case was some 40kg lighter than that of the DB9, while being around 39 per cent stiffer and 9 per cent larger, and was designed to meet the latest safety standards. The main difference from the VH platform was in the use of die-cast aluminium components and shaped panels with very complex designs.

The shaped panels, the main one forming part of the door frame, were formed using a technique called 'hot form quenching'. This technique was originally conceived in 2003 at the University of Birmingham in the centre of the UK automotive industry, and was further developed by Imperial College London and commercialized by Impression Technologies Ltd (ITL). The process is used to form aluminium parts with deep-drawn and complex geometry. It involves heating an aluminium alloy sheet up to around 550°C, then pressing the hot sheet in a cold punch and die tool to form the required shape. It means there is no cold working of the aluminium, and it can offer over 1,000 per cent elongation of the sheet within the press, which would be impossible with conventional cold forming. It also means that large and complicated one-piece pressings can be accurately produced, which would otherwise have to be formed from multiple pressings produced by conventional cold pressing.

The use of this technology means that the Aston Martin structure can be made up of fewer, larger and more complex elements, resulting in significant savings in assembly time. The DB11 was the first to benefit from this technology, using it in the 'A' pillar pressings that needed particularly tight radii to minimize the width of the pillar, thus increasing passenger vision while meeting the strength requirements.

The combination of these various manufacturing techniques means that parts can be bonded and riveted together to form the chassis, and, like the VH platform, allows for relatively easy modification of the basic design to provide variations in length, wheelbase and width, so the design can be adapted to a range of vehicles.

**The DB11 has some new styling features, such as the clamshell bonnet and roof strakes, that move the design on from the DB9.**

**The Vulcan is Aston Martin's hypercar, a track-only lightweight sports car.**

## Aston Martin Vulcan (2015–2016)

The Vulcan was a limited production, two-door, track-only lightweight sports car, costing around £2 million. Launched in 2015, it was designed by Marek Reichman. Based on an all-new carbon-fibre tub with carbon-fibre bodywork, the car was powered by a bored-out Aston Martin V12, displacing 7 litres, and pumping out a massive 820bhp, which was complemented by 575lb ft of torque. It was fitted with a six-speed manual transmission, pushrod-operated suspension, and large carbon-ceramic disc brakes. The car generated significant amounts of downforce thanks to a front splitter, rear diffuser and adjustable rear wing. This downforce was increased by some 27 per cent with the introduction of the AMR Pro package, unveiled at the 2017 Goodwood Festival of Speed. The package consisted of various aerodynamic add-ons, including a large dual-element rear wing, turning vanes to aid steering response, and dive planes. The cars were intended to be driven on 'approved' track-day events by the factory, along with driver training days.

## Lagonda Taraf (2015–2017)

With a 'list' price in the UK of over £600,000 it is really no surprise that very few Lagonda Tarafs were made. The limited-edition, hand-built Taraf was a full sized, four-door luxury saloon car based on a stretched Rapide VH chassis with a lengthened wheelbase of 810in (2,057mm) to give room for a truly sumptuous interior. It shared its mechanical underpinnings with the Rapide S. The exterior styling was designed to be modern Aston Martin but with a nod backwards to the angular lines of the 1980s Lagonda 'wedge'.

**The Lagonda Taraf was a luxury four-seater that was larger than the Rapide and built to very limited orders.**

The body panels were all carbon fibre, and a wide range of options was available, especially when specifying the interior. With a top speed approaching 200mph (321km/h) and a 0–60 time of 4.4sec, the Taraf offered a unique combination of pace and space. Offered for sale in 2015, the car was initially offered to Middle East customers, but was then subsequently also released in the European Union countries. The car was a limited edition of 200 (although it is not clear if all 200 were built), and was sold as a bespoke car, with the specification tailored to the customer's needs.

## Aston Martin DB11 (2016–)

The DB11 was the replacement for the DB9 in the Aston Martin range, and the first model to be launched as part of Andy Palmer's Second Century plan. The car was the first Aston Martin to be based on the all-new aluminium Second

**The DB11 was the range's 2+2 GT car. The clamshell bonnet and longer wheelbase distinguish it from the smaller Vantage.**

Century chassis, described above, and was initially powered by a new version of the Aston Martin V12. As with the DB9, the DB11 is a two-door coupé, with four seats and a conventional boot for luggage. The design of the New Century chassis gave the DB11 a longer wheelbase than the DB9, so the engine could be slightly repositioned to improve weight distribution (51:49 front to rear), as well as giving the car a roomier interior. The connection with Mercedes also enabled Aston Martin to fit more up-to date electronics, and the car benefits from Mercedes-derived electronics systems, including the built-in sat nav and infotainment system.

The V12 engine was a redesign of the unit seen in the DB9. Displacing 5204cc and with a reduced compression ratio of 9.3:1, the engine was fitted with a pair of twin scroll turbochargers and produced a healthy 600bhp at 6,500rpm and 516lb ft of torque between 1,500 and 5,000rpm, a significant increase over the final DB9's unit output of 510bhp and 457lb ft. It was also fitted with stop/start technology. As a result the new V12 DB11 not only has a significant performance boost over the outgoing DB9, it is also more economical to run.

**The DB11's rear view shows the sharp-edged aerodynamic 'blade' running across the back of the body.**

Transmission is an eight-speed ZF gearbox also used in the Vanquish and Rapide S, and incorporates a torque vectoring differential to aid traction. The suspension uses adaptive Bilstein dampers in a range of settings (GT, Sport and Sport Plus). The car is braked with steel discs, 400mm in diameter at the front.

As regards styling, the car has a very traditional 'floating' front grille incorporated into a clamshell bonnet. This is made from aluminium: it extends over the top of the front wings and is hinged at the front, opening forwards to give good access to the engine bay. The side strakes run all the way from the wheel arch to the door, and are aerodynamically designed to extract air from the engine bay and direct it out along the side of the car below the wing mirrors, which reduces drag and wind noise. The air is directed into the aero system at the back of the car, where it is directed into a duct at the bottom of the side windows and is ducted out along the back of the car, creating a blade of air at the back of the car. This patented system induces a good level of stability without any significant drag penalty. In comparison to the DB9 the front wheel is about 65mm further forward, and the front overhang is slightly less, while the rear overhang is about the same. Roof strakes delineate the roof from the lower body.

There are design elements seen before on the 100 roadster, the DBX (the Grand Turismo games car, not the SUV) and the Vulcan concept cars, including the treatment of the front wheels from the 100 and the DBX, and the 'discus' section on the rear seen on the Vulcan.

The all-new interior design was headed up by Matt Hill, and the concept was 'sporting comfort'. Retaining the traditional wood and leather, the interior was designed to be fully up to date and took advantage of the increase in interior space from the DB9. A notable feature is the single dial on the electronic dashboard, which has a circular analogue tachometer display incorporating a large digital speed reading in the centre.

In the summer of 2017 a 4-litre V8 DB11 was added to the range. Using the same engine as in the Vantage, the Mercedes M177 twin-turbocharged unit, with 503bhp, the V8 DB11 was otherwise very similar to the V12, although the smaller and lighter engine meant that the weight distribution of the V8 was 49/51 front to rear, and the overall weight of the car was some 254lb (115kg) less.

### *The DB11 AMR*

In May 2018 Aston Martin released the DB11 AMR. This model replaced the V12 DB11, sales of which had dropped after the release of the V8-powered DB11, and was designed to increase the performance gap between the V8- and V12-powered cars. To achieve this, the AMR's V12 engine was tuned to produce a healthy 630bhp, and the eight-speed gearbox was reprogrammed to give a quicker and sportier gear

**The DB11 Volante is very similar to the coupé from the front. With the hood the car loses the distinctive roof strakes.**

**From the side the Volante maintains the sleek lines with a subtle hood line.**

change. Stiffened rear suspension and 20in-diameter wheels enabled the chassis to cope with the extra power. The main cosmetic change was an all-black roof.

### *The DB11 Volante*

The DB11 Volante was released in 2018, and was based on the V8-powered DB11. As with the DB9, the Volante came with a power hood, made in mohair material. It was still a four-seater.

## The Aston Martin Vantage (AM6) (2017–)

The all-new Vantage announced in 2017 utilized the same Second Century chassis system as the DB11, and in a step away from Aston Martin's tradition of using its own engines, was fitted with a version of the Mercedes AMG V8 unit. Still maintaining its position in the marketplace as a sports car with two seats, two doors and a rear hatchback – which is aimed firmly at the Porsche 911 – the new Vantage is, like the DB11, an all-new design. While it shares some of its styling cues with the DB11, it is very much its own car and is a lot less similar to the DB11 than the original Vantage was to the DB9. One major change from the DB11 is a semi-clamshell bonnet. This is hinged on its rear face, and while it extends over the front wings, it is shorter than the DB11 unit, and at the front the bonnet line runs above the headlamps, leaving a separate panel running across the front of the car.

Overall the Vantage has a more aggressive look than the DB11: at the front a larger and wider grille aperture dominates the car's face, the traditional strakes of the side vents are replaced with a large rounded triangular vent on the front wing, while at the rear there is a continuous thin red LED rear light running across the width of the car.

To celebrate Aston Martin's return to Formula One, and the adoption of the Vantage as the F1 safety car, Aston Martin introduced the Vantage F1 edition. This was a modified Vantage with a 25bhp power boost (up to 535PS), along with

**The second generation Vantage shows the different nose treatment to the DB11 with its inset bonnet.**

**The side profile of the Vantage shows off its short wheelbase and aggressive lines.**

modifications to the suspension and aerodynamics, including a stiffer front end, reworked dampers and stiffer rear springs, along with wider and bigger diameter wheels – up from the standard 20in to 21in. Aerodynamic improvements included a full width front splitter, front dive planes, underbody turning vanes and a new rear spoiler. The car was available as a coupé and a roadster, and sits at the top of the Vantage range. At the end of 2021 Aston Martin announced that they were proposing to introduce a V12 version of the new Vantage.

## Aston Martin DBS Superleggera (2018–)

The DBS is the current top-of-the-range supercar, taking over from the Vanquish as Aston Martin's ultimate GT car, and resurrects a famous label from the past: 'Superleggera', or super light, which was originally applied to the construction method patented by Touring, and used on the DB4 and 5. In the case of the DBS it refers to the weight of the car, although as the car's dry weight is 3,733lb (1,693kg) it doesn't save that much weight over a standard DB11. Weight reduction is achieved by using carbon fibre on the body panels, such as the clamshell bonnet and deck lid, as well as the splitter and diffuser. Further lightening measures can be had as options, including a carbon-fibre roof panel. Otherwise the DBS follows the formula used for the top-of-the-range model: a two-door coupé body with boot, a luxurious interior with 2+2 seating, and a large V12 engine to propel the car at very high speed.

The car is broadly based on the DB11 Second Century platform, but has a large number of changes under the skin to enhance its handling and roadholding to allow for the increased performance. It also has all-new bodywork and styling to give the car a more aggressive and sportier look than the DB11.

The DBS is powered by a tuned version of the classic Aston Martin twin-turbo 5.2-litre 48-valve dohc V12 engine as seen in the DB11. In the DBS the unit produces 715bhp at 6,500rpm, along with 663lb ft of torque between 1,800 and 5,000rpm. This gives the DBS a class-leading performance of a claimed top speed of 211mph (340km/h) and a 0–62mph time of 3.4sec. Transmission is a rear-mounted ZF eight-speed transaxle.

Front suspension follows Aston Martin tradition with a double wishbone set-up, and a front track some 10mm wider than the DB11. At the rear, the car's subframe is rigidly fitted to the chassis, and the car is fitted with independent multilink suspension – and again, the track is wider by 20mm than that

**The DBS Superleggera is the current (2018) range flagship. Its bodywork is made from carbon fibre, and there is a traditional 'Superleggera' badge on the bonnet.**

**From the rear the DBS Superleggera has the corporate rear end with the aerodynamic blade complemented by a small lip spoiler.**

**The DBS Superleggera profile is sporting and aggressive.**

of the DB11. The car is fitted with the 'Skyhook' adaptive damping system, and the brake discs are carbon ceramic discs front and rear, 410mm diameter at the front and 360mm at the rear. The suspension is finished off by massive 21in forged aluminium wheels, fitted with wide 265/35 front and even wider 305/30 rear tyres.

Aerodynamics also play their part in the car's performance: an 'aero blade' system (as first seen on the DB11) is used to manage the airflow around the sides of the car, and in conjunction with the double diffuser – which accelerates the airflow under the car – creates a significant amount of downforce to help the car stick to the road.

Available as both coupé and soft top Volante, the DBS is the current flagship of the range, offering a classic Aston Martin Grand Touring car with a touch of brutality with its class-leading performance.

## Aston Martin DBX (2020–)

The DBX was Aston Martin's first sports utility vehicle (SUV) and was (and is) an essential element of Palmer's Second Century plan. The DBX opens up a third high volume (in Aston Martin terms) production model line, after the DB11 and Vantage, in a market that is already addressed by rivals Porsche, Maserati, Lamborghini, Bentley and of course Land Rover. As a capable five-seat, luxury four-wheel-drive SUV, the DBX gave the Aston Martin range a car that was a practical family wagon but added Aston Martin's own style and sporting character.

The DBX is a five-door, five-seat SUV and has an all-aluminium chassis based on the Second Century method of construction, but extensively reworked to provide a full five-seat SUV platform. Body panels are all in aluminium, apart from composites being used for the front and rear bumpers.

The DBX is powered by the Mercedes-sourced V8 as seen in the DB11 and Vantage. In the DBX the engine was reworked to adapt its performance to the DBX's all-wheel drive and off-road requirements, which meant changes to the induction system, turbochargers, exhaust system, compression ratio (down to 8.6:1) and firing sequence, all backed up with programming changes to the ECU to give 542bhp at 6,500rpm and 516lb ft of torque between 2,000 and 5,000rpm.

The DBX is fitted with an all-wheel-drive (AWD) system. It has a Mercedes-sourced nine-speed gearbox, and power is directed via a centrally mounted transfer case: this controls the power supplied to the front open differential mounted on the engine, and the rear electronically controlled limited slip differential. The centre transfer box automatically balances

**The DBX is Aston Martin's first SUV, introduced in 2020. The company has done a great job in giving it an unmistakably Aston Martin look.**

**The rear quarter of the DBX, showing how the design is very sporty and slim looking, unlike many rival SUVs. The boot is surprisingly spacious.**

the power feed between the front and rear differentials, which varies between 100 per cent power to the rear, to a 47/53 per cent split front to rear. The driveshafts front and rear are all the same length to minimize torque steer.

As with the other cars in the range, the DBX has twin wishbone front suspension and multi-link rear suspension. The car has air suspension all round, which enables the ride height to be changed by up to 95mm, along with electronic adaptive damper controls (ADS), set by the driving mode selected. There is an electronically controlled active roll control system (eARC). This is achieved using an electric motor fitted to the front and rear roll-bars used to control body roll. The system enables the roll-bars to counteract cornering forces to reduce body roll to a minimum. It also enables the roll-bars to be disengaged to enable full axle articulation when off road.

As well as the car, Aston Martin offers a wide range of accessories tailored specifically for the DBX to support the sporting lifestyle DBX owners are expected to follow – these include items such as bespoke luggage, ski bags, ski-boot warmer bags, and a temperature-controlled travel cup. If the car does not offer enough space, Aston Martin offers a roof-rack system, including fittings for bikes, skis, surfboards and roof boxes, as well as a tow bar.

The family pet is well catered for, with options including a dog bed, portable shower, a dog accessory kit and a partition to keep the animal comfortable, clean, watered and secure in the luggage compartment.

## The Aston Martin Works Continuation Cars

Since 2017, Aston Martin Works, based in the original Newport Pagnell works, has been specializing in the restoration and re-creation of various historic Aston Martins. The first batch of historic Aston Martins comprised twenty-five DB4GTs, the car an exact replica of the original cars. The number made was based on the thinking to bring the total number (seventy-five) of DB4GTs originally produced, up to 100, which was the original homologation target.

The success of this limited production run was followed in 2019 when Aston Martin works produced a further nineteen DB4GT Zagato cars. Like the DB4GT, these cars were built for track use only (although it is possible for owners to potentially get them road registered in the UK through the Individual Vehicle Authorisation (IVA) scheme), and like the four cars produced in the 1990s, are faithful copies of the cars produced in the 1960s. Unlike the 1990 cars, where the bodies were produced by Zagato and then finished at Newport Pagnell, the cars were all produced in-house, with bodies produced by the skilled craftsmen of the Aston Martin works at Newport Pagnell.

Following on from the DB4GT Zagato, the next project for Aston Martin works was the re-creation of the Aston Martin DB5 used in the Bond film *Goldfinger*, incorporating all the gadgets as seen on the movie car. The limited run was of twenty-five cars

## Aston Martin's Mid-Engine Supercars: the Valkyrie and Valhalla

### *The Valkyrie*

With an astonishing 1140bhp, the Valkyrie was the first of Aston Martin's 21st-century hybrid hypercars. The car was produced with, among other refinements, titanium con rods. The engine and transmission are used as a structural element at the rear of the car, carrying the rear suspension. Developed with Red Bull Racing Advanced Technologies, it is a track-oriented car that is useable and enjoyable as a road car. The car is claimed to be the fastest street-legal road car.

Codenamed AM-RB 001, the car is powered by a mid-mounted 6.5-litre V12 based on the existing Aston Martin V12 but tuned by Cosworth, along with an electric motor and

**With deliveries to customers starting in 2021, the Valkyrie was Aston Martin's first 21-century mid-engined supercar.**

lightweight battery pack developed by Integral Powertrain Ltd and Rimac, respectively. There is a Formula 1-style Kinetic Energy Recovery System (KERS) system fitted to store power generated from braking to boost power. The car's chassis and bodywork are made from carbon fibre, and are aerodynamically enhanced with an open underfloor to maximize downforce.

The car is available in coupé or open-topped spider versions. A higher-performance version, the Valkyrie AMR Pro which is fitted with a more powerful V12 engine, is designed purely for track use.

Customer deliveries started in November 2021, and there will be 150 units produced, with up to twenty-five being the AMR version. The limited-edition production run was sold out before production started.

### *The Valhalla*

Aston Martin's second twenty-first-century mid-engined hypercar, the Valhalla, was introduced as the 'son of Valkyrie' at the 2019 Geneva Motor show, and went on to appear in Q's workshop in the 2021 Bond movie *No Time To Die*. The car was originally intended to slot into the range below the Valkyrie and above the Vanquish. It was designated AM-RB 003, reflecting the collaboration between Aston Martin and the Red Bull F1 spin-off Red Bull Advanced Technologies, with Adrian Newey playing a big part in the car's design.

The car was originally intended to be a petrol/electric hybrid, with the front axle driven by one or two electric motors, and an Aston Martin-designed 3-litre twin-turbocharged V6 (designated the TM01 as a nod to Tadek Marek) driving the rear wheels. However, the use of a Mercedes hybrid powertrain was mooted in late 2020, as the company's collaboration with the German company grew closer and was confirmed in early 2021, with a Mercedes twin-turbo flat-plane 4-litre V8 substituting for the V6. The new set-up, with two electric motors (apparently one for each axle) has a combined power output of 937bhp, along with 738lb ft of torque.

## KEY FIGURE

### Andy Palmer

Andy Palmer was born in 1963, and has worked in the automotive industry all his life. He started with an engineering apprenticeship in 1979 with Automotive Products, a major supplier of components to many UK and worldwide manufacturers, and became a product engineer in 1983. He moved to Rover in 1991 when he took up the appointment of Chief Engineer of Manual Transmissions, but quickly moved to Nissan, having been appointed Business Administration Manager at the Cranfield, UK-based Nissan Technical Centre Europe (NTCE); here he was responsible for vehicle design and testing.

Palmer's career at Nissan went well: he became Deputy Managing Director at NTCE in 2001, following which he moved to Japan to become Programme Director for Nissan light commercial vehicles. Here he was promoted to be President of the Nissan Motor Light Trucks Company, and established the LCV Business Unit. In 2005, Palmer was promoted to Corporate

**The Valhalla was the second of Aston Martin's mid-engined hypercars, powered by a Mercedes hybrid system with a twin turbo V8 and two electric motors.**

## TECHNICAL DESCRIPTION

The DBX is Aston Martin's first mid-size luxury Sports Utility Vehicle (SUV). A five-door, five-seat, four-wheel-drive SUV, production started in July 2020 at Aston Martin's purpose-built plant in St Athen in South Wales. The DBX has an aluminium chassis based on extruded and bonded aluminium, and is powered by a 542bhp version of the Mercedes-AMG M177 twin-turbo V8. A nine-speed Touchtronic gearbox takes the drive via a transfer box to a part-time front differential and an electronically controlled limited slip rear differential.

The DBX has all-round independent suspension, with double wishbones in the front and multilink at the rear. The four-wheel-drive system has an active centre transfer case to automatically divert drive to the front wheels when needed. The dampers are electronically controlled, and springing is by air with triple-chambered air springs to provide a wide range of ride-height and spring-rate options. Five pre-programmed driving modes are provided: the default GT, Sport, Sport Plus, Terrain and Terrain Plus. A 48-volt electronic active anti-roll system controls body roll, and the active dampers provide variable-rate adaptive damping. Disc brakes are fitted all round.

## 2021 DB-X SPECIFICATION TABLE

| | |
|---|---|
| **Layout and chassis** | Front-engine, all-wheel-drive, five-seat sports utility car. Closed five-door body, bonded and extruded alloy chassis |
| **Engine** | |
| Type | Quad cam V8, twin turbos, water to air air-charge cooling |
| Block material | Aluminium alloy |
| Head material | Aluminium alloy |
| Cylinders | V8 |
| Cooling | Centrifugal pump with water/antifreeze mix |
| Bore and stroke | 83 × 92mm |
| Capacity | 3982cc |
| Valves | 4 valves per cylinder, operated directly via bucket tappets from chain-driven double overhead camshafts |
| Compression ratio | 10.2:1 |
| Fuel injection | Multi-point sequential fuel injection |
| Max. power | 542bhp @ 6,000rpm |
| Max. torque | 516lb ft @ 2,000rpm |
| **Transmission** | |
| Description | Four-wheel-drive system, with active centre transfer case |
| Gearbox | 9G-Tronic 9-speed automatic |
| Overall ratios | Not known |
| Reverse | Not known |
| Final drive | Electronically controlled torque vectoring, 2.93:1 |
| **Suspension and steering** | |
| Front | Double wishbone with air springs and adaptive dampers |
| Rear | Independent multilink system with air springs, adaptive dampers, anti-roll bar |
| Stability control | Electrically operated active anti-roll system |
| Steering | Electric power-assisted rack-and-pinion |
| Wheels | Front: 22 × 10J, rear 22 × 11.5Jin cast-alloy |
| Tyres | Front: 285/40, rear 325/35 |
| **Brakes** | |
| Type | Hydraulic front and rear vented and grooved semi-floating discs, incorporating anti-lock system, electronic brake force distribution, emergency brake assist, dynamic stability control, hill descent system, hill start assist, and traction control |
| Size (front) | 16.1in (41cm) diameter |
| Size (rear) | 15.4in (39cm) diameter |
| **Capacities** | |
| Fuel capacity | 18.7gal (85ltr) |
| Oil | Not known |
| **Dimensions** | |
| Wheelbase | 120.5in (3,060mm) |
| Overall length | 198.4in (5,039mm) |
| Overall width | 78.7in (1,998mm) |
| Overall height | 66.1in (1,680mm) |
| Weight | 4,940lb (2,245kg) |
| **Performance** | |
| Top speed | 181mph (299km/h) |
| 0–60 | 4.5sec |

Vice President in charge of the LCV Business Unit. Further promotion meant Palmer was appointed a senior vice president, giving him a seat on Nissan's executive committee. In 2010 his responsibilities were expanded to cover global marketing, and in 2011 he was named Executive Vice President and appointed as Chief Planning Officer. While at Nissan Palmer was an advocate of electric cars, and was responsible for the development of the Leaf all-electric car; he also supported the Zeod Hybrid Le Mans sports-car project.

In 2014 Palmer joined Aston Martin as CEO. His strategy for the company was dubbed the 'Second Century Plan', and during his tenure he was responsible for introducing the first Aston Martin SUV, the DBX. His tenure at Aston Martin as CEO ended in 2020.

Palmer set up Palmer Automotive Ltd in 2020 to exploit his experience in the automotive industry, especially his experience of electric vehicles gained at Nissan, to 'do something good for the planet' and to forward the drive for net-zero carbon emissions. He was also a non-executive vice chairman of Ino-Bat Auto, a Slovakian auto battery manufacturer. Since 2016 he has been an adviser to the British government for engineering education.

# INDEX